An Introduction to
French Classical Tragedy

Edited by C. J. Gossip

THOMAS CORNEILLE: STILICON

An Introduction to French Classical Tragedy

C. J. Gossip
Senior Lecturer in French
University College of Swansea

First published 1981 by
THE MACMILLAN PRESS LTD
London and Basingstoke
Companies and representatives
throughout the world

Printed in Hong Kong

British Library Cataloguing in Publication Data

Gossip, C. J.
    An introduction to French classical tragedy
    1. French drama (Tragedy) – History and
    criticism
    2. French drama – 17th century – History and
    criticism
    I. Title
    842′.051   PQ561

    ISBN 0–333–26168–2

For my mother

Contents

Preface

Given the aim of this little book, a deliberate attempt has been made to avoid encumbering it with references and footnotes. The majority of readers should find mention of a writer's name and the title of the work quoted a sufficient indication and guarantee. Unless otherwise stated, dates in brackets after a title are those of first performance in the case of plays, or of first publication in the case of prose works, including plays' prefatory material.

A study of this kind clearly owes a debt to many others, to far more than can be acknowledged here. The short list of further reading at the end indicates at least some of the major works on which I have drawn, not always, I hope, uncritically, but invariably with profit and pleasure. Professor John Lough's *Seventeenth-century French drama: the background* (Oxford, 1979) appeared only when the text of the present book was in final form.

I should also like to extend my thanks to undergraduate and postgraduate students here and in Aberdeen, who have taught me more about French classical tragedy than I can ever pass on to others; to Dr Peter Nurse and Mr Antony Wood for their helpful comments on some early draft sections; and to Professor Armel Diverres for his constant encouragement. I am particularly grateful to Professor Harry Barnwell for his friendship and the inspiration of his example, and for his careful reading of my final typescript. The deficiencies remaining in the work are entirely my responsibility.

Finally I would thank Jean for her forbearance and support, and for accomplishing what has come to be the academic wife's task par excellence: that of keeping the children quieter than they would have wished to be.

Swansea, 1979   C.J.G.

Introduction

This book does not aim to be another survey of serious drama in seventeenth-century France. That task has been tackled in one way or another in several recent English books, among them Will G. Moore's *The classical drama of France* (1971) and the relevant chapters of Geoffrey Brereton's *French tragic drama in the sixteenth and seventeenth centuries* (1973), as well as in Jacques Truchet's thought-provoking study *La tragédie classique en France* (1975). The need to reinterpret literature of the past, whether in the light of fresh evidence or because new critics or readers wish to set works in a different perspective, is an important and continuing one. For example, postwar criticism of Racine, often thought of as a difficult dramatist suitable only for the 'happy few', has been wide-ranging and innovative, bringing together conventional literary historians, so-called 'new critics' and others in-between these extremes. Although often quarrelling among themselves, they have given Racinian scholarship greater depth and breadth than ever before and have opened up whole new areas for discussion. Even the most traditionally-minded reader of *Britannicus* or *Phèdre* can no longer ignore the importance of sound—for example, the presence of noise of one kind or another and characters' awareness of it (or its absence, silence)—nor the way characters' looks can be more meaningful or deadly than a thousand words.

Textual criticism, then, is not the aim of this book. Nor is it concerned with establishing the sequence of events, the process of writing, performance and publication on which success or failure of both masterpiece and run-of-the-mill play so often depends. The nine large volumes of Henry Carrington Lancaster's *History of French dramatic literature in the seventeenth century* (1929–42) provided many of the nuts and bolts for this important initial job, and of course scholars before and since then have worked to

1

build up a sound chronology of individual playwrights or periods in the history of the seventeenth-century French theatre. Strictly biographical information, too, is usually necessary for the understanding of an author's output; at the very least it provides a yardstick by which to judge his or her concerns and achievement. Biographies of major and minor seventeenth-century dramatists—many of them preliminary, a few definitive—have been published in France and elsewhere since the last quarter of the nineteenth century.

But amid all the general and particular studies of seventeenth-century tragedy and writers of tragedy in France, there appears to be no introductory work which guides the new, English-speaking reader or playgoer towards a grasp of the basic issues which face him as soon as he picks up a text or enters the theatre. What, for instance, are the very aims of the genre? What made the seventeenth century the great age of French tragedies? What were the conventions which the contemporary French public accepted without question but which seem strange to a late twentieth-century foreign audience? What problems did tragedy at the time have to overcome? What were the effects of staging and publication?

This book attempts some answers to these and other questions. It has been written partly in the belief that the recent thoroughgoing reappraisal among specialists of many areas of seventeenth-century French tragedy has not, in the main, been accompanied by renewed awareness in schools and universities or among the general public. The present study does not seek to promote or popularise recent academic literary research, but rather to prepare the ground so that those whose interest is aroused can go on to enjoy and profit from the serious drama of the period.

French classical tragedy has long been the victim of outdated and unrigorous criticism, where too often the text itself as a dramatic entity has disappeared under a welter of comments. The play as a living thing, to be *staged*, not read like a novel, is easily forgotten. How many students have been taken through *Cinna* or *Bérénice* without truly grasping the inherent dramatic qualities of these works, the techniques the playwright uses, the limitations as well as the possibilities within which he was working? Linguistic line-by-line analysis kills a play dead as quickly as it does a poem or a novel, if not more so.

The present book's title employs the term 'French classical tragedy' as a convenient shorthand description for tragedy written and performed in the seventeenth century in France and does not imply any restriction to the period 1660–80. Indeed the use of the label 'classical' (as imprecise as several other similar epithets) lies behind many of the difficulties which have bedevilled proper appreciation of the plays of Corneille, Racine and their contemporaries. For too long seventeenth-century tragedy was seen as a monolithic entity, or at best as a remarkably short series of regular plays (by Racine), preceded by a number of less regular or 'preclassical' tragedies, by definition or implication inferior to the former. Such neat pigeonholing begs more questions than it answers and certainly does not do justice to the diversity of form and content in seventeenth-century French drama which is only now becoming fully apparent.

As the reader is assumed to be a complete or relative newcomer to seventeenth-century French tragedy, this book will deal mainly with the work of Pierre Corneille and Jean Racine, its two principal practitioners. It may now be helpful to place these figures in the context of the French theatre as it had developed from the Middle Ages onwards. Medieval French drama, like that of other European countries, initially had a liturgical basis, being performed inside church buildings, before moving elsewhere and incorporating secular elements. Plays dealing with saints' lives or offering panoramas of events from the Old and New Testaments were staged, not in makeshift or purpose-built theatres, but rather in the open air, in areas such as market-places or in front of churches. Alternatively they might cease to be static performances and become mobile pageants, offering different scenes of a play on a platform with wheels as a procession moved from one part of a town to another. Inevitably the purely religious content changed in such a secular setting, but it did not disappear: everyday lay elements and characters were added to the religious ones.

By the late Middle Ages there existed on the one hand miracle or mystery plays, cycles of Bible stories, and on the other farces; but morality plays (the secular equivalent of religious drama) and *soties* or topical satirical plays were also performed. The genres were becoming mixed, as were the individual programmes offered to the public. It was not until the middle of the sixteenth century that France produced what we would now recognise as its first tragedy, Etienne Jodelle's *Cléopâtre captive*, performed in 1552. As with his contemporaries Robert Garnier and Jacques Grévin, or Antoine de Montchrestien, who appeared some forty years later, Jodelle's inspiration came from classical Greece or Rome; they were true sons of the Renaissance.

But it is impossible to see in France in the second half of the sixteenth century the birth of a strong national dramatic tradition. None of these figures can rival Shakespeare in quality or range, or Spain's Lope de Vega in output (if nothing else). Indeed, some would say that the French tragedies of the last decades of the century are plays in name only, for they lack the tension and plot development which, it can be argued, are a prerequisite of true drama. Many of the plays no doubt were not performed, or even written to be performed; of those that were, not a few appeared in Latin rather than in French, as amateur productions staged by pupils in the Jesuit colleges. This is not to say that French Renaissance tragedies are inferior to later ones—those of the seventeenth century for example; they are simply different, and have to be accepted as such. Just as Shakespearian tragedy, with its mixture of tones and its wide-ranging use of time and space, is unlike the more formally restrained and unified tragedies of France one or two generations later, so the relatively active plots of French classical tragedy differ from the static lamentations of Renaissance drama. Shakespeare was unknown to Corneille or Racine; while the latter knew their predecessors in late sixteenth-century France through their published works, their aim was not the same and the form of their plays differed accordingly. For Garnier and his contemporaries writing in the 1560s and 1570s, the crisis for characters came early on in the tragedy: much of the five acts was therefore taken up, not with action as such but with reaction, with lamentation and commiseration rather than the pursuit of a possibly still attainable goal. To add to the elegaic, lyrical aspect of much of this drama, a chorus was still included, announcing and commenting on events as they affected the characters.

Establishing an indigenous tradition in tragedy can have been no easy task. It is obviously unfair to compare French Renaissance dramatists with those of the seventeenth century, and completely absurd to dismiss them with the label 'pre-preclassical', as if they could have been aware of how the genre would flower and develop in succeeding generations. Already, though, Jodelle, Garnier and, later, Montchrestien had made clear that modern tragedy could, indeed should seek its subjects in antiquity, taking secular themes from historians or mythology or Biblical stories from one or other of the Testaments. Another important point they accepted was the need for the unities to be observed, and for a unified tone where comedy did not explicitly mingle with the treatment of serious matters. All these important criteria were to be handed down to writers of tragedy in seventeenth-century France.

But the succession was not immediate, for the first quarter of the century saw few tragedies written or performed. It is possible only to speculate on the reasons for this, it being sometimes suggested that after a long period of wars of religion the French wanted relaxation rather than the intellectual demands of tragedy, while the assassination of Henri IV in 1610 did nothing to establish the stable social and political climate which appears to be the most favourable atmosphere in which serious drama can flourish. Be that as it may, the opening three decades and more of the seventeenth century were largely given over to dramatic forms other than tragedy, including pastorals and tragi-comedies (with a strong Italian influence) and heroic comedies. The range of drama enjoyed in France at this time is similar to Polonius's list in *Hamlet*: 'tragedy, comedy, history, pastoral, pastoral-comical, historical-pastoral, tragical-historical, tragical-comical-historical-pastoral, scene individable, or poem unlimited'. When tragedy as such was performed, it frequently contained violent, bloodthirsty scenes. For example, Alexandre Hardy's *Scédase*, published in 1624, depicts a double rape and killing, the rape being represented on the stage.

The need to produce escapist drama of various kinds and the establishment in Paris of companies of professional actors combined to give the French theatre the impetus it needed. The native tradition of tragedy was held in abeyance, and when the genre reappeared in the 1630s it had already advanced considerably, incorporating some of the aims and techniques, if not the form or tone, of the less dignified species it replaced. With the exception of a few years in the 1650s, tragedy was to hold the stage for over forty years, from Jean Mairet's *Sophonisbe* (1634) to Racine's *Phèdre* (1677), although tragi-comedies continued to be written in large numbers until the early sixties. It is conventional to split the period into two main parts: the era of Corneille, whose major tragedies date from 1635 to 1651; and that of Racine, whose nine secular tragedies span the years 1664 to 1677. Of course, literary history does not fall into neat sections, but it is feasible and useful to talk, in general terms, of the generation of 1630— Pierre Corneille and his contemporaries such as Jean Mairet, Tristan l'Hermite or Jean Rotrou—and the generation of 1660: Jean Racine and other writers of tragedy such as Thomas Corneille, the brother of Pierre, and Philippe Quinault.

This division is not merely chronological. As subsequent chapters will show, the concept of tragedy changes between the second and third quarters of the century. Again, it is possible to relate the difference to political and social pressures, although such parallels must always be drawn with great caution. Just as the aftermath of wars in the sixteenth century appears to have destroyed the mood for tragedy towards the end of the reign of Henri IV and during the regency of his mother, Marie de Médicis, so the civil wars of the Fronde (1648–53) may have had a decisive influence on the literature of the 1650s, ensuring that both the novel and drama concentrated, not on intellectually demanding issues, but rather on the sentimental story, the whodunnit and the thriller. In the theatre a perfect example is Thomas Corneille's *Timocrate* (1656), which with some eighty consecutive performances enjoyed the longest first run of any play in seventeenth-century France. This equivalent of *The Mousetrap* is labelled a tragedy by its author, but it shares with many other plays of the decade features which are at least equally tragi-comic. A skilfully constructed and constantly entertaining piece, it depends for its success on the dual rôle of the male lead, Timocrate, king of Crete, who, though committed to battle with Argos, appears there under the name of Cléomène in order to seek the hand of the Argive queen's daughter, Eriphile. Beneath the surface improbabilities of the plot are important studies of the widowed queen, torn between different courses of action, and of Eriphile, whose love for Cléomène is prevented by her scruples about his lowly rank until she learns of his true identity.

The 'tragedies' of Thomas Corneille and Quinault in the mid and late 1650s are exactly contemporary with the interminable, shapeless novels of the post-Fronde years, with their digressions, episodes and lengthy biographies. The *précieux* salons both spawned and then dissected the works of, for example, Madeleine de Scudéry, whose multi-volume romances are set in the Middle East (*Artamène ou le Grand Cyrus*, 1649–53, 13,000 pages) or Rome (*Clélie*, 1654–60, a mere 7000 pages) and consist of endless disguise, duels, rivalries, battles, oversubtle love plots ... and excessive decorum in attitudes towards the passions.

On either side of the divide of the 1650s pure tragedy flourishes. A later chapter will seek to define some of the issues raised by consideration of the tragic itself, but generally speaking it is convenient to see the plays of the 1635–50 period as based on a heroic ethic, a view of a man as optimistic, active, self-sufficient, yet still fallible and open to awareness of failure. By the late 1640s, with the last tragedies of Rotrou, the inactive non- or anti-hero has arrived, and it is possible to interpret the literature of the 1650s as an unconscious or possibly even deliberate parody of the self-mastering hero of Pierre Corneille. When tragedy proper returns around 1660, the mood is already different: forcefulness and criminality are accompanied by feelings of remorse and jealousy. The plays of the early 60s are thus an important lead-in to the thirteen years of Racine's main career and to his drama, where particular importance is now attached to the emotions, especially the passion of love, and from which any general code of values appears to be largely absent. Over the forty years or so during which classical tragedy (in our sense of the term) flourishes, it is quite possible to see a progression—not in the sense of a continual improvement in technique, although some would maintain this, but rather the evolution of a tradition, starting from what seems to us now, with hindsight, a surprisingly liberal, avant-garde view of the tragic and moving gradually, under pressure of events inside and outside the theatre, towards a more conventional interpretation.

That, then, is the background to our study. The chapters which follow this Introduction adopt a sequence which perhaps requires some explanation. Aiming as it does to provide preliminary reading for those approaching French classical tragedy for the first time, the book seeks— indeed is obliged—to take into account both material considerations and matters concerned with dramatic theory; a work of a different scope or prepared for a different audience might pursue just one or other of these two orders of problem. Our central purpose must be to contribute to an understanding of the major plays of the period in and for themselves, and to this end, after considering the purposes of tragedy, we begin by examining practical matters—conditions of staging, the nature and expectations of the public, and publication. These all explain, to some degree, the forms adopted. Thus the chapter on staging raises questions about the unities, the structure of acts, the need to maintain dramatic tension, the manner of the speaking of parts and hence (to some extent) the language of the play—items dealt with in subsequent chapters. The nature of the audience and its expectations help to account in some measure for the very subject-matter of tragedy, the changes in it in the course of the century, and the notions of verisimilitude and decorum treated later in the book. Even a matter like publication, which may seem extraneous to an appreciation of dramatic texts, is not to be neglected, for the play in performance is only one of two forms in which it appears, both in its own day and subsequently. Printing is a necessary corollary to staging and to an understanding of the playwright's total audience.

These three chapters (Chapters 2–4) are thus seen as a basis for the discussion of theoretical matters which, we would contend, should occupy the greater part of the work. Chapters 5 to 12 guide the reader gradually into the various aspects of a seventeenth-century tragedy, starting on the outside, as it were, with the sources and proceeding through the overall form and the three unities to individual considerations such as action and plot, characters, language, and proprieties and ending with a chapter which examines in some detail the tragic itself. A final topic, covered in Chapter 13, is criticism: not modern critical perspectives but, rather, seventeenth-century reaction to the staged or printed tragedies of the period. All of these discussions are related, wherever possible, to precise examples drawn from major plays, principally those of Pierre Corneille and Racine, written and performed in a half-century which saw very considerable and often heated debate about numerous matters of dramatic theory, some trivial but many crucial.

1 Purposes

Of all the various points raised in this book, perhaps the most tricky is that concerning the fundamental aim of tragedy. Now discussion here and later cannot claim to limit itself neatly to self-contained chapters; there is bound to be overlapping between subjects. Indeed such continuing discussion may be no bad thing, for it can help to emphasise the interdependence of the various component parts of a tragedy and the factors which have a bearing on its success. Nor can the treatment claim to be exhaustive; no one can explain different people's responses to a play or adequately define the enjoyment they, as individuals, should or do get out of it.

The most that subsequent chapters can hope to achieve is to touch on areas and topics which may, when taken together, form a picture of the conventions within which writers of French classical tragedies necessarily had to work, the practical restrictions and the opportunities they faced. In looking at these points, we are bound to touch, if only in passing, on the reasons why they wrote in the first place. Yet how explicit were even those aims which, three hundred years later, we now believe we can detect?

It was suggested in the introduction that the production of tragedy in seventeenth-century France could be related to fairly well-defined periods: the height of Cardinal Richelieu's ministerial powers in the late 20s and the 30s and then, after the gap formed by the civil wars of the Fronde, the two decades of the 60s and 70s, from the advent of Louis XIV as an adult king to, say, the death in 1683 of his queen, Maria Theresa. Not all good tragedies occur within these relatively stable periods, and by no means all the plays performed in those years were tragedies. Yet, while it is unwise to attribute the appearance of any literary form solely to the prevailing political or economic climate, a play in particular, as a spectacle to be mounted as well as a text to be read, can be seen as a means of celebrating and even explaining the contemporary mood and attitudes to life. At times it may go further and become a vehicle for political propaganda. Behind many writers stand patrons, known and unknown. The theatre, with the immediate impact of a first night followed by subsequent performances in the same or later seasons, is an ideal medium through which powerful men can express their influence.

Given the hierarchical structure of seventeenth-century society, we should expect to find much literary patronage. Almost all the major authors in France at the time were of bourgeois rather than aristocratic stock: certainly even the best writers of tragedy had no private income to fall back on. So it is that, at least while they establish their reputations, Corneille and Racine dedicate their plays to individuals who have shown financial or other practical interest in their work.

Almost always such dedications were to people other than the king. Yet the monarchy itself played a large part in theatrical life at the time. Henri IV, at the beginning of the century, had economic problems to cope with, and on his death the regent, Marie de Médicis, had other preoccupations, too. But when Cardinal Richelieu became Louis XIII's chief minister in 1624, things started to change. The emergence of tragedy as the dominant genre is in no small measure due to his influence. Of course, such encouragement was far from disinterested: Richelieu saw writers, including dramatists, as a means by which he, and the king he served, could exert political pressures and put forward a particular view of the state. However Richelieu was also a man with a genuine interest in the arts. His support of Corneille, Rotrou and other writers was in large part due to his fondness for literature. He approved an annual grant of 12,000 livres to the Hôtel de Bourgogne, the main Paris theatre operating early in the century, and was instrumental in setting up a rival to it, the Théâtre du Marais, providing a subsidy of 6000 livres, equivalent to twice the annual rent. In 1641 he established a theatre in his own Palais-Cardinal, and it is no coincidence that that same spring Louis XIII issued a declaration in which he ruled that actors should not have their profession held against them and that their public reputation should not thereby be affected.

It is difficult for us now, so long after the event, to separate the various pressures at work on, say, Pierre Corneille. How much was gratitude to Richelieu for his support of drama and for particular favours shown, and how much do Corneille's tragedies, like those of colleagues such as Rotrou, with their insistence on politics and political motives, simply reflect seventeenth-century man's acceptance of an authoritarian régime? In Corneille's case, for example, Richelieu's attacks on the style, the irregular structure and the 'improper' behaviour of Rodrigue and Chimène in *Le Cid* (1637), expressed through third parties, meant that his support was mixed with criticism. Richelieu died just five years later and Corneille's attitude to his benefactor remains ambivalent.

Of all forms of drama, tragedy is obviously the best vehicle for the spreading of political ideas. Imaginative literature can be a means to strictly utilitarian ends, which in Richelieu's and Louis XIII's case was the establishment of absolutism. *Le Cid* depicts a king whose power does not go unchallenged by one of his generals, Chimène's father Don Gomès. Although Corneille's next play, *Horace* (1640), shows a monarch dependent on one of his subjects—Tulle has to forgive the title-character's crimes so that Horace may serve and thereby save the state—the king is not without at least moments of decisiveness and he remains the final arbiter. The third play in this central tetralogy, *Cinna* (1642), ends with the self-mastery of Auguste and the acceptance by the defeated conspirators of both his clemency and his imperial authority. The change from this kind of political tragedy—widespread in the 1630s and 1640s, but later, after 1660, seen as at best an anachronism—to the more patently emotional tragedy of the Racinian period is not explained by just the desire for something new. The analysis of political actions, the establishing of political priorities, the resulting clash between public duty and private will, between reason of state and the desires of the individual, had all been aired by Corneille, Mairet and Rotrou, but this fertile seam had not been worked out. If, when tragedy returned around 1660, a new mood prevailed, it was partly because by then, almost twenty years after Richelieu's disappearance, absolute monarchy had become accepted as a way of life.

Drama, then, can act as a vehicle for political reform, or at least as a powerful means of commenting on current political attitudes. On the one hand we find Louis XIII, through his minister Richelieu, working towards a form of centralised government, and not hesitating to achieve this, where necessary, by the violent suppression of political opponents. On the other a playwright like Corneille, through Auguste in *Cinna*, appears to suggest (and it is not made more explicit than this) that absolutism need not be synonymous with dictatorship: the emperor, conscious of his own past crimes, arrives at an enlightened, essentially human form of control over his subjects.

The theatre could be an excellent social weapon too, a means towards changes in society. This is particularly the case with comedy, where the subject-matter is much less historical and the characters more middle-class than in tragedy. Molière's many farces and full-scale comedies contain criticism, at times satirical criticism, of the contemporary medical and legal professions, the state of the Catholic church, parent-child relationships within families and so on, as well as less specifically seventeenth-century attacks on hypocrisy, avarice, hypochondria and the like. Racine's one comedy, *Les Plaideurs* (1668), serves the same purpose. There is still much discussion about the extent to which comedies at this period contained 'ideas', 'messages' or 'theories' at all and how far they aimed at merely amusing the audience. Study of this, as well as of the influence of the literary salons and the prose fiction inspired by and then examined in them, falls outside the scope of this book. As far as tragedy is concerned, it is possible, as in other periods and countries, to notice how often the action turns on the difference in age between the characters and the misunderstandings this generation gap can cause. The youthfulness—and hence inexperience—of the children is contrasted with the often guilt-ridden and uncomprehending behaviour of their elders.

Richelieu's successor, Cardinal Mazarin, was of Italian extraction, becoming a naturalised Frenchman in 1639, only three years before Richelieu died. The new minister lacked his predecessor's wide interests and drive, and his preference in the arts was, naturally enough, for forms of stagecraft more in keeping with Italy: opera and spectacular productions. It fell to Nicolas Fouquet, the equivalent of a finance minister, to distribute patronage, which he did, for example, to the poet La Fontaine and to Pierre Corneille, encouraging the latter to return to the theatre in 1659 by proposing three subjects as suitable for tragedy. Fouquet's disgrace and Mazarin's death coincided with Louis XIV's assumption of full powers in 1661. Like his predecessors on the throne, the Sun King was understandably less interested in tragedy than in fostering more relaxing types of play, comedies, comedy-ballets and spectaculars. Yet although he acted as an avid supporter of Molière, who wrote many of his plays for court performance, he was also the patron of, for example, Quinault and Racine. In 1662, with the help of Jean Chapelain, among other things editor of *Les Sentiments de l'Académie Française sur la tragi-comédie du Cid* (1637), Colbert drew up for him a list of authors deemed worthy to receive annual subsidies. Pierre Corneille, as the 'first dramatist in the world', was awarded 2000 livres, his younger brother Thomas—also a prolific playwright—getting 1000 livres. The young Racine started more modestly with 800 livres a year, rising eventually to the 2000 livres his contemporary Quinault was also granted. It was only financial difficulties which caused the state to reduce the payments over twenty-five years later.

The monarchy was thus a vital patron of the arts in the heyday of classical tragedy, and it would be idle to suppose that motives were all disinterested. As with much more recent French heads of state, prestige was a factor: Paris as a cultural centre emphasised Richelieu's and Louis XIV's desire to centralise administration in the capital. But there appears to have been a clearer link between financial support and the ideological content of literary works in seventeenth-century France than there is in modern times. Although it would be unwise to attribute a particular tragedy, and the 'message' it may be thought to convey, solely to an individual patron's pressure, however indirect, this is an element which one cannot discount entirely.

If we look at the main tragedies of Corneille and Racine, we find that those in the first part of their careers were prefaced on publication, not only by the customary explanation 'To the reader' or its equivalent, but also by a dedication to an important individual benefactor. The practice died out once both reputations were well established. Corneille's earliest tragedy *Médée*, published in 1639, has a letter in which the dramatist reminds a certain Mr P.T.N.G. (otherwise unknown) that the play had pleased him when first performed four years previously. *Le Cid*, published a few weeks after its triumphal success in January 1637, is dedicated to Mme de Combalet, Richelieu's widowed niece, and in the dedication Corneille thanks her for her approval and support of the play and, through her, her uncle for recent political favours to his family. His next tragedy, *Horace*, he dedicates to Richelieu himself, despite (or because of?) the *Cid* affair. How can he ever show gratitude for all the minister's kindnesses? 'It is by [your goodness] that I have all that I am; and it is not without blushing that, by way of recognition, I make you a present which is so unworthy of you and so out of proportion to what I owe you.' Similar signs of gratitude can be found with *Polyeucte*—Corneille apologises for having waited so long before dedicating the play to the regent, Anne of Austria—*Pompée*, where Mazarin's Roman links are compared to the title-character's, and later *Oedipe*: here the ambitious Fouquet, who had suggested the subject, is regaled with eighty-four lines of verse.

Racine's first five tragedies have similar thank-you letters. After finding a protector in the duc de Saint-Aignan for *La Thébaïde*, he dedicates his second play, *Alexandre le Grand*, to the king, a latter-day conqueror but with a difference: 'Already your Majesty has reached the peak of glory by a newer and more difficult route than that taken by Alexander.' After addressing *Andromaque* to Henrietta of England, Louis's sister-in-law, who had helped him with the text and shed 'a few tears' when he first read it to her, Racine dedicates *Britannicus* to an influential young

Jansenist friend, the duc de Chevreuse, and finally *Bérénice* to the minister Colbert, Chevreuse's father-in-law and one of the dramatist's most important patrons.

The fulsome praise of so many seventeenth-century dedicatory epistles strikes the modern reader as quaint, even at times embarrassing. But in the light of a more highly structured society than our own it can be seen as largely conventional. Dramatists were genuinely grateful for financial support, and the younger among them need not be accused of obsequiousness in wanting to thank their elders and betters for showing an interest in their work. Of course, not all patronage was free from self-seeking. *Cinna*, published in 1643, is prefaced by a letter to the financier M. de Montauron, in which Corneille compares the generosity of the Emperor Augustus in the play to his benefactor's liberality. But it is now known that Montauron paid Corneille 2000 livres merely to have the work dedicated to him. By the late 1660s a critic like Gabriel Guéret could condemn the purchase of eulogies: in *Le Parnasse réformé* (1668) he advocates cutting lies out of literary dedications and banning 'panegyrics à la Montauron'. The practice of inserting *dédicaces* was dying out anyway, Racine's last being the letter to Colbert which prefaced *Bérénice* when it appeared in 1671. It would be quite wrong, in any case, to exaggerate the pressures brought to bear on dramatists. In very many instances, as we shall see, writers of tragedy appear to have chosen their subjects without any attempt at social or political comment, and patrons came to their aid in an often quite disinterested way.

A large number of authors of the period had, almost as their motto, the dual aim to please and instruct, *plaire et instruire*. As far as tragedy is concerned, how can we interpret the term 'pleasure'? It seems almost paradoxical to expect a literary form dealing invariably with human crises and often with death to arouse enjoyment and delight in the audience or reader. Yet both Corneille and Racine, in their critical writings, state that this is one of their chief goals. In this, they are merely following the example set by Aristotle, who stresses the aesthetic approach to tragedy: 'Though the objects themselves may be painful to see,' Chapter 4 of the *Poetics* tells us, 'we delight to view the most realistic representations of them in art,' while 'not every kind of pleasure should be required of a tragedy, but only its own proper pleasure. The tragic pleasure is that of pity and fear, and the poet has to produce it by a work of imitation' (Chapter 14). The dedicatory epistle to the tragedy *Médée* has Corneille saying that '[the aim] of dramatic poetry is to please, and the rules it lays down are only ingenious means to allow the dramatist to do so, rather than reasons by which the audience is convinced to like something when they dislike it'. Over twenty years later, Corneille chooses to open the first of his three discourses on drama (1660) with a reminder that pleasure is an integral part of a dramatist's aim. Eleven years after this, in a spirited and at times sarcastic reply to critics who had found the subject-matter of *Bérénice* rather thin, Racine says in the preface to that play: 'What more do they want? I beg them . . . not to think that a play which moves them and gives them pleasure can be entirely against the rules. The principal rule is to please and to move. All the others are only made in order that this first one can be fulfilled.'

The defence that Racine puts forward touches on a topic to be treated in a later chapter. For if the 'rules' governing subject-matter and structure allow a dramatist to fashion a moving play, it follows, he would argue, that a tragedy which pleases cannot be said to contravene these same rules. If so, the theatregoer's or reader's task is simplified: all he need do is trust his instinct. Pleasure can be gained either from the content of a play or from its form—it may satisfy by its dramatic qualities—or, most commonly, by a combination of both. As we shall see, the debate about the unities, about verisimilitude, about the observance of the proprieties is one which playwrights take part in but which major dramatists in the end find largely irrelevant. If Corneille comes to opt for a flexible, unconventional form of tragedy and sticks by his early beliefs despite critics' attacks, and if Racine, generally keeping closer to the 'rules', at times goes beyond them and creates an even stricter, more purified brand of tragedy, each has at heart the desire to write enjoyable plays, faithful in their different ways to the aim of showing man struggling against the odds or to the 'majestic sadness' which, the preface to *Bérénice* claims, 'constitutes the whole pleasure' of Racinian tragedy.

Racine, with his *plaire et toucher*, may not here specifically say that tragedy should instruct as well as please, but the omission is purely formal. Of course the call for 'tristesse majestueuse' reveals his preference for audience emotion, an approach which plays down the importance of didactic drama. As Maurice Descotes points out in *Le public de théâtre et son histoire* (1964), mid seventeenth-century France witnessed not just a shift towards love-plots suited to the growing bourgeois female audience but also the incidence of open weeping in the theatre. Nonetheless Racine's own criticism of his characters, as seen in his various prefaces, and in particular his remarks about vice and virtue in *Phèdre*, indicate that a moral code is at least implicit in his tragedies. Truly didactic literature, of course, is rare; claims to have produced such works sometimes merely hide a desire to escape censure, a wish to see a criticised or banned text printed or played. Molière's suggestion that the final version of his controversial *Tartuffe* fits in with comedy's aim of 'correcting human vices' is a case in point. More often, the notion of instruction is included because it is the done thing. Instead of explicit moral improvement, the most that authors can usually hope for is that their readers will see the message in the work and learn the lesson. In other words, the 'usefulness' which Horace, in his *Art of poetry*, added to Aristotle's 'pleasurableness' can rarely go beyond the point of view which Corneille adopts in his critical writings: moral purpose can perhaps best be achieved, the *Discours du poème dramatique* (1660) suggests, by 'la naïve peinture des vices et des vertus', where the audience is left to make up its own mind between clearly differentiated alternatives.

But even this presupposes a clear message, a single lesson, and few texts are as definite as that. Certain contemporary theatregoers, at least, saw as the centre of interest of Corneille's *Cinna* the emotional relationship between the two main conspirators, the leader Emilie and the more unwilling Cinna, rather than the unexpected clemency of Auguste, 'which one thinks little about', the prince de Conti said in his *Traité de la comédie* (1666), 'and which none of the audience gave a thought to praising as they left the theatre'. It is precisely the moral development of the emperor which many modern readers and audiences consider to be the highlight of the play. Or what is the lesson to be learnt from Corneille's *Horace*? Is there indeed only one, since even the title-character, innocent at the beginning, moves through the killing in battle of close relatives who are Rome's enemies to the murder of his own sister and, finally, in Act V, to a seeming unwillingness to repent? Is Curiace, his chief victim, 'innocent' or 'guilty'? How do we place Camille? Is her humanity to be preferred to the rigid patriotism of her brother Horace? And what of the other members of the family? What, again, is the correct focus by which we can judge *Polyeucte*, a tragedy whose main character appears to combine the Christian fervour of a neophyte and the self-centred pride of a mere human?

Although our knowledge of contemporary reaction to these tragedies—three of the most famous of Corneille—is severely limited by lack of documents, it is unlikely that audiences of the time were much less aware than we are of the different possible interpretations they contain. Plays of this kind, or those where moral conventions are flouted, aroused the anger of conservative critics. The Académie-Française's disapproval of *Le Cid* in 1637 extended to the apparently open ending (will Rodrigue marry Chimène eventually or not?) but turned on the unacceptable relationship between a girl and her father's murderer. Early on in the year's controversy over the play, before Richelieu stepped in and referred the matter to the newly-fledged Académie, Corneille's rival Georges de Scudéry, in his *Observations sur le Cid*, insisted on the didactic purpose of drama: 'Le poème de théâtre fut inventé pour instruire en divertissant'. Pleasure is secondary to moral instruction; the end must be to show virtue rewarded and wrong-doing always punished. Not long afterwards, in the first version of the *Sentiments de l'Académie Française sur le Cid*, Chapelain is less definite: the aim of drama is not clear, for the man in the street believes in pleasure as a goal, whereas others say that it is through pleasure that dramatic poetry 'imperceptibly purges the soul of some of its wrongful habits'. In *Le Cid* and in other plays, for example *Rodogune*, Corneille's portrayal of characters who overstep the commonly accepted limits of morality does not necessarily imply that we must take sides for or against. As we shall see later, the emotions which tragedy properly arouses in an audience are wide-ranging; few characters are so immoral or amoral as to have no redeeming features with which we can empathise or even identify.

Like the human life it represents, tragedy is rarely black or white. Shakespeare's King John or Richard III, for example, are not unmitigated criminals, characters with nothing to be said for them. Cléopâtre in Corneille's *Rodogune* descends to the depths of criminality, yet she has a quality of soul and a purposefulness which arouse astonishment at the same time as criticism. Racine's Phèdre may seem a clear-cut case—the dramatist maintains, in the preface to the play, that in no previous tragedy of his does virtue stand in a better light:

> The slightest faults are severely punished. The mere thought of crime is regarded with no less horror than crime itself. The failings of love are treated as real failings. The passions are offered to view only to show all the ravages they create. And vice is everywhere painted in such hues that its hideous face may be recognised and loathed.

But Phèdre

> is not altogether guilty, and not altogether innocent. She is drawn by her destiny and the anger of the Gods into an unlawful passion which she is the first to hold in horror. She makes every endeavour to overcome it. She chooses death rather than disclose it to anyone. And when forced to reveal it, she speaks of it with such shame and confusion as to leave no doubt that her crime is rather a punishment from the Gods than an impulse of her own will.

One could discuss at length what Racine understood by 'destiny' and 'the

Gods' in this particular case, but few readers would disagree that *Phèdre* offers in its title-character, and in some of the other characters too, a fascinating and very natural combination of guilt and innocence which it is well-nigh impossible to disentangle.

Blame can be widely attributed, then, and both playwrights and audience may be allowed to sit on the fence, as it were, drawing a number of apparently almost self-contradictory conclusions rather than just one message from a single play. Vices and virtues are shown within the same character—the guilt of Phèdre's stepson in his loving Aricie, for example, is matched by the innocence of his passion compared to that of Phèdre—or they can be distributed among different characters, and the audience makes up its mind in each individual case and in relation to the play as a whole. If instruction can be interpreted in this broad sense, then it is fair to claim that all French classical tragedy posited a moral function.

However, this aim is always secondary to the purely emotional response. Yet the area of the emotions to be worked on is limited, in theory if not in practice. The Church's opposition to the acting profession and hence to believers' attendance at the theatre meant that religion could rarely feature on the professional stage; sacred tragedies were largely confined to amateur performances in the Jesuit colleges or to schools like Saint-Cyr, for which Racine wrote *Esther* and *Athalie*. The appearance of Corneille's martyr-play *Polyeucte* in 1642–3 gave rise to strong criticism. Clerics such as the abbé d'Aubignac maintained, in *La Pratique du théâtre* (1657), that Christian subjects must be avoided, at least if insufficient time and skill were available to explain fully to men both the 'God-given marvels' contained in the plot and the thoughtless rejection of them by certain of the characters. Even a sceptic and confirmed Cornelian like Saint-Evremond could state around 1674 that 'the spirit of our religion is directly opposed to that of tragedy'. The humility and patience of our saints, he wrote in *De la tragédie ancienne et moderne*, were too contrary to the heroic qualities demanded of stage characters. This was indeed the problem: the combination of saintliness and the heroism necessary for drama often turned what was intended to be a religious play into a quasi-secular one. Religious tragedies, such as those on Christian themes written by Grenaille, La Serre, Baro or La Calprenède, decreased rapidly in number not long after 1640.

So far, various reasons have been suggested to account for the incidence of tragedy in seventeenth-century France. Along with other forms of drama, of course, it appears to have been stimulated by patronage or the desire for patronage, as well as by a wish to comment on and even change the current political and possibly social systems. Much more frequently tragedies were written for purely aesthetic reasons. But it is difficult to draw a clear distinction between pleasure or delight on the one hand and a utilitarian aim on the other, for although the concepts were used, they were linked by 'and' rather than by 'or'. Another purpose behind the writing of French classical tragedy must be mentioned, too: the down-to-earth desire to get the better of a rival dramatist, achieved either by choosing a *subject* previously treated by him or—more subtly—by invading the territory or *thematic area* occupied by the rival and attempting to beat him at his own game.

A good example of the latter approach is Racine's tragedy *Britannicus*, performed in 1669. Until then, the young dramatist had avoided Roman subjects, the preserve of his main predecessor Corneille. But after the great success of *Andromaque* in 1667, Racine appears to have decided to show he was a master of subjects other than those inspired by Greece. The comedy *Les Plaideurs* (1668) can be judged as a bid—and a successful bid—to match Molière in the field of comedy. The following year the story of the Britannicus episode in the early life of Nero gives Racine a chance to outshine Corneille. On this occasion, the purpose is made fairly explicit: behind the answers he gives to criticism of characters in the play, Racine, in his first preface of 1670, launches into a barely veiled attack on his chief rival and his methods:

> What must one do to satisfy judges who are so hard to please? It would be easy, provided one were prepared to deny common sense. All one would have to do would be to depart from the natural and plunge into the extraordinary. Instead of a simple action with minimal content, the sort appropriate to an action which occurs in a single day and which, gradually moving to its conclusion, is sustained only by the characters' interests, feelings and emotions, you would fill out the said action with a host of incidents which could only take place in a month, with a large amount of stage business, all the more surprising for being less and less credible, and with endless declamations by which the actors would be made to say the very opposite of what they should say.

Having tested the ground in this, his first Roman tragedy, Racine could go on in his next play, *Bérénice*, to construct five acts and some fifteen hundred lines on another Roman subject which, he boasts, has almost no content at all: 'I had long wished to see if I could make a tragedy with that simplicity of action which was so much relished by the Ancients . . . There are those who think this simplicity betrays lack of invention. They do not reflect that, on the contrary, the whole of invention consists in making something out of nothing.' So having mastered Corneille's favourite subject-matter, the author of *Phèdre* proceeds to eclipse him in the matter of structural simplicity. No other writer of French classical tragedy reaches quite the same level of brutal frankness. Yet it would be unwise to forget that the more important dramatists of the period, at least, were often moved to write by a fierce spirit of rivalry. For them, the task was particularly difficult. It is the job of a leading writer to innovate rather than copy, to set trends rather than merely follow them. As readers and audiences tend to be conservative, and prefer what is familiar, early plays in the new mould meet with resistance and, by a process of self-defence, the dramatist justifies his new approach by implied or direct condemnation of that of his predecessors or contemporaries. Neither Corneille nor Racine lacked false modesty in promoting their own individual brands of tragedy. Behind both the failures and the successes lay the constant need to update, to keep one step ahead of rivals and of public taste. It is in this relatively insecure context rather than in the world of the ivory tower that we must judge how well each coped with the task of writing 'pleasurable' and 'instructive' plays.

2 Staging

A play, we would maintain, only reaches its ultimate form when it passes from the final manuscript draft to the stage itself. Indeed, this order of priorities was followed, quite unconsciously, in seventeenth-century France, since plays were not printed or sold until their first run in the theatre was at an end. Yet it is precisely the transfer from text to live stage which the academic study of drama in school or university finds most difficult to achieve. All literature requires the imaginative response of the reader, but none more so than a comedy or particularly a tragedy, in which movement, groupings, silences, as well as the atmosphere of the stage setting itself, add to the words of the text and impinge on its meaning.

It is only fair to say that our knowledge of staging in seventeenth-century France is still far from complete. Much postwar research has given us a good deal of material on the two main Paris theatres in which the bulk of tragedies were performed: the Hôtel de Bourgogne, first established in the middle of the sixteenth century, and the Théâtre du Marais, which came into being in 1629 before moving finally, in 1634, to permanent premises in the Jeu de Paume du Marais, the scene of Pierre Corneille's first major successes until the troupe started diversifying into hybrid genres such as machine-plays. But information about the theatre in provincial France is still very sketchy and will inevitably remain so. Georges Mongrédien, researching the period, has found about one thousand professional actors in all and some two hundred wandering troupes, while the Lyonnais Samuel Chappuzeau, in his *Théâtre français* of 1674, indicates that at that time, towards the end of the vogue for tragedy in France, there were some twelve to fifteen provincial theatre companies, serving, as he says, as training-grounds for the Paris theatres. The repertory of these itinerant troupes was not, of course, limited to tragedy, or indeed to plays which have survived in print. The playwright Molière himself, as actor and manager of a group of players, toured central, western and south-western France for thirteen years from 1645, performing tragedies as well as his own and other people's comedies and farces. Although some towns in Italy, for example, already had proper theatre buildings, it would appear that throughout our period provincial France made do without purpose-built theatres. This at first sight rather surprising fact is of supreme importance for the subsequent design of seventeenth-century French professional theatres and the positioning and shape of the stage. As early as 1588 or very shortly afterwards, the author Montaigne, in the famous chapter 'On the institution and education of children' in the first book of his *Essais*, had suggested it would be (in the words of John Florio's 1603 English translation)

> reasonable, that Princes should sometimes, at their proper charges, gratifie the common people with plays, as an argument of a fatherly affection, and loving goodnesse towards them: and that in populous and frequented cities there should be Theatres and places appointed for such spectacles; as a diverting of worse inconveniences, and secret actions.

But his suggestion was not taken up. Wandering troupes would perform where they could, in inns, for example, as Paul Scarron recounts early on in his novel *Le Roman comique* (1651–7), devoted to the adventures of an itinerant group of actors who arrive one day in Le Mans.

A more permanent and suitable location was the local *jeu de paume* or indoor tennis-court, whose rectangular shape dictated the layout of theatre buildings for the whole of the seventeenth century. The chance visits of itinerant actors, coupled in many areas with the regular production of school plays at the Jesuit colleges, provided the only live dramatic fare which Frenchmen outside the capital could enjoy. It was an intermittent pleasure; as in so many fields, everything centred on Paris.

In Volume I of her book *Le Théâtre du Marais* (1954) Mme S. W. Deierkauf-Holsboer gives a description of the interior layout of the Marais theatre which more recent studies have only served to confirm. The company started life in various *jeux de paume* in the Marais district of Paris, on the right bank of the Seine near the Hôtel de Ville; by 1634, with a five-year lease, it occupied its own rectangular building—a former tennis-court measuring some 34.5 by 11.7 metres and converted rapidly, at no great expense. Ten years later, after a fire, a slightly larger version of the Marais theatre was constructed, probably measuring at least 38 by 12 metres. Inside, down both sidewalls, were two rows of *loges* or boxes, one above the other, each tier containing nine boxes. These measured 1.95 metres across, about 1.3 metres deep and 1.95 metres high, and each contained two benches and a folding seat. At the end of the theatre opposite the stage were two tiers of four *loges* with the same dimensions but containing three chairs rather than benches. Above the second tier of *loges* down each side of the building ran a *paradis* or gods, containing a long bench and a guardrail. The boxes at the far end were possibly surmounted by an *amphithéâtre*, 7.8 metres wide and 4.75 metres deep, with rows of benches rising steeply to the back, although some critics, quoting the definition given in Furetière's dictionary of 1690, see the *amphithéâtre* as occupying the rear of the pit or ground floor, raised above this floor level but with the double tier of four *loges* on top. Richelet's dictionary of ten years earlier is unhelpfully vague on the matter.

The gently raked main stage was raised at the front some two metres above the level of the floor of the building and measured 11.7 by 12.7 metres, although the depth of the playing area was only some 9.75 metres, extended to 12.5 in 1644.

But at the Marais, as in other converted tennis-courts or theatres built to that design, patrons who were seated made up only part of the audience. The area of floor in the centre bounded by the *loges* and the stage formed the *parterre* or pit; apart from a very narrow bench along the sides, holding at most perhaps eighty people, there was no seating there at all. The Marais pit measured some 11.7 metres across and 19.8 metres in length, and here the majority of the spectators stood and watched what they could of the performance.

The layout of the theatre's interior had its effect on the nature of the theatrical experience and, no doubt, on the audience's expectations. The modern traditional theatre, originated by sixteenth-century Italian designers such as Serlio and Sabbattini, consists of a fan-shaped or horseshoe auditorium, a semi-circular area of seats looking towards a stage outlined by a picture-frame proscenium arch within which hangs the curtain. Around the inner walls of the building are tiers of balconies. More recent theatre design may offer a different shape, a stepped auditorium with, perhaps, a gallery over the rear portion. Alternatively there is theatre-in-the-round, where the actors are enclosed by the audience on at least three sides. This was one form of staging in Shakespeare's England, for example at the Globe Theatre, founded in 1599. It was a hexagonal building on the outside, the inner courtyard which formed the theatre being circular. Running round the walls were three tiers of galleries for the audience, many of whom also stood at ground level in the yard or sat on stools on stage. The platform stage itself, almost square at 43 feet across and 39½ feet deep, projected out into the middle of the courtyard, a few feet above the ground. Over part of this stage was a thatched roof or 'heavens', carried on pillars. There was, of course, no proscenium arch but rather a permanent façade at the back of the stage, often of various levels.

Apart from the upper area in the heavens, above the stage and also at the rear, at the second level of the back façade, there existed an inner, curtained area or stage within the main structure of the building. All these locations, together with the fact that the stage projected out into the courtyard, gave the Elizabethan theatre a very flexible playing-area. Parts of the Globe, though, were open to the skies; winter performances had to be held at the Blackfriars Theatre in the City, a roofed, rectangular theatre probably measuring some 45 feet by 50–65 feet, and charging higher prices. Even so Shakespeare, as dramatist and actor, had the benefit of logical, adaptable theatre buildings, holding large numbers of people (perhaps two thousand at the Globe) in a remarkably small area and achieving a great sense of intimacy and audience involvement.

But in France the shape of the *jeu de paume* dictated that the stage occupied one end of the rectangle, with the audience, maybe numbering fifteen hundred at a full house, stretching back along the rest of the length, looking at the stage straight ahead from the pit, the end *loges* and the *amphithéâtre* or from sideways on if they occupied a seat in the lateral *loges* or the gods. The main consequence of this layout—retained when the Marais *jeu de paume* was destroyed by fire in 1644 and subsequently rebuilt—was that more of the audience were at a greater distance from the action on stage than in the case of a modern theatre. One effect, as we shall see, was to turn the level pit, occupied in part by the lower classes, into a rowdy and at times dangerous area. For, quite apart from the type of person who went there, visibility was poor: the top of the tallest spectator's head was still lower than the front of the stage. Indeed one can only wonder whether even the occupants of the distant *loges* and *amphithéâtre*, as well as spectators in the rear section of the *parterre*, were not more interested in social intercourse than in the text of the play being acted out a good way from them.

The main Paris theatre for tragedy—indeed the only theatre which existed in the capital at the start of the seventeenth century, compared with the four regular ones in London—was the Hôtel de Bourgogne near Les Halles and Saint-Eustache, set up by the Confrérie de la Passion in 1548. One of a number of societies of players made up of small merchants and tradesmen, the Confrérie laid down strict guidelines about which troupes could perform in Paris and at what profit, but by the turn of the century the theatre building was being let out to occasional visiting companies. The Comédiens du Roi, headed by Valleran le Conte, established themselves at the Hôtel by 1610, but they did not have exclusive use; it was not until the late 1620s that their chief rivals, the Comédiens du Prince d'Orange, under the actor Guillaume Montdory, gave up the struggle and yielded their ground there. The Comédiens du Roi, now led by the actor Bellerose, took over the Hôtel and five years later, by order of the king, saw six actors transferred to their company from that of Montdory at the Marais.

Unlike the Marais, the Hôtel de Bourgogne was purpose-built, but on the same model. The latest research suggests that the theatre measured approximately 33 by 13.6 metres. Depending on the number of *loges* along the sidewalls and the short end wall (probably two tiers of seven, with five *loges* on each tier facing the stage), it would seem that in 1647, when internal structural alterations were carried out, the entire stage depth at the Hôtel was 10.7 metres, but provision for a passage backstage would have limited this to 8.75 metres. The possible width of 13.6 metres would be reduced by supporting columns on both sides, leaving a proscenium opening of some 9.7 metres net. Thus the usable space on stage, the effective playing area, was virtually a square, just under 32 feet across and 29 feet deep at most. This may seem small in comparison with some modern panoramic stages, such as that of the former Théâtre National Populaire at the Palais de Chaillot in Paris, but in fact it corresponds closely to the area commonly available on present-day British provincial and even London theatre stages.

Recently a very rough diary sketch made by the English history painter and set designer Sir James Thornhill after a visit in 1717 to the old Hôtel de Bourgogne building has been cited as proof that perhaps the last three *loges* on each side of the theatre furthest away from the stage were angled so as to give their occupants a better view of the actors. But the evidence is slim and it is perhaps safer to assume that the pattern of the boxes when the Hôtel was remodelled in 1647 followed the rectangular shape of the building rather than breaking with French tradition and moving towards the Italian horseshoe-like layout.

Although theatre design in France did not change until the very end of our period, the concept of what constituted an appropriate set did. We are fortunate in still having the original book in which the stage-designer at the Hôtel de Bourgogne, Laurent Mahelot, sketched the sets of certain plays performed there just prior to 1635. It is clear from this and other evi-

dence that early seventeenth-century French plays took place in a composite décor inherited from the Middle Ages—a series of small,
canvas-covered, wooden-framed compartments juxtaposed horizon-
tally, after the manner of some medieval mystery plays, or, much more frequently, in a semi-circular pattern round the three walls of the stage and
each representing a different setting. Hence the term *décor simultané*, since
various places could be indicated on stage at one and the same time. These
compartments or *mansions*, even more than a modern full-scale set, were
only symbolical representations, of course: given the reduced scale, the
actor, when he moved downstage from inside or in front of a compartment, was assumed to be still related to the setting which that particular
mansion suggested. Subsequent locations might be hidden, then revealed
at the appropriate moment, by small curtains—what in Corneille's time
were called *tapisseries*. When in position these could themselves be taken
to represent a different setting. The central upstage location may on
occasions have been a painted backcloth rather than a three-dimensional
compartment.

By the late 1630s, the multiple set was being seen as having major disadvantages. Replying over twenty years later to criticisms of *Le Cid*,
Corneille admits in an *Examen* that the action of that play requires at least
four different locations: the King's palace, the Infante's apartments,
Chimène's house, and a street or square. While many of the separate
scenes are easy to place in one or other of these, those parts of the play
which have sets of closely-linked dialogues are almost impossible to
situate properly. If the Count and Chimène's father exit from the palace
into the street in the middle of Act I, for example, can the latter still be
outside in the street following the blow the Count gives him? It would
surely be more proper and credible if he were able to react to this event
inside his house, as in the Spanish source (Guillén de Castro's *Las moce-
dades del Cid*), 'so that he could give free rein to his feelings'.

Given the state of the theatre in France at the time, most of the plays for
which Mahelot designed the sets were not tragedies but pastorals, comedies or tragi-comedies. Among them, though, was the set for Rotrou's
Hercule mourant, an influential tragedy staged at the Hôtel de Bourgogne
sometime between 1630 and 1634. The *décorateur* emphasises the need for
magnificence, and certainly the description indicates a heightened interest in the willing suspension of disbelief. One side of the stage represented the temple of Jupiter, with an altar and various ornaments, while
the other was a climbable mountain made of wood, with at its foot 'une
chambre funèbre remplie de larmes, le tombeau d'Hercule superbe'.
There were various pyramids, and vases with painted flames coming out

of them. A fourth site was the 'middle' of the stage, representing an ornately decorated room, and a final location was the prison near the tomb, making five sites in all. Thunder was called for in Act V, when Hercules comes down to earth on a cloud; and Mahelot tells us that the temple and tomb were to be hidden, that is, by a *tapisserie*.

It can be seen how, on the very eve of the first 'regular' tragedies, scenic effects were still required which are more reminiscent of the machine-play than of conventionally serious theatre. It may well be that, as at the rebuilt Marais, the Hôtel de Bourgogne theatre called for the occasional use of a second, smaller stage of sorts, temporarily fixed on top of the stage proper and brought into use when spectacular effects or extra locations like the heavens were required. The one at the Marais was almost four metres above the main stage, supported by eight pillars and reached by a spiral staircase. At the Hôtel, another of Rotrou's tragedies, the Christian play-within-a-play *Saint-Genest* (1645–6), calls for the sky to open. It contains a rare and fascinating account of contemporary staging when, in Act II, the character taking the part of the saint in the internal play scolds the hard-pressed scene painter for the rather mediocre set he has produced. To quote from Peter Arnott's partial translation,

> It's good enough, but yet, with small expense
> You could improve on its magnificence.
> Let in more daylight. Take away the gloom.
> Add stature to the trimmings of the room—
> Marble façade and jasper colonnade,
> Pillars with drums and capitals arranged . . .
> And on the backdrop where you paint your skies
> Make them appear more natural to the eyes.
> They look somewhat funereal to me!

The painter retorts that time was short and in any case it was better to leave things as they were: the foreshortenings and perspectives were best seen from a distance and colours appeared brighter.

By the date of Corneille's *Horace* (1640)—five years after his first tragedy *Médée* and three after the performance of his tragi-comic tragedy *Le Cid*, with its multiple décor—the single set was beginning to be introduced in France, although it did not immediately oust the older form. This move coincided, as we shall see, with the increasing use of the two other unities, those of time and action. The unified place, the *lieu vague*, was later, in Racine's day, to be called the *palais à volonté*. Both terms indicate the all-purpose nature of a neutral set, which in most instances could conventionally be taken to be the common meeting-place of the various factions within a play. *Horace* takes place at Rome, inside one room, and the external action, including a small-scale battle, is conveyed by eye-witness reports. The only prop required, as Mahelot's successor at the Hôtel de Bourgogne, Michel Laurent, notes in the late 1670s, is an arm-chair in Act V. Similar unity of place occurs in two of Corneille's other tragedies of the early 1640s, *Polyeucte* and *Pompée*. Two years after *Horace*, the conspiracy play *Cinna* is set in Auguste's palace, but calls for two rooms, given the nature of the action. Again, the props are minimal—an arm-chair and two stools, then later, in Act V, an armchair and one stool.

By Racine's time the single-set *palais à volonté* was established as the only possible décor. Michel Laurent tells us that minimal local colour, according to the theme of the play, was added to the standard setting. *Andromaque* (1667) needed 'a colonnaded palace and, in the background, a sea with ships'. Racine's next tragedy, *Britannicus* (1669), set at Nero's court, required as props two doors, two armchairs for Act IV and curtains. Three years later *Bajazet*, set in Constantinople, called for 'a Turkish-style drawing-room', plus two daggers.

Not only the single set but the earlier *décor multiple*, too—indeed, the *décor multiple* particularly—appears to have done without a stage curtain for some considerable time. The composite set had individual curtains masking the various compartments, as we have noted. But in the first half of the century at least, there are very few references to a main curtain being raised at the start of a play or lowered at the end, and what reports there are suggest that the practice was unusual, perhaps dictated by the content of a particular play, especially its closing scene. Richelieu's theatre at the Palais-Royal had one when it was inaugurated in 1641 with Desmarest de Saint-Sorlin's tragi-comedy *Mirame*. In the following few years both the Marais and the Hôtel de Bourgogne probably acquired a stage curtain, although it was by no means regularly used. What is certain is that no curtain rose or fell to mark the beginning or the end of the separate acts. The reason is a straightforward one: seventeenth-century technology, and that of the eighteenth century too, for that matter, simply could not cope with the frequent movement of a large, heavy curtain. In a sense, then, this problem had an important influence on the set erected on the *jeu de paume*-type stages. Once the public—and the playwrights—had tired of the essentially medieval idea of a composite décor, far removed from any semblance of naturalism, and in the absence of a stage curtain, one unchanged setting had to be the order of the day. Dramatists and managers made a virtue out of necessity and wrote or staged plays which relied on a single, all-purpose location. Of course, the best playwrights turned this apparent restriction to their own and our advantage.

As we shall see, costume in tragedy corresponded broadly to this fairly lax stage setting. But it would be wrong to suppose that contemporary audiences would necessarily have benefited, had the sets (multiple or single) been more faithfully reproduced. For one thing, the lighting in seventeenth-century theatres bore no relation to the powerful stage or house-lights of today. An anonymous painting surviving from Racine's period and depicting French and Italian farce players shows a stage lit by six chandeliers of about ten tallow candles each, the chandeliers being hung in a slightly curved pattern which illuminates the middle of the stage but not the upstage area, the distant part of a street scene. Along the edge of the stage are early versions of small footlights, eighteen candles in a row in the middle, with another eight on each side. In the late 1680s a drawing depicts a set at the Comédie-Française, lit by six chandeliers in a line along the front of the stage, with a further three on each side of the décor, following the line of the perspectives. But however numerous the individual candles, defects in the stage set would not have shown up as much as we might expect. Nor was the audience's relationship to it the same as in the twentieth century. While nowadays the spectator is used to sitting in what G. B. Tennyson calls 'the darkness of his own private world', the auditorium in seventeenth-century France was kept lit throughout the performance, meaning, among other things, that less attention was focused on the set than is the case in a modern theatre.

Before we leave the stage itself and pass to the remaining problems raised by staging, mention must be made of a practice which may strike modern readers as distinctly quaint. In the seventeenth century and indeed on into the second half of the eighteenth, it was common for certain members of the audience, usually from the nobility, to be seated on the stage itself. The custom was not restricted to France. In Shakespearian England, the dramatist Thomas Dekker tells us in his *Gull's Hornbook* of 1609, 'on the very rushes where the comedy is to dance ... must our feathered ostrich, like a piece of ordnance, be planted valiantly because impudently, beating down the mews and hisses of the opposed rascality'. Several advantages are gained by a stage seat:

> First, a conspicuous eminence is gotten ...
> You have a signed patent to engross the whole commodity of censure ...
> If you be a knight, you may haply get you a mistress; if a mere Fleet Street gentleman, a wife ...
> You may with small cost purchase the dear acquaintance of the boys; have a good stool for sixpence ...

Many French writers and dramatists comment, usually critically, on this habit, of which the first attested account concerns the opening performances of *Le Cid* in 1637. In the late 1650s Tallemant des Réaux, in a portrait of the actor Montdory, recounts how both sides of the stage in Paris were filled with young people seated on straw-bottomed chairs, the reason being that they feared the rabble in the pit 'even though there are often soldiers on the door, and the pages and lackeys [in the pit audience] do not wear swords'. Seats in the *loges*, Tallemant reports, were expensive and had to be booked well in advance; some extra cash ensured a seat on stage. A year or two later Eraste tells his valet in the opening scene of Molière's comedy *Les Fâcheux* (1661) that he had been in just such a position at a play when an overdressed, loud-mouthed man had arrived and demanded a seat to the disturbance of the actors, and had eventually placed it downstage in the middle, thus blocking the view for 'three-quarters of the pit'.

The practice, while inconvenient, was not without its amusing consequences. At times actors had difficulty getting from the wings on to the stage, or spectators arriving late were mistaken for members of the cast, so that the audience's identification with the characters must have been sorely tried. Of course, being seated on stage avoided the dangers of the pit, but it was largely a social phenomenon. Just as presence at Court meant little if one was not noticed there, so seats under the chandeliers fulfilled the nobles' craving to be seen, whatever the incidental merits of the play.

And what of the actors themselves? We have seen how groups of them played a vital part in developing the two main Paris theatres: Bellerose and company at the Hôtel de Bourgogne, Montdory and his associates at the Marais. Yet neither group had an entirely easy start, particularly the Marais players, since they had to move from *jeu de paume* to *jeu de paume* before finding their permanent home in the rue Vieille-du-Temple. If this was so with companies initially specialising in tragedy, the same was true of Molière's company, the Illustre Théâtre, forced by lack of success when founded in 1643 to tour the provinces for thirteen years before returning to Paris.

Much is often made of the alleged dissolute life of seventeenth-century actors. This may have been the case with some of the itinerant troupes, but those based in Paris had the same morals as anyone else. Their reputation was perhaps partly due to rumours spread by the Catholic church which, like the Protestants, strongly disapproved of theatregoing and the acting profession. In theory actors were excommunicated; Molière, for example, as actor, playwright and manager combined, was at first refused Christian burial, although eventually he was buried with minimal ceremonial and at night. In practice, actors were often married in church and had their children baptised.

The companies or associations of actors which came into being in seventeenth-century France are an interesting example of self-help and democratic control. Usually consisting of only nine to a dozen members, drawn more from the bourgeoisie than from the lower classes, the troupes worked out mutually acceptable conditions and had these duly formalised by a deed of association in front of a lawyer. Points laid down included length of service (a year, sometimes two or three), financial terms and, often, the kind of parts a member would have to agree to take in plays mounted during his time with the company. Breach of contract, as for example when an actor departed early, might incur a fine; in the 1670s there are examples of such payments rising to 2000 livres, at a time when the average daily wage of an artisan ranged from three-quarters to one-and-a-half livres (fifteen to thirty sous).

Thanks to the survival of legal documents, we know quite a lot about the composition of the main seventeenth-century companies, particularly those of the Hôtel and the Marais. So even when our information about individual plays remains sketchy—if, for example, we lack contemporary accounts of an opening night and the reception a play got then—it is often possible to deduce from the association contracts which person took which part at a given time. Similarly we can speculate on how often a dramatist may have written a play with a particular actor or actress, or indeed with a specific group of actors, in mind. Racine, we know, chose Mlle du Parc (wife of the actor René Berthelot, called du Parc) for the title rôle in *Andromaque* at the Hôtel de Bourgogne in 1667. Admittedly she was his mistress. Equally, the famous Mlle Champmeslé had specific parts written for her at the Hôtel in the 1670s. The number of male and female rôles, and the distribution of parts throughout the five acts, were often not due to chance but depended on the current membership and acting abilities of the troupe for whom the play was destined.

There was, of course, a *directeur* or leader in each company, but decisions were taken by consensus or majority vote. The financial arrangements were also democratic, if rather rudimentary. After a performance, theatre expenses would be met and then the takings would be shared out among the actors. Sometimes, as we shall see later, the author was entitled to his cut as well during an initial run—often a double share. The leader, too, might get a double share (there are examples of this at the Hôtel de Bourgogne) or he would make do with what each of the others received. It was a precarious existence in some ways, since all income was distributed; nothing was put aside to meet future expenditure. But actors were not in general impoverished, to judge by what evidence exists. In his retirement, Montdory of the Marais was able to make several gifts to his daughter and sister, while Bellerose had a country house. Moreover, costumes—if often unrelated to the period of the play—were apt, even in the early part of the century, to be ornate and made of expensive cloth. The rumoured extreme poverty of the urban acting profession is largely a myth which some of its members probably found it in their interest to foster.

Naturally enough, the various seventeenth-century companies tended to specialise: the Hôtel de Bourgogne in tragedy, the Marais—after starting in tragedy in the 1630s and 40s—moving over to spectaculars and machine-plays once Pierre Corneille began giving his plays to the rival company. Molière's troupe played tragedy (badly, common opinion had it) but obviously preferred comedies, particularly those of its leader. Yet to this day, despite much research, we still lack firm details of who played what. The *Mémoire de Mahelot*, with its stage sets and lists of plays, tells us about at least part of the repertory of the Hôtel de Bourgogne, while La Grange, actor, secretary and treasurer of Molière's company, has left behind an invaluable manuscript register of performances, receipts and staff changes at the Palais-Royal theatre from 1659 to 1672. But we are not entirely sure where some of Corneille's major tragedies were first put on; no conclusive contemporary evidence has survived.

Once they had taken a part, actors and actresses—for women were admitted from early in the seventeenth century at both the Marais and the Hôtel—tended to keep their rôles for life. This could lead to problems and at times to hilarity, as when an elderly actor, still playing Rodrigue in *Le Cid*, had to claim, somewhat inappropriately, that his valour was greater than his youthful appearance might suggest, or fell at his beloved Chimène's feet and was physically unable to get up again. In modern eyes much of the action—and much of the tragic effect—in Corneille's four early major tragedies, to take only them, depends precisely on the naivety and inexperience of the young characters involved: *Le Cid*'s Chimène and Rodrigue, Horace and his sister in *Horace*, Cinna and Emilie in *Cinna* and Polyeucte in the play of that name. To be sure, it is not only the seventeenth century which thought that the actor's age mattered little: Maurice Descotes, in his book *Les grands rôles du théâtre de Corneille* (1962), reminds us that Albert Lambert, playing Rodrigue in 1931 after forty-five years in the theatre, aroused ironic comments such as 'He's still holding the sword! He's even managing to move it about!'

Corneille as well as Racine seems to have been quite unaware that realism in certain areas of a production might be an added advantage. Montdory was twice Rodrigue's age when he played the part for the first time in 1637. Thirty years later, at the opening performance of *Andromaque*, only Mlle du Parc, who took the title-rôle, was, at thirty-four, about the right age for the part. Mlle des Oeillets, playing her rival Hermione, was forty-seven, while the part of Pyrrhus was given to Floridor, then fifty-nine, and that of Oreste to the obese Montfleury, who was at least the same age. By 1677, it is true, the company had been renewed with younger actors, so those playing Phèdre, Thésée, Hippolyte, Aricie and Oenone in Racine's masterpiece were then thirty-five, thirty-five, about twenty-three, thirty-five and twenty years old respectively.

These anecdotes can serve as a lead-in to one final point about the staging of French classical tragedies. Elementary make-up, even if it was not tested by bright stage-lighting, could not adequately disguise an actor's age, and physical infirmity was unable to cope realistically with youthful parts. The conclusion to be drawn is that seventeenth-century audiences were not looking for—or did not get—interpretations in which the performer appeared as of the same age as the stage character. A similar discrepancy occurred with costumes. In Elizabethan England actors in tragedy wore a mixture of contemporary clothes and Roman-style dress, an idea imported from Italy: breastplates, tunics, kilts, helmets. The same was true of the two Paris theatres. Just as local colour was absent from the set or at best suggested in very general terms, so there was no attempt to reproduce accurate period costume. Contemporary frontispieces, prints and drawings are a useful guide to us: they show Louis XIII and Louis XIV dress—doublet and hose for example—with extra finery to represent what was thought necessary for the dignity of tragedy.

Much of this garb, whether supplied by the troupe leader or provided by the actors and actresses from their own wardrobes, is highly anachronistic. For example, the frontispiece to Tristan l'Hermite's tragedy *La Mariane*, staged at the Marais in 1636 and dealing with the victim of Herod the Great, shows a group of characters with a wide variety of clothes and a range of exotic headgear: hats, turbans, plumes. Ribbons, lace, plumed hats, even on occasions white gloves, are difficult to reconcile with ancient secular or Christian subject-matter. The point does not seem to have worried the contemporaries of Corneille. Indeed, despite murmurings from some commentators, the same carefree mixture is to be found in later seventeenth-century tragedies. Only in the eighteenth century were serious attempts made to fit stage characters out with faithful period costume.

Despite numerous and often daunting problems, the actual staging of plays came a long way during our period. The search for suitable buildings, their conversion into theatres and the attempt to act in far from ideal conditions and before a very mixed audience less than comfortably installed were only the first of many difficulties which actors had to overcome in interpreting some of the most important tragedies of all western literature. It is paradoxical that in 1689, when the young Comédie-Française company, formed nine years earlier by the union of the Guénégaud theatre (Molière's old company, together with the Marais) and the Hôtel de Bourgogne troupe, was forced to seek a different home, it moved just up the road from the Guénégaud on the right bank into a new theatre building whose interior was no longer rectangular but semi-circular shaped. For by that date all the best regular tragedies had been written, with the practical handicaps of a small stage awkwardly sited in an oblong building very much in mind.

It is difficult to determine now exactly what effect these conditions had on the acting of plays. For example, the declamatory style used by actors, mentioned in a later chapter, was presumably due, in part, to the need to reach out to the audience, both the style itself and the tirades which it conveyed going back to the earliest days of French tragedy. To complement the set pieces, words, gestures and looks will be important on a stage where much physical movement is not possible or may not be desired. If the Italian troupes of actors in Paris could successfully put over their comic foreign-language texts through gestures, mime and diction, it is not unreasonable to suppose that writers and actors of tragedy in the vernacular would use the same devices, albeit much more sparingly and to more subtle effect.

On the other hand the acting conditions did not prevent major technical developments, especially regarding the type of set within which the action took place. Indeed, the physical constraints of the stage and the auditorium may well have hastened the move towards the single set and the generalised use of a front curtain. The multiple set did not, of course, preclude observance of the three unities of time, place and action which we shall examine in a subsequent chapter. In a play like *Le Cid*, the characters have an excessively busy twenty-four hours, although events beyond the minimum necessary are not shown on stage but are relegated to the four intervals and to places offstage during the acts. The play may have several locations, but these are limited to adjacent areas of the same town. The single set which first appeared around 1640 will not lead specifically to a much shorter timespan—even so-called 'crisis tragedy' needs rather more than the two hours of the performance to develop the plot with its necessary background—but, among the best dramatists at least, to a more noticeably claustrophobic setting, with its attendant psychological and emotional pressures on the characters. This unified décor could also be said to fit in with the call for verisimilitude which, as we shall see later, is widespread among both critics and practising dramatists in seventeenth-century France.

3 Public

As the previous chapter has shown, our knowledge about the performance of tragedies in seventeenth-century France is confined in the main to Paris, with one principal theatre at the beginning and another towards the end of the century, and at no time more than two playing tragedy with any regularity. Since we know little about the repertory and acting conditions of itinerant companies working the provinces and even less about those who came to see their plays, it is on the evidence of the Hôtel de Bourgogne and the Marais, supplemented, where appropriate, by details of the Palais-Royal theatre where Molière's troupe were the main performers, that we have to rely for information about theatre audiences.

Although France in the seventeenth century, with some twenty million inhabitants, was the most populated country in Western Europe (England had only a quarter of that number), Paris was still proportionately smaller than it is today. Yet its population, estimated at some five hundred thousand in the 1680s, far exceeded that of any other town in France, which remained predominantly rural. How far did theatre facilities in the capital satisfy its half-million inhabitants? How many of them attended the theatre? Did they exert any influence on the content of tragedies put on? And how were performances organised?

Despite the researches of Professor John Lough, notably in his book *Paris theatre audiences in the seventeenth and eighteenth centuries* (1957), it is difficult to agree with his objection to the traditional view, according to which audiences in the early part of our period were largely drawn from the lower classes. As in so many matters concerning the seventeenth-century French theatre, our information here is scanty. What accounts have survived about theatre attendance are often vague and may not give a truly representative picture, since critics of rowdyism in the pit or other aspects

35

of alleged mismanagement were more likely to rush into print than theatre-goers (perhaps the silent majority?) who found their experience a satisfying one.

We have seen how a seventeenth-century Paris theatre offered basically three types of accommodation: *loges* or boxes, the pit and the stage itself. Above the *loges* were the *paradis* and (possibly) the *amphithéâtre*, with their cheaper seated accommodation. Just as the lateral *loges*, fitted out with benches, provided a side-on view of the stage, while the end *loges* were more luxurious, having comfortable seats and a better view, so the rows in the *amphithéâtre* rising to the roof at the end opposite the stage outclassed the single long bench in the gods down the sidewalls. Accounts of the disturbances caused by spectators on stage imply that the troublemakers there were usually members of the minor aristocracy, those who had most to gain through social prestige by sitting (or in some cases standing) where they did, and given the cost of a place on stage we can safely assume that this category of patron came from the nobility. The middle or upper-middle class of bourgeois would tend to choose the boxes.

Which leaves the pit. Was this the preserve of plebeian theatregoers? As Professor Lough usefully reminds us, the word *peuple* had several shades of meaning in the seventeenth century, including both 'plebs' and 'public', and it is virtually impossible to determine to what exact social level users of it are referring at any particular time. Several contemporary accounts mention pages, lackeys, clerks (meaning, for example, lawyers' clerks) and shop-assistants as members of the *parterre* audience. One of the best-known descriptions is by a character in Charles Sorel's *La Maison des jeux* (1642):

... the pit is extremely uncomfortable because of the crowd of a thousand rogues mingling with the respectable people, whom they sometimes try to insult. Having provoked quarrels for a mere trifle, they then draw their swords and stop the whole play. At their quietest they never cease speaking, whistling and shouting, and since they have paid nothing at the entrance and only come because they have nothing better to do, they hardly bother to listen to what the actors are saying. This is proof that the theatre is dishonourable, in that it is patronised by such people, and it is clear that those who wield power in the world think little of it, since they do not prevent all this rabble from going in, without paying, with a view to stirring up trouble.

His words are echoed fifteen years later by the abbé d'Aubignac, who says in his *Pratique du théâtre* that performances are constantly interrupted by young libertines who only attend in order to display their insolence, who strike terror in everyone and often commit murders . . . Nowadays the galleries and pit are very uncomfortable, because most of the boxes are too far away and badly positioned, and the pit is on the level and without seats. As a result, since safety cannot be guaranteed, respectable people do not want to lay themselves open to pickpockets, women are afraid of seeing drawn swords there, and many people cannot tolerate the discomfort.

Even in Racine's day, critics mention unauthorised entry to the theatre without payment: the abbé Michel de Pure writes in his *Idée des spectacles anciens et nouveaux* (1668) about 'this group of ruffians who turn up from all directions, without interest, without knowledge and without money'. Better control would mean that 'the endless noise they make would cause less disturbance to those who give their attention to the play and want to listen'.

It is clear, even from these brief excerpts, that the pit audience did not consist *exclusively* of troublemakers, but that, given the physical conditions, a number of them could, if they wished, create a disproportionately large disturbance among at least the other patrons standing there. Since two of the three authors quoted might be said to have a vested interest in attacking rowdyism in the theatre (both the abbé de Pure and the abbé d'Aubignac, as well as being critics and prose writers, were minor dramatists), we may want to treat the detail of their accounts with some caution. What appears certain from the available evidence is that the pit audience was by and large a popular one; if this is so, then the number of patrons from among the lower classes was far from negligible. After all, as we have seen, the layout of both the Marais and the Hôtel de Bourgogne meant that the pit and the cheaper seats in the *paradis* or even the *amphithéâtre* provided room for certainly more theatregoers than could be accommodated in the *loges* or on stage.

But while *le peuple* did not in general frequent the boxes, there are several reports of the more socially advantaged watching plays from the pit. Indeed on occasion even dramatists went there (as another character in Sorel tells us), believing that it was a good vantage-point from which to judge the success or failure of their works. Noblemen, if unaccompanied by their womenfolk, and male foreign visitors would congregate there, too. Bourgeois in particular, though—well-to-do Paris merchants and other professional people—seem to have found the pit a congenial place. Taken together, the reports of this social mixing perhaps help to put accounts of killings and gross misbehaviour into a truer perspective. Theatres, like other areas of cultural life, have never lacked their conservative or critical snobs. Early in the century it seems that women attended the theatre infrequently, and then only if they had seats in the *loges* and wore masks or veils. Nobody challenges the view that women would not be seen in the pit at this time. Yet a well-known engraving of a performance at what is believed to be the Hôtel de Bourgogne might suggest the opposite. Attributed to Abraham Bosse, one of the great engravers of the century who lived until 1676, it is unfortunately not dated, but a fair sprinkling of women can be seen among the predominantly male audience standing in the front section of the pit which, along with the stage, is the only part of the theatre shown. The drawing may well date from around 1630 and by then, when Corneille and his contemporaries were beginning to write, it was accepted that women could attend the theatre freely. In 1666 d'Aubignac could write that fifty years previously women were present only if veiled and 'quite invisible'; even so, such people were wanton in his eyes. But Mairet, in the preface (1636) to his comedy *Les Galanteries du duc d'Ossonne*, informs us that 'the most respectable women now go to the Hôtel de Bourgogne with as few qualms as they would to the Hôtel du Luxembourg' (now the palace of the same name, inhabited in the early seventeenth century by Marie de Médicis, Gaston d'Orléans and others).

The self-imposed ban on regular female attendance at the theatre in the first two decades of the century was no doubt due to two closely interrelated factors: the crudeness and violence of many of the plays performed and the lack of control over the kind of people admitted, with resulting rowdyism. It is interesting to speculate on which of these two features changed first and what influence this exerted on the subsequent switch away from hybrid types of play into pure comedy and tragedy. Certainly by the 1670s admission to the theatre was more stringently and effectively, although unobtrusively, controlled. Chappuzeau, in his *Théâtre français* (1674), recounts how, because of Louis XIV's strict instructions about curbing gatecrashers, 'door-keepers' were recruited to prevent possible disturbances. One of their main attributes, Chappuzeau says, should be the ability to distinguish between 'respectable people and those who don't look respectable. They stop those trying to get through without a ticket and warn them to get one at the box-office. They do this politely, since they have instructions to be civil to everyone, provided all violence is avoided.' The Hôtel de Bourgogne, according to the *Théâtre français*, had a door-keeper only at the entrance (the implication being that other such janitors or bouncers might patrol the pit); when necessary, and with the king's permission, soldiers from among the royal guard were used to police the theatre. The Marais company still used door-keepers (in the plural) but could also call on troops if need be. 'Thus it is that all disturbances have been done away with, and the middle-class person can attend the theatre with greater enjoyment.' But Chappuzeau's comment, weighed against the abbé de Pure's remark a few years earlier, is certainly not sufficient proof from which to conclude that theatre audiences became socially less mixed in the second half of the century, or that the pit audience in that period was composed solely of men. In a recent book *Writer and public in France from the Middle Ages to the present day* (1978), Professor John Lough states his conviction that since, from the middle of the seventeenth century until the closing decades of the Ancien Régime, one finds hardly any written references to the presence of lower-class spectators, 'it would seem as if the cheapest part of the various Paris theatres, the parterre, was largely a middle-class preserve'. Again, the presence of certain professional people and noblemen in the pit leads him to believe that, well before Racine's time, this part of the theatre was filled with 'all male spectators'. The existing positive (rather than negative) evidence does not appear to warrant such conclusions.

Best estimates put the capacity of both the Hôtel de Bourgogne and Marais theatres at about 1500, while the Palais-Royal theatre, shared by Molière's company and a troupe of Italian actors, probably held some 300 less. But what were attendances at plays like? Once again we lack all the necessary statistics. La Grange's register, mentioned previously, gives us precious information about the activities of Molière and his troupe between 1659 and 1672, but for each performance only the total receipts and the actors' shares are listed. So although we have a good idea of what the admission charges would be, it is obviously impossible to say how many seats or places were paid for in each part of the theatre and hence what the overall attendance was. For the last year before Molière's death in 1673 and the merger with the Marais to form the Guénégaud theatre, the Palais-Royal register was kept by André Hubert, and by chance he provides rather more detailed statistics. The 131 performances at the theatre attracted some 52,000 spectators, and at over 86 per cent of them more people bought tickets for the pit than seats in all other parts of the house combined. The largest number of pit admissions during the 1672–3 season was 514, on a day when the total attendance reached 925, still well short of capacity, as far as we can tell.

We have no information of any consequence at all about the two theatres which interest us the most, the Hôtel de Bourgogne and the Marais. On the other hand, the archives of the Comédie-Française, the theatre formed by the union of the Guénégaud and the Hôtel, provide us with raw figures about annual attendances from 1680 onwards. A typical year, 1682–3, saw a total of some 150,000 admissions to the daily performances, but given the wide number of plays staged, perhaps a hundred each season, most of them not brand new, it is impossible to say exactly how many people attended on each occasion, far less how many *different* patrons turned up each time. Presumably many people attended the theatre and its various productions regularly, while some might go two or more times to see the same play.

If we discount additional people admitted free of charge for various reasons (perhaps 10,000 in an average year), we are left with widely varying estimates of the number of different patrons frequenting the Comédie-Française in one of its early years. Professor H. C. Lancaster (1942) believed that the 150,000 paying spectators of 1682–3 might represent about '100,000 individuals who attended', while in 1957 Professor Lough reduced the figure by almost two-thirds. He calculated that 1000 people might have turned up on thirty separate occasions during a season, a further 1500 on twenty occasions, 3000 ten times, 5000 five times, 10,000 on two occasions and 15,000 at only one performance. Thus the gross total of 150,000 was whittled down to 35,500 people.

Both calculations, and in particular the latter, are necessarily based on inspired guesswork. Our lack of firm information on this score is all the more frustrating since detailed statistics about performances and theatre attendance would help to counter the view of French classical tragedy as an arid, intellectual exercise, to be read rather than staged.

We must remember that when the Comédie-Française company was formed towards the end of the century, it was once again the only theatre in France regularly performing tragedy. In addition, by the 1680s, the best tragedies had almost all been written, so that the repertory consisted of new good, average and poor plays, together with revivals of earlier masterpieces or favourites by Corneille, Racine and their contemporaries. Corneille's last play, the tragedy *Suréna*, was performed in 1674, while after *Phèdre* in 1677 Racine was to produce only two tragedies, in 1689 and 1691, both dealing with Biblical themes and initially written for performance in a girls' school. In the last decade of the century, only a quarter of the tragedies staged at the Comédie-Française were new plays.

But although the Comédie in effect restored the monopoly held in the opening years by the Hôtel de Bourgogne and so restricted public choice, there was a major development in 1680: daily performances. Until then it appears that the two main Paris theatres operated on only two or three days a week. By the second half of the century, the Hôtel and the Marais gave performances on Fridays, Sundays and Tuesdays, as did the Italian troupe at the Palais-Royal; Molière, on his return to Paris in the late 1650s, shared the theatre with them and had to make do with the remaining, less favoured days. First 'nights' were normally on a Friday, to allow for the hoped-for success to draw in big crowds at the subsequent Sunday performance. If the word 'nights' has to be in inverted commas, this is because all seventeenth-century public performances in France were in effect matinées—as they were at, for example, the Globe in London, but for the different reason that the pit and part of the stage there were open to the sky. Only invitation performances at the French court or possibly in private châteaux would take place in the evening. The official starting-time of 2 p.m. was chosen in order to allow even winter performances to end in daylight and the audience to get home before dark, since street-lighting in the capital left much to be desired. Needless to say, then as nowadays, Paris theatregoers found it impossible to bring themselves to arrive on time, so that performances would often start one-and-a-half to two hours late.

When a play was particularly popular, additional performances could be arranged. In 1661, for example, the tragedy *Camma* by Pierre Corneille's brother drew such crowds that the Hôtel de Bourgogne actors decided to play on Thursdays as well as the three normal afternoons. But the usual way of coping with success would be to extend the run. Of course nowadays in the theatre we are quite used to seeing certain plays staged for a fair length of time. West End hits can run for months and sometimes years, transferring from one theatre to another when prior commitments require this, while touring companies may take a play round a number of towns and cities, so that by the end of their travels it has been performed on a large number of occasions. In contrast, and although we sadly lack comprehensive information, seventeenth-century runs in Paris seem to have been short indeed. By all accounts it was not a tragedy by Pierre Corneille or Racine which had the longest opening run in the seventeenth century, but the romantic so-called tragedy *Timocrate* by Pierre's younger brother Thomas, first put on at the Marais in November 1656. It lasted a whole winter, which, as we shall see, at the rate of three performances a week, would give a total of about eighty. No conventionally serious tragedy had anything approaching this level of exposure on first performance. Dramatists would be delighted with twenty or thirty consecutive performances, and most made do with ten or twenty. If one can assume that a well-made play was doing well to attract perhaps 800 patrons early on in its run and that that figure would tend to drop rather than rise later, the number of people who saw even a major tragedy when it first came out is remarkably small—6–8000 for a modest success, 15–17,000 for a striking one, perhaps 10–12,000 for an average first run. The social mix of the audience may well have been considerable quite far on into the second half of the century, but at no time can more than a tiny minority of Parisians have had direct experience of a new production.

To stir up interest in potential theatregoers, announcements about forthcoming performances were made, often some weeks in advance, in the various gazettes, both in Paris and abroad (in the *Gazette d'Amsterdam*, for example). Each theatre troupe also had an *orateur*, probably one of the actors, who at the end of a performance would try to 'sell' subsequent productions to that afternoon's captive audience.

Immediate publicity for new plays was in the form of small posters, which soon replaced the proclamations of street-criers current in the early years of the century. Each theatre had a different coloured poster, but from an age which preserved ephemera less methodically than our own only a handful of them have survived, more or less intact. These few scraps of paper do, however, provide important insights into seventeenth-century attitudes to theatres and the acting profession. The complete text of a 1658 Hôtel de Bourgogne poster runs as follows:

LA SEULE TROUPE *royale entretenue de Sa Majesté. Vous aurez demain Mardi xviie jour de Décembre, le Feint* ALCIBIADE, *de Monsieur* QUINAULT; *C'est tout ce que nous vous dirons sur ce sujet puisque vous savez la vérité de cet Ouvrage.* [*Gap*] *A Vendredi prochain sans aucune remise, la* TOLEDANE, *ou* CE L'EST CE NE L'EST PAS. *En attendant le Grand* CYRUS, *de Monsieur* QUINAULT. *Défenses aux Soldats d'y entrer sur peine de la vie. C'est à l'Hôtel de Bourgogne, à deux heures précises.*

While the name of the author of the tragi-comedy *Le feint Alcibiade*, Philippe Quinault, is given (this was not always the case, especially early in the century), there is no indication of who is taking each part; actors in seventeenth-century France were not the objects of veneration they often are today, or at least their names seem not to have been thought worthy of special mention. The reason may be, of course, that with a relatively stable company at each theatre during a season, the probable cast-list would be common knowledge anyway. The official starting-time is given, and the military are warned to keep out. In addition, trailers for subsequent productions are given: for the unknown *la Toledane ou Ce l'est, ce ne l'est pas*, to be mounted a few days later, and for another Quinault play, the tragedy *La Mort de Cyrus*, staged at the Hôtel sometime during the 1658–9 season. It is taken for granted that readers of the poster know the background to the first of the Quinault plays; all we know nowadays is that it was played before Queen Christina of Sweden at the end of February 1658 and that the December performance was presumably its first commercial one.

Another poster, at the Marais, advertises plays for February 1660, including 'la plaisante COMEDIE' *Jodelet maître* by Paul Scarron (3 February), first performed in the mid-40s, and a revival on the following Friday of Pierre Corneille's *L'Illusion comique*, dating from the 30s. The same author's *La Conquête de la Toison d'or*, with its 'superbes Machines', is announced; in fact this will not be publicly performed in Paris for another year. On other occasions the posters are printed with the date left blank for later insertion—a wise economy.

The 1660 Marais poster had started with the explanation 'Since joyful amusements are seasonable, we believe we are giving you a treat in promising for tomorrow Tuesday 3 February . . .' This refers to the *carnaval* season, which filled the period each year from Epiphany (6 January) to Ash Wednesday, the first day in Lent. Apart from this, for psychological or other reasons, different kinds of plays were staged at different times of year. The theatre season ran from just after Easter to the beginning of Lent of the following year; the break allowed for religious observance and, more mundanely, the hiring of actors or the renewal of contracts. It appears that tragedies were, on the whole, performed in winter, while the better weather was thought a suitable time for comedy. Thus Corneille's *Le Cid* opened at the Marais early in January 1637; *Horace* appeared in March three years later, after a private performance for Richelieu in February; *Cinna*, by way of exception, was probably first performed in the summer of 1642, although some believe it was during the winter of 1640; and *Polyeucte* was staged in December 1642 or January 1643. Racine's dates are better established than at least Corneille's early ones: *Andromaque* opened in November 1667 at the Hôtel de Bourgogne, *Britannicus* in December 1669, *Bérénice* in November 1670 (followed a week later by Corneille's rival 'heroic comedy' on the same theme) and so on.

At the beginning of the seventeenth century admission to the pit cost 5 sous and seats elsewhere 10 sous. By the middle of the century inflation had pushed the pit price up to 15 sous, while the cost of seats in other parts of the theatre tended to vary but was considerably higher—3 livres (60 sous), for example, in the best *loges*. These were the prices still being charged at the Comédie-Française in 1680, when a place on stage cost all of 6 livres. For the first few performances of a new play, it was customary to charge double, to ensure that high initial expenditure was at least covered. Outside tragedy, plays which required elaborate sets or stage-machinery habitually ran at increased prices. Of course, it is necessary to relate these charges to then current costs. As we have seen, 15 sous represented a typical workman's daily wage in the second half of the century, certainly in provincial France; a Parisian craftsman might earn up to twice that sum. In comparison, a pound of bread cost one to two sous, a pound of butter five to eight, a dozen eggs about ten sous and a pair of shoes about three livres, four times the price of normal entry to the pit.

What conclusions can we draw concerning audiences and their possible effect on the drama they saw performed? For all the isolated and perhaps unrepresentative criticisms which have come down to us in print, it seems that then, as now, Parisian theatregoing was on the whole a fairly restricted but certainly enjoyable experience. The number of individual citizens who set foot inside the Hôtel de Bourgogne or the Marais, to say nothing of the Palais-Royal or the Opéra, is impossible to determine accurately, as is the presence of visitors from provincial France or other countries; but such evidence as there is suggests a wide social mix. Whatever the precise details about spectators may have been, one thing which appears to have changed little in seventeenth-century theatregoing is the theatre building itelf and its facilities. If the Palais-Royal theatre, opened in 1641, provided a revolutionary stepped *parterre*, with better sightlines, the abbé d'Aubignac could still, sixteen years later, lead a crusade for both an inclined pit and fixed seats for its occupants. 'And for the comfort of the audience,' he wrote in his *Projet pour le rétablissement du théâtre français*, 'the pit should be on an incline and filled with fixed seats, until some other provision is made. This would prevent those present there from fighting, since they would have no room to do so.' Indeed. Prices might have been raised, too, to match the greater comfort. But large numbers of those who had formerly paid their 15 sous would then have seen no play. Authors and actors might have been slightly better off, but Paris would have been the poorer for the abolition of what was a forum for both critical discussion and social intercourse.

This truly popular setting and the relative cheapness of access to it must be contrasted with the restricted overall size and overwhelming Parisian bias of the audience which saw an average play during its initial run. It would be fair to assume, then, that writers of tragedy in particular were aiming their works principally at a literate, urban élite, one which had a sound knowledge of earlier and contemporary French plays, the material on which these were based and the traditional forms adopted, and one could argue that such an audience was unlikely to favour radical change or encourage an unorthodox approach to tragedy-writing. Whether this was so or not, one new factor must have exerted some influence. By the end of the first quarter of the century, with the general acceptance of women, the potential theatre audience had never been greater, and there is no conclusive widespread proof that women of all social levels, not just the highest, did not attend plays with their husbands. Certainly it is not coincidence that the attested presence of more and more women in the audience was accompanied by increasing restraint in the subject-matter of tragedy. One might go further and try to trace back the greater importance of love, and the analysis of love and other emotions in tragedies in the second half of the century, to women's influence. Of course elsewhere, in the salons and in prose fiction for example, the same topics were being examined, and one cannot put the discussions and their products into separate watertight compartments. But for much of the seventeenth century French novels and short stories, frequently written by women, could be said to have catered for a predominantly female readership. No such claim, of course, can be made for tragedy, written exclusively by men. Yet the very existence of women both as an important segment of the live audience and as potential readers of the printed text must have had its effect on both content and form.

4 Publication

We saw in the previous chapter the possible extent to which a new tragedy reached its Paris audience during a first run at the Marais or the Hôtel de Bourgogne. Even assuming a good series of twenty or so performances and reasonably full houses at the first two or three of these at least, the number of people who witnessed the play remains relatively small—a few thousand at most. In a total population of twenty million, three-quarters of them country dwellers, this is a drop in the ocean. But for a city of half a million inhabitants it is no mean feat and probably differs little from the proportion of Parisians who actually see the opening run of an important new play staged today. Then as now, theatre attendance was a minority interest.

But what about publication? How was the printing of plays arranged and what size and kind of reading-public was likely to have first-hand knowledge of the great tragedies of Corneille and Racine? Indirect, second-hand knowledge by means of critics and correspondents is an important matter we shall look at later. But the printed text of the play, on which subsequent commentators and others interested in French classical tragedy have had to depend so largely, offers readers a direct experience, different from a live performance, but valuable nonetheless.

As has been mentioned, certain seventeenth-century dramatists were to all intents and purposes attached to particular theatre troupes: Hardy and Rotrou, for example, wrote many of their plays specifically for the Hôtel de Bourgogne and got paid accordingly. A fellow-playwright, Tristan l'Hermite, tells us that Hardy, only a fraction of whose plays have survived, turned them out for thirty livres each. But this practice of hired authors, *poètes à gages*, began to die out around 1630. The alternative system was for companies to buy new plays from dramatists. This could be done in one of two main ways. Either a single payment was made or, as we noticed earlier, the author could be given a share (sometimes a double share) of receipts from performances, after deduction of costs, during the initial run. Subsequent performances, if the play was put on again later, might well produce no return at all for the dramatist. This system became commonplace in the early 1650s, but it was only in the closing years of the century, however, that an author's rights to one-ninth of net receipts for a five-act play were established by royal decree, and even this system did not apply if takings fell below a certain sum (e.g. 500 livres) on two consecutive or three separate occasions.

Both systems—the once-and-for-all payment or the percentage scheme—raised obvious difficulties for actors and authors alike. Companies could not afford to buy only new plays from dramatists, and in their repertory had to combine new works with older, published plays. For the author, an outright initial payment, calculated on a variety of factors, could be a severe injustice if the play later turned out to be a great success, while the share scheme, apparently more equitable, had uncertainty built into it from the very start. Either way, the playwright was unlikely to come off well financially.

According to seventeenth-century practice, a play was not printed until its initial run was complete. Once printing took place, the play became public property and could be acted by other companies with no further return to the author. It was therefore in his interest, as well as in that of the troupe staging a play for the first time, to extend the run as long as possible and to make sure that demand for performances was satisfied before allowing the play to be published. Chapelain, a spokesman for the critics of *Le Cid*, wrote to Guez de Balzac early in 1640, just before performances of Corneille's *Horace* were due to begin, saying that it would be some time before he received a printed copy of the play, since prior to publication 'it will have to provide six months' living for the actors'. (In fact *Horace* appeared ten or eleven months after the first public performance in Paris.) In view of what we have seen of short seventeenth-century opening runs, it is not surprising that most plays were printed within a matter of months, sometimes weeks, of their first night. However, a gap between first performance and date of publication is not always a safe guide to a play's success or failure. Even when we are sure of performance dates—and for Corneille's early, major tragedies and the plays of many of his contemporaries this is not the case—extraneous factors such as political unrest or problems with other authors may serve to explain why publication is apparently brought forward or, on the other hand, delayed. Corneille's *Agésilas*, for example, which aroused little enthusiasm, was printed within five weeks of its opening night at the Hôtel de Bourgogne in February 1666, yet *Oedipe*, seven years earlier, had met with a favourable response and was still published less than nine weeks after its appearance at the same theatre. Racine's *Bérénice*, first performed on 21 November 1670 at the Hôtel and a great success, appeared in print just over two months later, whereas Corneille's *Tite et Bérénice*, staged on 28 November, was published on 3 February 1671, in the middle of its initial run of twenty-one performances at the Palais-Royal theatre, where it alternated weekly with Molière's *Le Bourgeois gentilhomme* until the Easter break on 17 March.

Not all plays performed were published, of course. Only thirty-four of Hardy's six hundred or so (some say eight hundred) have come down to us in print, while it has been calculated that almost half the tragedies performed at the Comédie-Française in the last twenty years of the seventeenth century were never published. But in both these cases an explanation can be found. Early in the century, before the arrival of Corneille and Rotrou, the nature of the plays being written and the low cultural level of the population, which enjoyed—and perhaps imposed—the scenes of violence and physical action, meant that live performance was more appropriate than publication. On the other hand, by 1680, as we have seen, tragedy was starting to decline. Racine's withdrawal after *Phèdre*, Louis XIV's second marriage to the pious Madame de Maintenon, who disapproved of the theatre, and largely sterile debates about the respective qualities of Greek and Latin literature and modern writers (the so-called Quarrel of the Ancients and Moderns) coincided with a reduction in both the number and quality of tragedies and led to the stagnation of the genre. The closing decades of Louis's reign, beset as they were by wars, natural disasters and economic collapse, proved to be, in Geoffrey Brereton's words, a period of 'stocktaking in the arts, of a disinclination to innovate, of a certain lassitude . . . but particularly of a tendency to cling to acquired values'. The storehouse of tragedies played or printed over the previous fifty to sixty years provided a first-class repertoire with which the second-rate or merely derivative could not compete. As in the opening years of the century, but for different reasons, a process of natural selection appears to have dictated what moved from stage into print.

Provided we bear in mind, then, that at each end of the century figures for plays printed do not correspond closely to the number of works staged, it is instructive to see the breakdown of plays published in France during the seventeenth century. Jacques Scherer, in his book *La dramaturgie classique en France* (1950), had tabulated the total of tragedies, tragi-comedies, comedies and pastorals which appeared in print during each of the nine decades from 1610. His statistics for tragi-comedy include heroic comedies, the total of comedies excludes farces and one-act comedies, while pastorals cover various kinds of play with the word 'pastoral' in the designation provided by the dramatist. Tragedy, which concerns us most, is the category with the least overlap, although even here some hesitation occurs, at least in nomenclature. *Le Cid*, with its flouting of the unities and certain moral conventions and its 'happy' dénouement, is called a tragi-comedy when it first appears in 1637, but Corneille alters this to tragedy just eleven years later, with no significant change to his text. The often-quoted distinction—that tragi-comedy is a tragedy with a happy ending—is not an adequate guide, as later chapters will show. In considering Scherer's figures, we should bear in mind that there is some difference between the melodramatic, romantic tragi-comedies of the opening decades of the century and plays of serious import like *Le Cid*, just as we must remember that some of the so-called tragedies of Thomas Corneille and Quinault in the 1650s and early 60s might well be labelled tragi-comic.

In the 1610s 25 tragedies were published, more than all the other three types of play put together. But from 1620 to 1629 23 tragi-comedies and a similar number of pastorals (plays dealing with nymphs, satyrs and courtly, if sometimes despairing lovers, all set in a bucolic landscape) appeared, alongside 33 tragedies and 4 comedies. In the 1630s, one of the great periods for drama in any European literature, the number of plays printed more than doubled, from 83 to 182. The most startling increases were in tragi-comedies (passing from 23 to 80) and in comedies, which jumped from 4 to 33. Pastorals, which rose dramatically in the 1620s, were slightly more popular (31) but there were only 5 more tragedies (38 as against 33). Published tragedies soared to 69 during the 1640s, while tragi-comedies dropped to 67, comedies remained in the low thirties and pastorals disappeared. The second half of the century saw new patterns established: tragedies fell by more than half to 32 in the 1650s but maintained this level fairly well in the remaining decades (40, 39, 25, 30). Tragi-comedy dropped steadily out of favour from the 1650s (30) to the 1680s (2) and none was printed in the 1690s. Comedies, having come into prominence in the 1630s, reached a peak of 52 in the 1660s, when Molière was active, and after a decline came back strongly in the closing decade (56). Pastorals followed the same pattern as tragi-comedies, with single-figure publication rates throughout the last five decades of the century.

The heyday of serious and semi-serious drama—the period from around 1630 to the end of the 70s—thus yielded a crop of 218 printed tragedies, backed up by 198 tragi-comedies, in all over 400 plays of this type in 50 years.

Once the initial run was finished or coming to an end, the author's manuscript would normally be acquired by a bookseller for what appears nowadays to be a very small sum. The average price paid was 150 to 200 livres: the latter figure, for example, was the sum Racine may have got for his third play and first major success, *Andromaque*, performed in 1667 and printed the following year. On occasions, though, a controversial play or an important author could command much higher terms. Molière received 2000 livres for *Tartuffe* at the height of his career and Corneille was paid the same amount for both *Attila* and *Tite et Bérénice*, performed in 1667 and 1670 respectively. The next stage was the obtaining of a *privilège* or licence to print. For new works as well as reprints of old ones this was granted indirectly by the king and constituted, some would say, an early form of censorship. (Perhaps surprisingly, there appears to have been no pre-censorship of plays *in performance* in seventeenth-century France.) The system, a further indication of royal power, can be justified, though, since it not only controlled what was printed but also stipulated which publisher had exclusive rights to a text for a given period of time. The manuscript registers in which details of *privilèges* granted were recorded can still be seen in the National Library in Paris. They show that licences were awarded sometimes to authors, sometimes to *libraires* or booksellers—the word publisher was not yet current—and they lay down the period, usually five to ten years, during which no one else could legally print or distribute the text. Licences, though, could be transferred to one or more other booksellers and their validity was commonly extended, often for long periods. All in all, it was a tidy system with inherent advantages for booksellers and perhaps their customers, if not for authors.

Most provincial towns in France were poorly off for printers in the seventeenth century. Few had more than one or two, exceptions being Lyon and Rouen, towns which had important cultural and trade links with Italy and Spain respectively. The most recent research indicates that the number of printers available in Paris in the years during which tragedies were actively produced varied between forty-odd and seventy-odd, not all of whom, of course, would print works of fiction. In 1644 there were seventy-five, but two-thirds of these had only one or two printing-presses. By 1666 the number had risen to seventy-nine, with a slightly higher proportion of large firms. In 1679, only a third of the sixty-three printers still worked with less than three presses, and thirteen years later single-press printing-houses appear to have been eliminated. So although by the time Racine withdrew from the stage the industry was on a more commercial footing, the capital appears to have been well provided with printers in the heyday of classical tragedy.

Virtually all publishing was centred on Paris, where *libraires* occupied two main areas: the rue Saint-Jacques in the Latin Quarter, around the Sorbonne and the colleges, and the Palais de Justice, with its galleries of small shops, some of which had been occupied by booksellers for several centuries. Corneille, in an early comedy *La Galerie du Palais* (published in 1637), sets part of the action in this forerunner of a shopping centre, with a *libraire* among the three trades represented. At the Palais could be found some of the main publishers who brought out tragedies in addition to other works: Augustin Courbé, whose list included Corneille's *Le Cid*, *Horace* and *Polyeucte* as well as plays by Tristan l'Hermite, Mairet and La Calprenède; Antoine de Sommaville, who published some La Calprenède and Corneille, too, along with plays by the latter's brother Thomas, Du Ryer and Rotrou; Toussaint Quinet, the publisher of *Cinna*, his son Gabriel and his son-in-law, Guillaume de Luynes; and Claude Barbin, who started publishing in the late 1650s and brought out the main tragedies of Racine.

Although these half-dozen names represent the main publishers of tragedy, there were several other firms in Paris. At the turn of the century it would appear that seventeen publishing-houses brought out, over a three-year period, some 330 literary works of all kinds, representing perhaps two-thirds of total book production during that time (the remainder of the texts have not survived). By the early 1640s, twenty-four publishers can be found, offering some 610 surviving works—perhaps less than half the total printed—during the three years 1643–5. At both sample periods, eight or nine large firms captured most of the market: almost two-thirds of the titles in 1598–1600, as we have seen, and about 350 of the 610 in the early 1640s. In a normal year an average seventeenth-century Paris publisher might expect to bring out fifteen new titles.

His task was not made any easier by the pirating of texts. Just as theatre companies occasionally snatched as yet unfinished plays from a rival troupe and put them on in direct competition—Molière's company as well as the Hôtel de Bourgogne did this to the Marais, who had staged Corneille's *Sertorius* in 1662; and the Hôtel, perhaps at the author's instigation, put on Racine's *Alexandre* in 1665 while Molière was still performing it—so pirate presses, many of them foreign, brought out their own editions of plays which had first been properly published in Paris. Holland was one of the main centres of this trade in French-language texts. Strictly speaking, the procedure was not illegal, since the restrictions of the licence to print did not extend beyond the borders of France, but clearly Paris publishers did not greet the dumping of quantities of rival editions with any enthusiasm. It did not help their sales and, of course, it was of no financial interest to the author. It was not only foreign competitors who were thus actively discouraged; Paris booksellers set themselves up as a trade association and tried to impose a cartel, making strenuous efforts to prevent copies of their publications being sold in other Paris outlets—for example the very popular stall-type shops which, in the seventeenth century, lined both sides of the Pont-Neuf across the Seine, in the heart of the city.

As happens today, plays, like other texts, were produced in a variety of formats. The largest book-size was folio, made from sheets of paper folded only once and thus each bearing four sides of print. For practical reasons this format was rarely used for books other than dictionaries and the like, and when it was, it denoted a particularly important text or series of collected works. Individual plays early in the century were usually printed in quarto size, made up of sheets folded twice and carrying eight sides of print. This resulted in pleasantly-sized pages, usually adorned with a reasonable quantity of roman or italic type, with good margins. Later in the century, partly for economic reasons, smaller formats like octavo and duodecimo—sheets folded three or four times, producing sixteen or thirty-two sides each—became the norm (the change in Corneille's plays comes between 1651 and 1653, for instance); this, together with smaller, denser print, resulted in more convenient but in some ways less attractive books.

What is of particular interest to us nowadays is to know not just the format of printed plays but also the number of copies printed. As with other matters raised in previous chapters, available data are less than adequate. It is really necessary to start with the printing process itself, for this had a direct influence on book production. Two operators were required on each hand-press to carry out the various manoeuvres. Printing-workers, like other trades in the seventeenth century, worked on average a fourteen-hour day, and surviving records suggest that an individual press would be expected to turn out 3000 full-size sheets (single side) a day at the beginning of the century, the number dropping to around 2500 early in the second half. This gives a rate of some 200 sides an hour or an astonishing three to four every minute.

An average octavo-size book of the time consisted of 240 pages, i.e. fifteen sheets with sixteen pages printed on each. (Even five-act plays, of course, would be considerably shorter, half that length or less.) As far as we can tell, a typical print-run for a seventeenth-century text would be 1000 to 1500 copies. We know, for example, that two tragedies from the end of Corneille's first period, *Nicomède* and *Pertharite*, were each thought worthy of between 1200 and 1500 copies when first published in the early fifties. If for argument we take an average of 1350 copies as typical of a seventeenth-century literary work's first run, a printing-press might produce one whole sheet, printed on both sides, in a day (given the expected rate of 2500 to 3000 sides). Production of all copies of the book could thus be expected to take several days for the printing and binding process alone, significantly reducing the often short gap between the last performance and what we would now call the publication date.

Actual printing charges would not normally have much exceeded the price paid by the publisher to the author. An unexceptional run of 1000 copies of an average 240-page book printed on good quality paper would have cost a publisher about 190 livres in the middle of the century: 100 livres for the paper itself and 90 for the printing. Retail selling prices varied, of course, according to the format, number of pages and quality of binding, but a full-scale folio volume might have set a purchaser back five livres, a quarto one two livres, while a calf or morocco-bound octavo or duodecimo book would cost about 1½ or 1 livres respectively. The cost of a slim individual play should not have cost the purchaser more than a few sous, certainly much less than the price of a modest theatre seat or *parterre* place at a first performance.

Although print-runs were small by modern commercial standards, it would be wrong to think that large numbers of copies circulated due to subsequent impressions. A run-of-the-mill dramatist could not expect more than two printings of any one play, so probably less than 3000 copies would be available for sale during his lifetime. Major playwrights, such as Corneille and to some extent Racine, were in a different position. *Le Cid*, for example, first printed in 1637, appeared again that same year and then in 1639, 1644, 1645 and 1646. However it is interesting to note that of Racine's eleven tragedies only four had more than one individual printing during his lifetime. Of these, *Esther* appeared in two formats soon after performance in 1689, *Andromaque* was published in 1668 and reprinted in 1673, while *Athalie*, printed in 1691, appeared again the following year. Only the early *Alexandre* (published in 1666) enjoyed three further editions, in 1672, 1681 and 1689. In addition, Corneille and Racine, unlike most other dramatists of the time, benefited from collected editions, which gave plays previously printed separately yet further exposure. Editions bringing together the works of Corneille published until then appeared, for example, in 1644, 1648, 1652, 1654, 1655, 1656 and 1660, while Racine's plays up to *Iphigénie* appeared together in 1676, with further collected editions in 1687 (incorporating *Phèdre*) and 1697, two years before his death (adding *Esther* and *Athalie*). But such lavish treatment by publishers was the exception rather than the rule.

While a publisher's costs in acquiring a manuscript and having the play printed may appear modest, the return on his capital was also slight. For although many of the copies would be sold from his shop in Paris, he had to distribute his wares to outlets not just in France but in the main cities of Europe, too. As early as the end of the sixteenth century Amsterdam had become the biggest centre of French-language publishing after Paris, bringing out pirated texts as well as copies of books banned within France. Holland and, to a lesser extent, towns like Antwerp, Brussels, Cologne and Geneva flourished as producers of pirate French editions largely because of poor transport facilities, and these hindred the satisfactory distribution of Paris-printed books as well. The sheer weight of consignments of texts, the risk of their getting damaged in transit, and the difficulty of arranging suitable methods of paying for them are all factors which directly explain the small print-runs of the seventeenth century. In addition, as has been noted, Europe in general and France in particular had few large towns; sales to a population dispersed throughout the countryside posed very considerable problems.

Publication had undeniable advantages, as it still has. For all the dangers of reading more into the text than the author intended—a danger not peculiar to the study of drama—the printed play was a desirable and helpful complement to the play in performance, providing a permanent version of its rapidly moving action and soon-forgotten language. At times the text was a necessary adjunct, allowing events which appeared complex or simply obscure on stage to be unravelled later at the audience's leisure. In other cases, printing was particularly called for. Racine's two religious tragedies, *Esther* and *Athalie*, written for the girls' school at Saint-Cyr, were put on there in 1689 and 1691 but not staged by professional actors in Paris until thirty-two and twenty-five years later respectively. Without printing, which in each case occurred shortly after the Saint-Cyr performances, even the ordinary Parisian would have had no first-hand knowledge of what Racine had achieved on his return to the theatre after twelve years' absence.

Yet all the available evidence suggests that the number of copies of a text circulating during a normal dramatist's lifetime must in many instances have been lower than the number of people who saw the play live on stage. Of course, a great many copies would have been read by more than one person, but equally some, although bought, will never have been opened, and inventories taken on a bookseller's death in the seventeenth century invariably record sizeable batches of plays awaiting distribution and sale. In addition, many theatregoers, having seen a tragedy performed, will have later purchased a copy, and while their appreciation of the text may thereby have increased, the extent of the play's direct influence would not. It is hardly surprising if some of the less successful tragedies have survived the last three hundred years in only a handful of copies. Neither author nor publisher had an easy job. The dramatist in particular, in releasing his manuscript for a fixed and usually very modest price, enjoyed none of the modern advantages—or at least safeguards—of percentage royalties on sales or foreign reprint, translation and other rights. In the absence of manuscripts of plays by Corneille, Racine and their contemporaries, we cannot be sure, particularly with one-edition works, that it was not the printer rather than the author who at times decided matters like punctuation and capitalisation, with a consequent lack of uniformity that still creates minor problems for editors today. In many ways it would have been in an author's interest to publish at his own expense, but publishers naturally did all they could to discourage this.

It was, we must remember, an age of low adult literacy. Although well-meaning investigations have been carried out, sampling the percentage of people able to sign their names or just put their mark on documents of the period (for example, marriage contracts), the results remain fragmentary and provide no realistic estimate of the numbers of seventeenth-century Frenchmen and women who could read works of fiction. Certainly, though, a large market for texts was simply not there; or if more copies could have been sold, their commercial distribution presented almost insuperable obstacles. It is little wonder that the average playwright, offered inadequate terms by his actors or reduced to the uncertainty of a percentage of the takings, and then fobbed off with a token payment by a publisher, felt he had to demean himself by writing fawning *dédicaces* and seeking or accepting patronage, which was to remain a necessity for most writers until well into the eighteenth century. This precarious financial state reflected the low social standing of writers in seventeenth-century France, looked down upon by those who enjoyed greater social rank, wealth or influence. In the circumstances it is perhaps surprising that so many good tragedies were ever performed, far less printed.

5 Sources

Like any other author, the tragic dramatist cannot fail to be influenced in what he writes by the world round about him: by current events and social conditions but also by happenings in the near or distant past, recorded in the history books. Yet it is difficult, indeed dangerous, for the modern reader to try to draw parallels between literature and what we at present know of contemporary events, between characters in fiction and named individuals who existed in real life at the time. For one thing, although recent scholarship has begun to reveal the full diversity of life in seventeenth-century France, its varied periods and social patterns, there are still enormous gaps in both our general and our detailed knowledge of the age. Then again, literary history itself is being constantly updated. Until the early 1960s, for example, some critics tried to see the action of Corneille's tragedy *Cinna* as a comment by the author on Louis XIII's handling of a peasant revolt in Normandy in the second half of 1639, just months before the supposed date of the play's first performance. The latest scholarship places the appearance of *Cinna* in the summer of 1642, making any connection with the Norman *nu-pieds* even more improbable. The same general problem arises in attempts to link fictional situations with events recorded in past rather than recent history, although para-doxically the difficulty here is perhaps not so acute.

As later chapters of this book will stress, tragedy in general, and not just seventeenth-century French tragedy, tends to find its subject-matter among a restricted number of more or less well-known persons, historical, mythological or sometimes Biblical. The events and characters depicted by Aeschylus, Sophocles and Euripides in their plays of the fifth century B.C. were taken up and developed by Seneca in his first century A.D. Latin tragedies and then by European dramatists from the Renaissance onwards. Part of the reason for this continual repetition lies, perhaps, in what Eric Bentley, in *The life of the drama* (1965), sees as the theatre audience's need to recognise the familiar. 'A good storyteller aims at the effect of re-telling,' he writes, 'a good dramatist at re-enactment'. Yet this ritual element, which is surely part of the dramatic experience, cannot by itself explain the very small number of subjects generally recognised as worthy of the name tragedy. Books have been written with promising titles such as *Les trente-six situations dramatiques* (by Georges Polti in 1895) and *Les deux cent mille situations dramatiques* (by Etienne Souriau in 1950). While the runaway numerical inflation here may seem worrying, the main point to note is that, whereas actual situations and plots can be numerous, the range of historical *characters* capable of providing these to a dramatist is severely limited. We shall have to ask ourselves later why this should be so; for the moment it might be helpful to set this first point in a wider context.

Seventeenth-century French readers and theatregoers, like those of any other period, were tempted to find 'keys' to some of the figures they saw depicted in tragedies then being performed. In this, they merely applied to tragedy a method used in the same century by, for example, audiences who saw Molière's comedies or by readers of the *Caractères*, a series of portraits and maxims published by the *moraliste* La Bruyère from 1688 onwards. Many authors, however, specifically disclaimed any intention to describe or criticise their contemporaries. Molière himself, for instance, has the character Brécourt say of the author of *L'Impromptu de Versailles* (1663):

> He said that nothing displeased him so much as being accused of having an eye to some particular person in the pictures he draws; that his design is to paint the manners, without touching the person; and that all the characters he represents are airy characters, and properly phantoms which he dresses according to his fancy to delight the spectators.

But at least comedy is principally concerned with depicting, commenting on and poking fun at ordinary, contemporary man or perhaps at such a figure as being representative of middle-class man of all time, while in their prose works La Bruyère, La Rochefoucauld and others dissect the human condition in general, with particular and obvious reference to the society of their own day. Even if not aimed specifically at seventeenth-century France, such literature can still be seen to fit in closely with that society's mood and aspirations; the gap between fictional character and reader, between fictional situation and reader's situation, is quite a narrow one.

Not so with tragedy, at least on the surface. Very few tragedies in seventeenth-century France dealt explicitly with modern subjects; those that did fell into two main categories—plays with a Turkish theme or setting and those treating more or less contemporary British history. Events in French history, however, were avoided; there is no equivalent in French classical drama of the 'historical tragedies' of Shakespeare, for example. It may be that this difference explains attempts, then and now, to identify characters in seventeenth-century French plays with figures in real life: an audience feels an instinctive need to situate its material, to make it in some way relevant to itself. Indeed, as we shall see later, 'identification' is a *sine qua non* of successful tragedy and one of its distinguishing features. Faced with situations and characters from other cultures and periods rather than from national history, French readers and especially critics have been tempted to draw analogies which are at best uncertain, at worst unhelpful or anachronistic.

Of course any study of 'sources' in literature is fraught with difficulty. For one thing, few writers feel the need to 'show their workings', and those who do appear to provide hints or even forthright statements about their sources of inspiration are perhaps deceiving themselves as well as us, albeit often unconsciously. In this respect as in others, the content of prefaces and forewords to plays must be read with caution, dramatists being partial critics and incomplete exponents of their own work. Again, the painstaking tracing of influences, a hunt undertaken at times even by commentators who pour scorn on the method as such, can in the end be quite unrewarding. In looking at the range of possible sources for seventeenth-century French tragedies, we must proceed circumspectly.

If only because they are few in number, we can start with the plays built round modern subjects. Of these, perhaps only one—Racine's *Bajazet* (1672), set in Constantinople—is a main-line tragedy of the kind this study is dealing with, but the others contain competent and at times exciting material, important for the development of classical tragedy as represented by the two major dramatists, Corneille and Racine. Events in recent English history were of obvious interest to a French audience: a nominally Catholic country could not fail to be aroused by the struggle between a coreligionary and a Protestant queen, while the treason, trial and execution of Essex, with its Irish connections, showed another, damaging side of Elizabeth's character. The general question of religious tolerance was given additional focus by Henri IV's granting of limited Protestant rights through the Edict of Nantes of 1598, a privilege gradually eroded during the minority and early reign of Louis XIV until the Edict was revoked in 1685. This perhaps accounts for the appearance of various sets of English tragedies in France, early in the century (Montchrestien's *La Reine d'Escosse* dates from 1601), then around 1640 (notably La Calprenède's *Le Comte d'Essex* of 1639) and again in the late 1670s (plays on the same subject by Thomas Corneille and Claude Boyer). French interest in the eastern Mediterranean may seem more difficult to explain, at least in relation to the subject-matter of tragedy. Yet, as Margaret McGowan, the most recent British editor of *Bajazet*, points out, Turkey was far from being a totally unknown land to Paris audiences.

Their weekly newspapers . . . faithfully recorded the *minutiæ* from the Turkish court, which ranked second to Versailles as far as public interest in its affairs was concerned . . . In addition to topical news and political history, a long literary tradition had kept the Turks and their affairs in the forefront of men's minds. Their love of war had, for two centuries, made them a power to reckon with in Europe. Plays, novels, *ballets de cour* based on Turkish themes constantly attracted authors.

Mlle de Scudéry's immensely popular novel *Ibrahim ou l'Illustre Bassa* (1641) and the finale to Molière's comedy *Le Bourgeois gentilhomme*, performed in 1670, are cases in point; the latter is a burlesque treatment of a topical event, the visit of a Turkish diplomatic mission to the French court.

If we look more closely at *Bajazet*, we find Racine pointing out in the preface written for the first edition in 1672 that, although the story is not yet available in print, it is nonetheless authentic, an adventure which occurred in the seraglio not more than thirty years ago. Made aware of all the details concerning Bajazet's death, the French ambassador in Constantinople had on his return related the episode to the French court where, Racine says, his informant, the Chevalier de Nantouillet, had first heard it. Indeed, it was Nantouillet who gave him the idea to write a tragedy about Bajazet in the first place. Four years later, in an extended preface, Racine dubs the incident 'tragic' and says that Cézy, the ambassador, not only learned about the affair of Bajazet and the Sultana, but actually saw the former several times when he was allowed to 'sometimes walk on the seraglio cape, along the Black Sea channel. The comte de Cézy used to speak of the prince's good looks.' This insistence on an eyewitness account, even one passed on at second hand, underlines Racine's concern to prove the historical 'truth' or accuracy of his play's subject-matter. It is a concern he shows in other tragedies, too, and it soon becomes a target for his critics' attacks.

But the details of the death of Bajazet are only part of Racine's problem; he feels the need to have both a genuine plot and a credible setting. 'The main thing I was concerned with', he writes in the early preface, 'was not to alter anything in the manners or customs of the nation.' This general requirement is expounded more fully in 1676. Criticisms that his heroines are too knowledgeable about love or too gentle for people considered in France as barbarous Racine wards off by citing the well-known attributes of the seraglio, where women have nothing better to do than to please and be loved. Bajazet, on the other hand, must be shown to have a true Turk's ferociousness. In both these respects information could be obtained from recently-published accounts of Turkey, including Rycaut's 1669 *History of the present state of the Ottoman empire*, which had just been translated into French.

Such claims to historical accuracy, however, should not mislead us. There is next to no local colour in *Bajazet* or indeed in the other tragedies with a contemporary foreign background. Conventional staging did not allow it, and in any case dramatists are more concerned with psychological interest than with topographical accuracy or scenic *vraisemblance*. The atmosphere of the Elizabethan court or of Amurat's oriental seraglio is conveyed by the clash of personalities rather than by a detailed décor, by what is said (and not said) more than by what is shown.

Finally in his preface to *Bajazet* Racine comes to perhaps the key point that concerns us: his choice of a modern subject. Looking back four years after the play's first performance, he believes that there are indeed dangers in trying to stage a more or less contemporary episode, especially if it deals with characters who are from the same country as the audience or known to the majority of them. But Turks and other foreigners are a special case: 'Their manners and customs are so different. We have so few points of contact with the princes and other persons who live in the seraglio that we regard them, as it were, as people who live in a different age from ours.' In other words, geographical distance and, to some extent, social class (the princes) and unusual beliefs compensate for the lack of historical perspective. Together they help to provide the distancing which creates the aura necessary for tragedy (what Racine calls *reverentia*) and which—perhaps paradoxically—both separates ordinary members of the audience from the characters on stage and allows them to identify with those characters. This argument raises many questions, some of which will be examined in later chapters. It could apply not just to the Turkey of *Bajazet* but also to the tragedies dealing with Mary Queen of Scots and Elizabeth I; for the Channel, then as now, kept British and

French cultures almost as decisively apart as the much greater distance separating Paris from Constantinople did the French and Turkish.

The vast majority of seventeenth-century secular tragedies in France, though, are based on ancient history or mythology rather than on more recent events. Greek tragedy offered a fund of profound dilemmas which dramatists in our own day—Giraudoux, Anouilh and others—have still found worth treating in their particular idiom. Many French classical tragedies, on the other hand, draw their inspiration more or less directly from Roman history. Indeed in the period 1634 to 1669 over seventy tragedies staged in Paris—almost half the total—have Roman themes.

It is often pointed out that the plays of Corneille and his contemporaries in the 1630s, 40s and early 50s are largely Roman, while Racine, writing in the late 60s and the 70s, chooses Greek subjects. Of course, this distinction is only partly valid, for Corneille treats Greek subjects in *Médée* and *Oedipe* among others, and topics that are neither Greek nor Roman in *Le Cid*, *Rodogune, Pertharite* and *Suréna*, while Racine, in his nine secular tragedies, included three Roman plays and a romanesque account of Alexander the Great in addition to the Turkish *Bajazet*. Yet the difference in inspiration remains an important one. It can to some extent be traced back to the education each writer received. Corneille, brought up by the Jesuits, knew Latin but could not read Greek in the original, whereas Racine, educated by the Jansenists, was one of the few in seventeenth-century France who could.

But this is only part of the story and should not be exaggerated. Considering the intellectual and political climate of their respective generations, we see that authors of the 'generation of 1630', dramatists like Corneille and Rotrou and the novelists, too—Gomberville, La Calprenède, Mlle de Scudéry—are a product of their heroic age, the era of Louis XIII and Richelieu, culminating, a few years after the death of both king and prime minister, in the civil wars which extend into the early 1650s and whose end marks the temporary death of tragedy as a genre in France. The revival of tragedy around 1660 coincides, as we have seen, with the coming of age and accession to full power of Louis XIV. The study of the passions, good and bad, which will occupy Racine and contemporaries like Quinault and Thomas Corneille in the theatre, La Rochefoucauld in his *Maximes* and Mme de Lafayette in her novels and short stories, is the other side of the coin from that on which the splendours of the Sun King are conventionally engraved.

The optimism, then, in peace and war, of the first half of the century, with its emphasis on individualism, is replaced early in the second half by the growth of absolutism and court ritual and the rise of a new wave of literary salons, where attitudes to the emotions are discussed and analysed at length. Beyond the distinction which can be drawn between Latin literature and Greek, or even between the Jesuits' liberal brand of Catholicism and the Jansenists' much more restrictive version, there is, then, a more fundamental, if less tangible difference in mood and atmosphere at all levels of French society. In these circumstances it is not at all easy to say what attracted a particular dramatist to a given tragic subject.

Two examples of the treatment of historical or mythological source matter in very different sorts of tragedy may help to indicate the range of opportunities open to dramatists in seventeenth-century France. Typical of the Roman tragedies of the 1630 generation is Corneille's *Horace*, performed in Paris early in 1640. The story of how two sets of brothers, the Horatii and the Curiatii, are chosen by Rome and Alba respectively to take part in a representative combat, which replaces an all-out war between the two armies, is recounted by the first century B.C. Latin historian Livy and by his Greek contemporary Dionysius of Halicarnassus. If we look at these two accounts, we find that Corneille in his play has retained much that is common to both versions; but it is also clear that he has omitted many details, some of them potentially dramatic, while adding others which affect the nature or order of events or the characterisation.

The account given by Dionysius stresses the claims and initiatives of Alba and its dictator, who sees the balance of power in a different light from the Roman king Tullus and who proposes the three-man combat after having sounded out the Curiatii. The same historian's Tullus seeks a truce that will allow him time to reflect, while later he handles the trial of the surviving Horatius, accused of killing his sister, much more expeditiously than does Livy. Whereas in Livy's *Roman History* (and in Corneille's play) the sole remaining member of the Horatii takes on the three injured Albans in turn, Dionysius shows the eldest brother on each side killed first, with the two younger ones fighting on until the last Horatius dispatches the surviving Albans, including an as yet uninjured one. Finally, both Livy and Dionysius, in their separate versions, differ from Corneille in the mechanics of the trial: in particular Livy says that Horatius, guided by Tullus, appeals against his conviction for murder, whereas in Corneille's *Horace* he specifically refuses to do so but is pardoned nonetheless.

More modern historians such as Scipion Dupleix, the first volume of whose *Histoire romaine*, containing an account of the incident, was published in Paris as late as 1638, merely present and summarise Livy and Dionysius. So, when constructing his five-act tragedy, Corneille is able to pick and choose. He prefers, for example, the arithmetic of Livy's battle as being neater and potentially more dramatic than that of Dionysius. He omits Dionysius's note that after the combat Horatius is surprised on seeing his sister approach and also the Greek historian's comment about her love for one of the Alban triplets being a well-kept secret. He also heightens certain characteristics and polarises attitudes, for example showing the Albans as dependent from the start, almost inevitable victims of the Roman war-machine.

These details underline the dramatist's concern for a clear-cut plot and for people who act with full knowledge of the situation they are involved in. But Corneille also likes a well-filled play; he incorporates new characters, giving Horace a wife, Sabine, to match Camille, fiancée to the Alban Curiace, and providing the latter with a rival, Valère. Yet the issues are not clouded. The additions and changes of emphasis not only draw attention to the close-knit family relationships within which tragedy develops and heighten the audience's awareness of a situation inspiring fear and pity; they are designed also to increase the dramatic tension without radically altering the well-known historical episode.

Indeed this is one of the dramatist's main difficulties. Although it is now too easily assumed that the seventeenth-century French public had an intimate knowledge of ancient history and would therefore object to plots which differed significantly from the familiar accounts, restrictions of this kind must have influenced the way plays were conceived. Usually, however, if the end had to accord more or less with history's accepted version, the means used to reach that end were within the dramatist's discretion. In *Horace* and in similar tragedies of the 1630s and 40s, selection and simplification of source material are needed in order to bring out what can be seen as the underlying theme of these plays, the clash between private desire and public duty in all the characters. The former, expressed usually through love, often requires the addition of new characters, who help to focus the play on the emotions. Sabine, for instance, or Emilie in *Cinna*—women who, Guez de Balzac says in a 1643 letter to the dramatist, are the 'principal ornaments' of these two tragedies—serve this purpose, and Corneille, in the 1647 *Avertissement* to *Rodogune* and the 1660 *Examen* to *Nicomède*, argues that changes he has made in these stories have the same effect. Tragedies of the next generation, including some by Corneille, will seek to incorporate additional characters who play a rather different rôle—that of providing not so much a distraction from public duty but quite simply a new, unhistorical love interest, of the kind called for by audiences in the 1660s and 70s.

Almost forty years after *Horace*, Racine chooses to end his run of nine secular tragedies with *Phèdre*, performed in Paris in 1677. There were two ancient versions of the Phaedra legend for the dramatist to draw on: the *Hippolytus* of Euripides and Seneca's *Phaedra*, a play written to be read in public rather than actually performed. For Euripides the story is basically a struggle between two goddesses, Artemis and Aphrodite, chastity and sexual love. Aphrodite, angered by Hippolytus's refusal to adore her, uses him to punish Artemis, employing Hippolytus and Phaedra, relatively passive victims, towards this end. After Phaedra's nurse informs Hippolytus of his stepmother's love for him, Phaedra in shame hangs herself. Both despite and because of this feeling of guilt, she incriminates her stepson, who is put to death by Poseidon, invoked by his father Theseus. Seneca's tragedy, as the title suggests, gives greater prominence to Phaedra, who now takes the initiative, confesses her love, incriminates Hippolytus and dies only after news of her stepson's death is announced. Remorse has become the culminating emotion of Phaedra's career.

Now Corneille, in drafting *Horace*, was charting new territory; no tragedy of any importance had been written on that subject in France before. Racine, on the other hand, had several examples to imitate or avoid—and this brings us to a third area of source material, contemporary plays on similar themes. Garnier's early *Hippolyte* of 1573 follows Seneca closely, while La Pinelière in 1635 writes a *Hippolyte* also directly based on Seneca but with updated characters and quasi-courtly setting and language. By the mid-1640s, however, when the salon dramatist Gabriel Gilbert brings out his *Hypolite ou le Garçon insensible*, the emphasis has changed: Phèdre is now only the fiancée, not the wife of Thésée, and Hypolite, despite the sub-title, responds to her advances. Thésée, thus becomes a guilty party, by trying to prevent such an apparently legitimate relationship. Thirty years later, in Bidar's tragedy *Hippolyte* (1675), the title-character loves Cyane, a fact which arouses jealousy in Phèdre, again only Thésée's fiancée.

It is clear that in writing *Phèdre* Racine had a wide range of immediate source material to choose from, ancient plays and more modern stage versions of the legend. The seventeenth-century adaptations in particular provide interesting, if often anachronistic, nuances: the very French *dames d'honneur* and *lieutenant des chasses* in La Pinelière; the reduction of Phèdre from wife to fiancée in Gilbert and Bidar—a change which perhaps maintains the proprieties but only at the expense of important emotions; the introduction by Bidar of a rival to Phèdre. While some of these changes merely reflect current taste, others can now be seen as important stages towards the concept Racine had of his subject: the jealousy which consumes his heroine in 1677, for example, can be traced back to the humble

Bidar's play of just two years earlier.

In choosing their ancient subjects, Corneille and Racine adopted rather different procedures. As Jacques Truchet reminds us in *La tragédie classique en France* (1975), Racine's preference for well-known topics and previously-treated characters was quite exceptional in seventeenth-century France. Of his eleven tragedies, ten deal with main-line themes from history, mythology or the Bible. Only *Bajazet* does not fit into this pattern, and we have seen how the author seeks to justify and compensate for his choice of a modern subject. Most other writers of tragedy, including Corneille and Rotrou, and later Thomas Corneille and Quinault, working alongside Racine, drew their inspiration from minor historical figures or at least from lesser-known areas of the lives of famous ones. *Cinna*, for instance, deals with the conspirator who is the title-character and with the woman he loves, Emilie. But their joint plot to overthrow the Roman emperor serves to focus attention also on Auguste himself, who gives his name to the sub-title of the play; the tragedy concerns the Cinna episode in Augustus's career.

By often taking fairly obscure figures as their starting-point, dramatists like Corneille not only wanted to avoid duplication of subject-matter; they felt less constrained to adhere slavishly to the detail of their source, rightly believing that audience or reader would not notice omissions or additions as long as these were consistent with the overall subject. Now this free approach may seem to run contrary to what we shall see in a later chapter, namely Corneille's desire in particular to give pride of place to what is historically true (the *vrai*) over what is 'probable' (the *vraisemblable*). But there is in fact no paradox here. Corneille's preference is always for the *beau sujet*, and if he rejects the need to make his initial subject-matter 'probable', it is because he relies on history to provide him with attested facts and situations, however improbable, as a starting-point. Once the play is off the ground, his characters, their emotions and their dilemmas develop in an acceptably logical way.

Racine's technique is different in some respects from Corneille's. Starting with a well-known and usually probable character or situation, he ensures that his plot contains only the minimum number of people and developments for the emotions he wishes to portray: *Bérénice* is a case in point. But this tragedy is also an exception, a wager, since Racine never again chooses to fill five acts with just three characters and their renunciation of each other.

Nothing, indeed, could be further from the truth than the still widely-held belief that he merely reproduces historical or mythological situations. New love plots, for instance, are grafted on to *Britannicus*, *Mithridate* and *Iphigénie*, while of course Antiochus, Titus's rival in *Bérénice*, is an invented character. Or again the emotional struggle is given a fresh twist by changes to the Andromache and Phaedra stories. In *Andromaque* he makes Pyrrhus less violent than in Seneca or Virgil and, as he points out in the second preface of 1676, Andromaque's position is radically altered. She is no longer, as in Euripides, fearful for the life of Molossus, a son she there had had by Pyrrhus and whom Hermione wished to have put to death. Rather she is trying to protect Astyanax, her son by Hector, against her captor Pyrrhus and the Greek demands conveyed by Oreste. Indeed, Racine reminds us, 'Andromaque knows no other husband than Hector and no other son than Astyanax.' It is her resistance to Pyrrhus which now makes the plot.

A sense of seemliness may well underlie these last changes and also the insertion of a fresh love interest into the Nero, Mithridates and Iphigenia plays mentioned earlier. This is not surprising, since attention to *bien-séances* or the proprieties has close links with respect for *vraisemblance* or verisimilitude. Such a concern is made more explicit still in Racine's remarks on *Phèdre*. He claims to have shifted some of the blame from the title-character to her nurse, Oenone, in order to spare Phèdre who else-where, the preface says, has 'such noble and virtuous feelings'. Hip-polytus is accused in Euripides and Seneca of having actually raped his stepmother; in Racine the stepson is said only to have intended to violate Phèdre. But since the ancient versions of the legend may have suggested too perfect a character, the Hippolyte of 1677 is given a defect: he loves Aricie, his father Thésée's avowed enemy. Equally, the dramatist seems to be saying, Hippolyte's relative innocence—at least in relation to Phèdre—helps to spare the feelings of Thésée, whom the audience would otherwise have found a less acceptable character.

We shall have to return to the matter of the proprieties later. But what-ever the truth of the statements by Racine just quoted, a declared concern for his audience's sensibilities lies behind, if not the initial choice of subject, then at least its subsequent development as a play. Closely allied to this are a desire for verisimilitude (or for 'truth' which is *at the same time* probable), a nuancing of character and a sense of the dramatic (as well as an awareness of other seventeenth-century treatments of the story) which all call for a relative complexity of structure and motivation. In the end, paradoxically, the two approaches to both subject-matter and its exploi-tation require from dramatists as fundamentally different as Corneille and Racine a degree of flexibility and inventiveness which is remarkably similar.

We have seen, then, something of the thematic debt which the greatest

French classical dramatists owe both to their predecessors in Greece and Rome and to their near contemporaries in the French theatre. But the influence of immediate rivals is greater than has been indicated so far. It is important to stress the number of occasions in the century when two plays on similar themes appeared within a very short time of each other. Racine's *Phèdre* was first performed on 1 January 1677; two days later Pradon had his *Phèdre et Hippolyte* also staged in Paris. A few years earlier, on 21 November 1670, Racine's *Bérénice* appeared at the Hôtel de Bourgogne theatre, followed exactly a week later by Corneille's *Tite et Bérénice*, put on by Molière's company at the Palais-Royal. These are just two of the most obvious examples of coincidence of subject-matter. To this day we do not know whether, in the latter instance, Racine copied Corneille or Corneille Racine: it would be dangerous to assume, just because *Bérénice* soon dominated Corneille's play, as later *Phèdre* was to eclipse Pradon's tragedy, that in each case Racine had chosen the subject first and was then unsportingly imitated by a rival. But contests of this sort, whether deliberate or fortuitous, are a feature of the French classical stage, inspired by the absence of effective copyright and by companies' cut-throat competition for successful plays.

The influence which such rivalry exerted on dramatists is difficult to gauge, partly because it was so rarely admitted at the time. Neither the dedication nor the preface to *Bérénice*, for example, breathes a word about Corneille; Racine cites Suetonius as his main source and then goes on to discuss the rather exceptional structure and content of the play. Corneille, for his part, offers no preface at all, just some relevant quotations from Xiphilinus, whose summary of Cassius Dio's *Roman History* contains elements of his tragedy's plot. The practice was common: contemporary sources are very rarely mentioned. At best a conscientious dramatist will acknowledge previous stage treatments of a subject and point out, perhaps, where he differs from them, but even then his comments may amount to little more than special pleading in favour of an unsuccessful work. For example, Corneille, publishing *Sophonisbe* in 1663, tells his readers he is acutely conscious of Mairet's successful play on the same theme almost thirty years earlier: his aim has been to avoid his predecessor's plan so as not to be accused of falling short of him or trying to excel him: 'If I have kept the events he has changed and changed those he has kept, it has been with the sole intention of doing something different, not aiming to do something better.'

Besides contemporary events (almost always foreign), ancient history or plays from classical antiquity, and borrowings from living, rival French dramatists, there are at least two further sources which seventeenth-century playwrights tapped in their search for themes. The first of these is school drama. Corneille, as we have seen, was educated at a Jesuit college, and many of his contemporaries in the theatre were, too, for the Jesuits had a dominant rôle in secondary education in France at the time. One of the annual events in Jesuit colleges throughout Europe was the mounting of a Latin play, performed by some of the pupils for their parents and friends at the prize-giving ceremony each summer. Only very few texts of such plays have come down to us, but rather more printed pro-grammes have survived, giving a summary of the plot in Latin or in French.

Recent research has begun to show the debt which many dramatists owed to subjects which they saw staged in this way, either during their own schooldays or perhaps when they had occasion to attend a perform-ance later in life or to get hold of a script. As Félix Gaiffe and Emile Des-chanel have shown, Rotrou borrows from Father Cellot's *Sanctus Adrianus* (1630) for the core of his play-within-a-play *Saint-Genest* and from the same Jesuit's *Chosroës* for his own tragedy *Cosroès*, performed in Paris in 1648, while Racine's last tragedy, *Athalie* (1691), may, according to Raymond Lebègue, owe something to a Latin *Athalia* put on for the prize-giving at the Collège de Clermont in Paris in 1658. As it happens, two of the three examples just quoted are religious or quasi-religious rather than secular, but the Jesuit influence was by no means limited to Christian tragedies or Biblical themes, for college drama, with its didactic aim, dealt with lay figures as well as with saints and martyrs.

A second important mine for tragic subjects is one mentioned pre-viously in passing: the prose fiction of the seventeenth century. Novels and short stories from France and elsewhere in Europe provided material for all forms of drama in our period, comedies, tragi-comedies and tragedies. No doubt tragedy draws on this source rather less specifically than do the other two kinds, although it is helpful to note how prose and drama at any given time have very similar preoccupations and create similar moods. Just as authors cannot be cut off from the general atmos-phere of their period, so various types of writers interact on each other, sharing the same ideas, reflecting the same attitudes. Thus the heroic characters in the tragedies of Corneille, Rotrou or Tristan l'Hermite stand in close relation to the figures in the multi-volume adventure novels of the 1630s, 40s and early 50s. Outwardly these works seem the very anti-thesis of regular drama: the shapeless novels of Gomberville, La Calpre-nède and Mlle de Scudéry include lengthy accounts of past events and interminable digressions in the course of the main narrative, in a vain attempt to transfer a flexible version of the three unities from stage to fiction. Although chance encounters and concealed identities are common features of tragedies of the period, serious dramatists do not regale us with the hotch-potch of shipwrecks, abductions, battles and duels which the characters in Gomberville's *Polexandre*, La Calprenède's *Cassandre* and *Cléopâtre* or Madeleine de Scudéry's *Le Grand Cyrus* and *Clélie* find to their liking. But behind the obvious formal differences and the improbabilities of the plot lie very similar ideas and motives. For we find aristocratic characters (in La Calprenède's case set in allegedly historical surroundings) indulging in what could be called courtly love, facing up to moral conflicts of love versus duty or love versus revenge, moved by what Corneille's generation termed *gloire* or *générosité*, greatness of heart, and imbued above all with that unquenchable energy and optimism which are part and parcel of contemporary tragic characters. The psychological study may be relatively superficial: as Henri Coulet says, an author like La Calprenède, unlike, say, Corneille, remains on the surface, taking the mask for the face, unable to penetrate into his characters' souls. Nor can the influence of fiction on tragedy be pinpointed in any detail—the debt is often the novelist's, not the dramatist's. But the two genres, despite necessary differences, have the same concerns at the same date.

Equally the subject-matter of Racinian tragedy coincides with the more subtle of Mlle de Scudéry's later accounts and in particular with the introspective short stories and novels of Guilleragues, Mme de Villedieu and Mme de Lafayette among others in the 1660s and 1670s. Here again the link is implicit rather than explicit, general rather than particular, although there do exist situational parallels from earlier fiction, between, for example, J-B. Du Pont's *L'enfer d'amour* (1603) and *Andromaque* (1667) or Segrais's short story *Floridon* (1657) and *Bajazet* (1672). But the tortured, pessimistic yet often lucid analyses of passion and jealousy in Guilleragues's *Lettres portugaises* (1669) or in Mme de Lafayette's *La Princesse de Montpensier* (1662), *La Princesse de Clèves* (1678) and the posthumously-printed *La Comtesse de Tende*, together with the restricted number of characters and the austere form, are precisely what Racine will show in tragedies such as *Andromaque*, *Bérénice* (1670) and *Phèdre* (1677). The title of Mme de Villedieu's work *Les désordres de l'amour*, published in 1675, sums up exactly the atmosphere in which both the 'classical' novel and the last (some would say the greatest) of the 'classical' tragedies are bathed.

Our discussion so far has been concerned with how dramatists discover and re-work earlier or contemporary material relating to the characters or episodes they intend to stage. This presupposes that the playwright always starts with a subject or theme—the killing by Rodrigue of his beloved Chimène's father (Corneille's *Le Cid*), the young Nero's plot to get rid of Britannicus (Racine's *Britannicus*) and so on—that he finds sufficient subject-matter and then disposes it suitably into (usually) five acts and about eighteen hundred alexandrines. But very often, rather than starting with a definite historical or mythological episode, he will begin at the other end, as it were, choosing a framework or structure, a pattern of characters or relationships, to create a certain effect, and then fill this out, putting flesh on its bones by finding individuals to fit his structure. In other words, his inspiration can be, say, a previous play dealing with a quite different *subject* but having a similar basic *structure*.

Two examples may help to show what is meant. In preparing *Phèdre*, Racine, as we saw, could call on not just Greek and Roman tragedies about Phaedra but a number of seventeenth-century French ones as well. Yet in the ten years between La Pinelière's *Hippolyte* and Gilbert's *Hypolite*, two plays appeared in Paris which are almost certainly important steps towards Racine's version. Both François Grenaille in 1639 and Tristan l'Hermite in 1644 offer us tragedies dealing with Crispus, son of the emperor Constantine, who has married Fausta after the death of his first wife. Fausta falls in love with her stepson, but in each play Crispus already has an *amante*—Adélaïde in Grenaille, Constance in Tristan— and this ultimately arouses jealousy in the stepmother. The tragedies vary in the details, of course, the later one being especially melodramatic, but the main point is that the basic situation in both of them is remarkably similar to that of the Phaedra legend, as is the psychology of the characters, in particular the emotional responses of the guilty stepmother Fauste.

The other example also concerns Racine. His third play, *Andromaque* (1667), deals with the fate of Andromache, widow of Hector, after her capture by Pyrrhus, king of Epirus and victor at Troy. The author dutifully refers his readers back to the *Aeneid*, to Euripides and to Seneca, but says nothing about another French play which has come to be seen as an important stepping-stone: Corneille's *Pertharite*, performed almost sixteen years earlier, at the end of 1651 or early in 1652. The tragedy flopped, partly, it would seem, because of the outlandish names of some of its characters. Yet it has exactly the same linear structure as *Andromaque* will have. Garibalde loves Eduïge, who loves Grimoald, who in turn loves Rodelinde, but she remains faithful to her husband Pertharite, king of the Lombards, believed dead. Racine will, exceptionally for him, choose this rather than his usual 'eternal triangle' pattern, so that in *Andromaque* Oreste loves Hermione, who is in love with Pyrrhus; Pyrrhus loves Andromaque, who holds dear the memory of her late husband Hector and lives on in him through their son, Astyanax. In *Pertharite* the title-character returns from the 'dead'. Racine avoids this melodramatic device—although he does not hesitate to profit from it later, in *Mithridate* and *Phèdre*—and uses his rival's earlier failure to achieve his first masterpiece and assert his supremacy over the Paris stage.

This chapter has sought to raise questions, to give pointers rather than suggest a set of final guidelines. If nothing else, it has perhaps indicated the scope and variety of the material from which dramatists have chosen their subjects, ranging as it does from the great Greek tragedies and myths through the Bible, the Latin dramatist Seneca and Roman historians like Livy to plays and novels by contemporaries and rivals in seventeenth-century France. A good deal of this source-material is mentioned by playwrights themselves; indeed they often helpfully supply us with extracts of it in their prefaces. But much remains hidden, including some which throws a penetrating light on the intense and at times debasing competition for survival on the Paris stage. Of course, we shall never fully understand the process which takes a dramatist from the initial conception of his subject to its final, staged form, and perhaps we should not expect to. But by realising the range of possible inspiration, we can perhaps better appreciate both the opportunities offered to practitioners of French classical tragedy and the very considerable problems they faced.

6 Form

Once the dramatist has decided on what he will incorporate into his play—both 'source' material and ideas of his own invention—he comes to the disposition of this matter into a form suitable for the stage. The present chapter and the next two deal with some of the problems a seventeenth-century French playwright had to face when carrying out this transformation. There is, of course, a fair amount of overlap between the items to be covered here, but on balance it seemed sensible to restrict the section dealing with form to what one might describe as the more external or general aspects of a play, then move inside the structure to discuss, in chapter 7, the famous three unities before examining in chapter 8 the terms action and plot and the distinction between them which is all too rarely made. I believe that these last two items, action and plot, are going to be conditioned by the conventions regarding the outward shape of the play and the restricted time and place, although others would argue differently. Jacques Scherer, for instance, in his influential book *La dramaturgie classique en France* (1950), maintains that the creation of characters comes first in a playwright's list of priorities, and he studies that and the unities of action and time among the 'internal' items before turning to an examination of the 'external' structure, where he includes discussion of the third unity, that of place.

The tragedies of Corneille and Racine, and those of virtually all their contemporaries, are in five acts and in verse, the twelve-syllable alexandrine line. Once more, the position is different from that of comedy, where fewer acts and plays written in prose were, if not common, at least accepted. Some of Molière's best-known comedies, for instance—*Dom Juan, George Dandin, L'Avare, Le Malade imaginaire*—are prose plays, either because the dramatist did not have time to turn his drafts into alexan-

drines or (a view rarely put forward by commentators) because he may
have felt that certain topics or characters came over better if they were not
expressed in verse. The length of comedies varied, too. Most had five acts,
but many were three-acters or one-acters; indeed Molière again wrote
more of these shorter kinds than he did full-scale comedies. Comedy, with
its essentially bourgeois and lower-class characters and its contemporary
concerns, no doubt called for greater flexibility as regards both the length
and the means of expression. The 'loftier' genre of tragedy, on the other
hand, required verse and a full five acts; only very minor dramatists,
usually provincials who were out of touch with what was happening in
Paris, broke this convention.

One may speculate on why French seventeenth-century drama preferred an uneven rather than an even number of acts, though Horace, in
his *Art of poetry*, had noted early on that 'a play which is to be in demand
and, after production, to be revised, should consist of five acts, no more, no
less', a remark about tragedy which is echoed by the fourth century
Roman grammarian Aelius Donatus in his treatise *De tragœdia et comœdia*,
well-known in sixteenth-century Europe. There are, perhaps, more
mundane reasons which explain the overall length of plays and their
further division into scenes. Shakespearian drama, with which readers
may be familiar, commonly runs to 3000 lines of verse or the equivalent in
prose: his tragedies and histories, for example, average between 2900 and
3000 lines. In France, and a generation later, things are very different. By
the time Corneille had his first tragedy, *Médée*, performed in the mid-
1630s, tragedies of well over 2000 lines had come to be seen as excessively
long; 1800 lines is normal for Corneille, as can be seen from the well-
known quartet *Le Cid, Horace, Cinna* and *Polyeucte*, which run to 1840, 1782,
1780 and 1814 lines respectively. By the next generation Racine will have
pared this down still further: of his nine regular tragedies, from *La Thébaïde* to *Phèdre*, three have less than 1600 lines and the longest, *Iphigénie*,
has only 1796. But although there is a clearly discernible tendency, at
least among major dramatists, to shorten the overall length of tragedies as
the century progresses, the difference is not a major one. What the contemporary public was left with was a text which, in performance, would
last between two and two-and-a-half hours.

The five acts of a tragedy were, again partly by convention, designed to
be of approximately equal length. As we shall see shortly, various means
could be adopted to relieve what might seem to be excessive uniformity,
for example by variation of the pace of an act through the number of scenes
and characters it contained. But there was also a practical explanation for
the standardisation of an act in tragedy to around 350–380 lines. This was

about the maximum time a tallow candle would last without trimming, and since seventeenth-century French theatres depended entirely on candle-power for the lighting of both the stage and the auditorium (which was not darkened during performance), intervals had to be worked in to the sequence of scenes at these regular points.

The individual acts, the first four of them always followed by intervals, thus had an identity which many modern plays only partly share. Each act, in turn, was divided into a number of scenes. In the previous century this was not usually the case, but by the middle of the seventeenth century it was normal in France for a new scene to be called for whenever there was a change of character, that is whenever a person left or came on to the stage. This convention, which applied even with minor characters like confidants or soldiers, may seem unimportant, and to a theatre audience it was much less obvious than the changing pattern of the acts. But to the reader, then as now, the practice clears up any doubts about who is or is not on stage at a particular time. For although some characters speak in a scene, others are often just silent observers, while the dramatist, restricted, as we have discovered, by a small stage often encumbered with members of the audience, may have welcomed this minor check on the range of characters he might otherwise have been tempted to introduce, not always necessarily.

The convention of starting a new scene whenever a character arrives or departs was not allowed to lead to fragmentation, however. While the duration of the action, as we shall see, might be spread rather unevenly over the five acts and four intervals, continuity within each individual act was ensured through *liaison des scènes*, the rule by which, basically, at least one person remained on stage to link a scene with the following one. Before unity of place was established in the seventeenth-century theatre, it was to be expected that characters in one location would be different from those in another. Even when unity of place appeared, around 1640 or earlier in some cases, continuity was not always guaranteed, although breaks in it were unusual by mid-century.

This desire that the stage should not be left empty between scenes was not just a theoretical matter. There were practical problems for the actor in gaining access from the back of the stage, down through (in many instances) a noble audience to the front of the stage itself, from where the lines, in order to be heard, had to be declaimed. And only there, as Jacques Scherer reminds us in *La dramaturgie classique en France*, would the characters be seen clearly and in correct perspective against the set, particularly in relation to the details painted on the backcloth several metres behind them. Entrances and exits thus took some time; it was excessively difficult, as well as clumsy, to change a group of characters completely between one scene and the next; even the convention of linking scenes in the manner described often entailed a character on stage filling in time by telling others and the audience that he could hear or see a new character arriving or an existing character departing. There could be no—or no regular—voids in a seventeenth-century tragedy.

Whereas the play length and especially the number of acts were fixed by tradition and circumstance, we find that the number of scenes, as defined above, varies considerably from tragedy to tragedy, with most having between twenty-five and forty. Corneille, who in the six comedies early in his career, prior to *Le Cid*, averages out at forty-two scenes per play, drops to twenty-seven when his tragedies and so-called 'heroic comedies' are considered. Racine, in his ten five-act tragedies (*Esther* is a three-acter), has rather more—an average of just over thirty scenes per play. Given the generally shorter length of Racinian tragedies, the difference is all the greater. The reader may well ask, 'So what?' The point is that the number of scenes in relation to a fairly stable overall length is a good indication of the movement of characters, whose number remains fairly stable from play to play, and hence of the type of action within any given play or individual act. A high proportion of short scenes, or a series of short scenes at some point within a tragedy, suggests a different pace from that in a play where characters change less frequently. Any indication of this kind is particularly useful to someone who is only able to read the text of a play and is deprived of the entrances, movements and exits of actors discernible in a stage performance.

One or two examples may serve to clarify the point. In its final form Corneille's *Le Cid* has thirty-two scenes, ranging from eight in Act II to five in Act IV, the other three acts having six, six and seven. The overall number is thus above average for the dramatist (indeed only his early romantic tragedy *Clitandre*, with thirty-five, and, later, *Nicomède*, which also has thirty-two, can match it), and although part of the reason may be the play's origin as a tragi-comedy based on Spanish source-material, the fact remains that what in Corneille's eyes later becomes a tragedy is a play with a large cast-list of twelve and a plot which requires a rapid throughput of these characters. In only four of the thirty-two scenes does the number of lines reach treble figures, the longest (just over 150 lines) being the well-known meeting of Chimène and Rodrigue in Act III. The plot calls not just for action offstage (the killing of Chimène's father, the battle with the Moors, the duel with Don Sanche) but for plenty of movement from those, other than Rodrigue, who are left behind, on stage as it were, in Seville.

Five years and two plays later, Corneille's *Cinna* (1642) is a very different matter. The second of a number of tragedies based on Roman history, *Cinna* has a respectable nine characters but only twenty scenes in its 1780 lines, the smallest total in Corneille's production apart from his last play *Suréna* (1674), performed at a time when he may be thought to have been aiming at Racinian 'simplicity'. Three of the five acts of *Cinna* have fewer scenes than any in *Le Cid*, Act II having but two. Of these the first, the famous consultation scene between the emperor Auguste and his would-be assassins Cinna and Maxime, lasts for 292 lines, virtually one-sixth of the play and the longest scene in Corneille's theatre. The subject-matter explains all.

While *Le Cid*, and the intervening tragedy *Horace*, had depended on the preparation, execution and aftermath of a series of physical acts, *Cinna* is a play where such busyness is concealed beneath scenes of conspiracy and deliberation. We shall return in a later chapter to the rhetorical nature of the set pieces which adorn a scene like *Cinna*, II.1. But it is no coincidence that the other two Cornelian tragedies (apart from *Suréna*) with a particularly low number of scenes—*La Mort de Pompée* (1642–3) and *Sertorius* (1662), each containing twenty-two—have Roman subjects and consultation scenes not unlike *Cinna*'s: in *Pompée* the opening discussion between the Egyptian king Ptolomée and his three advisers, reflecting on what can be done with the title-character (who will never have a chance to appear on the stage), in *Sertorius* the meeting in Act III between the rival Romans Sertorius and Pompée, a scene which lasts for over 240 lines.

No act in Racine has less than four scenes in it. What might, from the author's own remarks, appear to be his 'simplest' tragedy, *Bérénice* (1670), runs to twenty-nine scenes in a mere 1506 lines, and this in a plot which is almost entirely devoid of external action. As we shall note subsequently, neither the absence of physical movement and outside events which impinge on the characters nor the restricted number of characters necessarily results in static tragedy. Rather the nature of the episode covered in the play, and the date of composition of the latter, will determine the average speed at which scenes are presented to the audience and reader.

Linked to these particular factors is the general requirement, formulated by Aristotle, that to be successful a tragedy must have a beginning, a middle and an end. Such an apparently self-evident truth can be translated, in seventeenth-century French terms, into the words exposition, *nœud*—that is the knot, core, complication or development of the play—and dénouement, where the knitting is unravelled and the plot resolved. Once again, this desirable division of a tragedy into its main component parts will have an effect on the numbers of scenes and characters to be found at different stages. As a general rule, the smallest number of scenes in a tragedy of our period is to be found in the opening act or two acts, at that part of the play when the story-so-far is usually being presented to us and we are meeting most, if not all, of the principal characters. The exposition does not necessarily coincide with the limits of one or more acts: sometimes it requires only a scene or a couple of scenes, on other occasions the information comes to us, not in a more or less continuous sequence but in small doses. Be that as it may, the opening act of a tragedy is bound to contain much material essential to the audience and the pace must not be too rapid.

Once the subject-matter and main characters have been presented, the initial situations are then developed in the central and what is usually the longest section of the play, the *nœud*. Here the rhythm will be geared to the nature of the plot and the material distributed accordingly over two or three acts. The untying of the knot, normally confined to all or just part of the last act, was seen by contemporary dramatists to call for an increased rate of scenes and hence greater pace, for just as the exposition had to contain at least a mention or basic details of all subsequent main characters and possible lines of action, so the resolution of the *intrigue* called for a careful tidying up of loose ends, leaving the theatre audience in no doubt about the fate of those to whom it had been introduced.

In the case of Corneille, then, *Médée, Polyeucte, Pompée, Théodore* and all subsequent serious plays except *Pertharite* and *Tite et Bérénice* have as many scenes in their last act as in any previous act, if not more. But there are notable exceptions: *Horace*, where the aftermath of Horace's killing of his sister Camille, including his trial before the king, is compressed into three scenes in a final act which the dramatist, in an excess of self-criticism, later came to see as separate from the main action of the play, or *Cinna* again, where three scenes are enough to allow Auguste to confront in turn the title-character (V.1), the instigator of the conspiracy, Emilie (V.2), Maxime, Cinna's fellow-plotter, and finally himself (V.3).

Racinian tragedy is slightly different—only in *La Thébaïde*, *Bajazet* and *Phèdre* is the last act as busy (in this sense) as any of the previous ones. Normally it may be true to say that Act IV sees the key decision, the moment of resolution of doubt (Andromaque's decision to marry Pyrrhus, then commit suicide; the Agrippine-Néron interview in *Britannicus*; the monologue of Mithridate), with the physical events of the dénouement coming later. The play that stands out among the ten five-act tragedies Racine wrote is *Bajazet*, with twelve of the thirty-six scenes allocated to the closing act, as the fate of Bajazet and Atalide is finally sealed by Roxane within the seraglio in Constantinople, the feverish pace of the scene-changes mirroring perfectly the plight of the sultan's victims as they try, but fail, to escape death.

Generally speaking, a five-act tragedy can be expected to reach a climax in the final act, at the moment when the crisis prepared earlier in the action reaches its point of solution. With obvious exceptions, the overall pattern can be represented by a graph rising through the first four acts (taking its origin, in some cases, before the play starts, as many tragedies throw us into the middle of the situation from the opening scene) and then falling away in the last scene or two of Act V. When acts are examined individually it is sometimes possible to detect a similar rise-and-fall pattern within them. According to Professor Scherer, many of Corneille's acts in tragedy are centred on one major scene, whereas in Racine's theatre the pattern is often less clear-cut. *Andromaque*, according to the author of *La dramaturgie classique en France*, can be said to have two major scenes per act, the first dealing with Oreste or Hermione, the second with either Pyrrhus or Andromaque herself, while *Phèdre* is a mixture, the first three acts each containing a single *scène à faire*, the final two having a couple each. Of course, some scenes are more important than others, just as some pages in a novel or stanzas in a poem have more significance than others. But it may be straining symmetry too far to want to find meaningful patterns of this kind within a single dramatist, far less within a particular play. Is the *récit de Théramène* scene in *Phèdre* (V.6) as important as Phèdre's declaration to Hippolyte (II.5)? It is certainly very different in many respects. How can one judge?

Which is not to say that the statistical analyses which have been hinted at in this short section, and a concern for the general mechanics of a play, are not perfectly legitimate aims for someone approaching a seventeenth-century tragedy for the first time, especially when the play is being read rather than seen. Indeed, we must never hesitate to take apart and attach figures to the various elements of a play, thus enabling us in some measure to see the number and condition of the individual bricks from which the dramatist constructed what Jacques Truchet, in an extended analogy, describes as the castle of tragedy. For, as Leo Spitzer wrote in his *Linguistics and literary history* (1948), 'the critic should be so familiar with the play he is studying as to be able to reconstitute the interplay between all the characters and situations, to release all the springs which the author has built into the structure of his play'. These individual items will form the subject of subsequent chapters of this book.

7 Unities

Tragedy, Aristotle tells us in Chapter 6 of his *Poetics*, is

> the imitation of an action that is serious and also, as having magnitude, complete in itself; in language with pleasurable accessories, each kind brought in separately in the parts of the work; in a dramatic, not in a narrative form; with incidents arousing pity and fear, wherewith to accomplish its catharsis of such emotions.

Some of these terms will be taken up in later sections of this study. But imitation, which we shall need to look at again in Chapter 11, is what lies behind the three unities, a set of rules (so-called) which was to exert some influence on the way seventeenth-century playwrights conceived of their task and which continues to puzzle English-speaking readers of French classical tragedy to this day. If for no other reason, it is worth devoting a few pages to the unities of time, place and action.

The idea that drama in general and tragedy in particular aim to create in the audience an illusion of reality was one commonly held by both sixteenth and seventeenth-century playwrights and critics, in Italy and France. The theory of *ut pictura poesis* mentioned by Horace in his *Art of poetry*, that poetry is like painting, is re-expressed as late as 1660 by Corneille, writing in the third of his *Discours*: 'The dramatic poem is an imitation or, to put it better, a portrayal of men's actions; and it is beyond doubt that portraits are better, the more they resemble the original.' But conveying to an audience in the course of a performance lasting at most three hours this representation of an action, this 'imitation not of persons but of action and life, of happiness and misery', as Aristotle puts it, again in Chapter 6, poses inevitable problems. No fictional work is able to mirror 'actual life': the writer, whether novelist or dramatist, must be highly selective, giving priority to certain details and playing down more everyday events. Faced with the need to entertain and perhaps instruct his audience by showing them 'a dramatic action in which personages above the common have to react to a situation above the common, in that it involves a danger, usually of death' (to use Professor R. C. Knight's minimal definition of French seventeenth-century tragedy), the playwright is obliged to think seriously about the amount, range and nature of the material which he will choose to depict on the stage, in front of an audience which is almost certainly seeing the play without the advantage of studying the text beforehand and whose disbelief it is his task to try to suspend.

Discussion of the first two of the unities mentioned above—time and place—will be important, since such restrictions appear rather unnatural to some modern, non-French readers or audiences. But the notion of unity of action, perhaps more difficult to circumscribe, must be looked at first.

Towards the end of the main period of French tragedy, just three years before *Phèdre*, Boileau published his *Art poétique* (1674) which contained a two-line summary of the three unities:

> 'Qu'en un lieu, qu'en un jour, un seul fait accompli
> Tienne jusqu'à la fin le théâtre rempli.

The unified place and time are to be the product of 'a single action' occupying the whole play. Now if we go back to Aristotle, we find that the definition which opened the present chapter mentions 'an action that is . . . complete in itself', certainly one which has a beginning, a middle and an end and which can be simple or complex depending on the number of discoveries and reversals of intentions which are called for in the course of it. Three centuries after Aristotle, Horace's *Art of poetry* requires the action of a play to be both simple and one, where it appears that the 'unity' of the second term is not necessarily limited to the 'simplicity' of the first. As René Bray has pointed out in *La formation de la doctrine classique en France* (1927), Renaissance critics interpreted Aristotle and Horace in this liberal fashion and called for several strands of action in tragedy, provided always that there was some necessary link between them.

Commentators in the first half of seventeenth-century France realised that the unity of a plot in drama could not be built on an inadequate amount of action. Thus Sarrasin, in his *Discours de la tragédie* (1639), or La Mesnardière, in his *Poétique* of the same date, who compares the necessary structure of a tragedy, with its 'continuous assembly of several incidents', to the 'infinity of parts' which together go to make up the magnificent palace at Fontainebleau. Other critics of the 1630s, among them some who attacked Corneille over *Le Cid*, adopt a similar approach. Both Chapelain, in his *Discours de la poésie représentative* of 1635, and Scudéry, in his *Observations sur le Cid* (1637), realise that a dramatist requires a certain amount of material, without which his play cannot hope to sustain the public's interest.

For Scudéry, the plot of Corneille's tragi-comedy is all too obvious, lacking variety and complication: 'the least perceptive spectator guesses, or rather sees, the outcome of this adventure as soon as it has begun'. The abbé d'Aubignac, writing about 1640 (although his work, *La Pratique du théâtre*, is not published until 1657), would agree that *Le Cid* is not to be criticised because of its excessive complexity.

Was Boileau, then, an isolated example of a commentator calling—or seeming to call—for maximum simplicity in tragic plots? It is normal to back up his statement by quoting one or two of Racine's remarks from just a few years before. In the first preface (1666) to his second tragedy, *Alexandre*, he reminds us belligerently that the main criticism his play has aroused is that his material is 'too simple and too sterile'. Has he not filled every scene, linked the scenes together properly, justified every entrance of every character? If so, and if, as he believes, his audience has been enthralled from beginning to end, then the small amount of subject-matter is not a valid objection. He prefers to note the disarray of his critics, who cannot agree on the merits or otherwise of some of the characterisation. Four years later, the first preface (1670) to *Britannicus* suggests that for a dramatist wishing to heed requests for the extraordinary rather than the natural,

> instead of a simple plot burdened with little matter, such as a plot that takes place in only one day must be, a plot which progresses step by step to its end, which is only sustained by the interests, the sentiments, and the passions of the characters, it would be necessary to fill this very plot with a heap of incidents, which could take place only in a month, with a great number of theatrical tricks, all the more surprising for being less probable, with countless declamations in which actors were made to say precisely the contrary of what they should say.

Finally, the famous preface to *Bérénice*, published just over two months after the tragedy's first performance at the Hôtel de Bourgogne in November 1670, states defiantly:

> I had long wished to see if I could make a tragedy with that simplicity of action which was so much relished by the Ancients. For it is one of the principal precepts they have left us. 'Let what you write', says Horace,

'be always simple, and be one'. They admired the *Ajax* of Sophocles, which is nothing else than Ajax killing himself for grief, because of the rage into which he had sunk after being refused the arms of Achilles. They admired the *Philoctetes*, the whole subject of which is Ulysses coming to filch the arrows of Hercules. Even *Oedipus*, full as it is of recognitions, is less loaded with matter than the simplest tragedy of our day.

Racine's repeated calls for simplicity are not disinterested, however. The preface to *Alexandre*, his first piece of self-criticism or self-defence, was published when he had just turned twenty-six. Having scored a hit with *Andromaque*, a Greek subject, in 1667, he appears to have chosen the material for his next tragedy, *Britannicus*, with an eye to beating Corneille on his home ground of Roman history. The tone of the first preface, and a number of allusions in it, show that he is making a confidently blistering, personal attack on what he sees as his failing predecessor. In that context *Bérénice*, Racine's second Roman tragedy, is a wager, a one-off attempt to go beyond *Britannicus* and to find a plot based on 'nothing', consisting of 'a simple action, sustained by the violence of the passions, the beauty of the sentiments and the elegance of the expression'. Having won that battle by the time he was thirty-one, he could relax and return to normal, as can be seen in the rather more twisting, less austere plot of a tragedy like *Bajazet*.

Although, as we shall see, the nature of Racine's tragedies is far from simple, both the theory and practice of Corneille show the latter's preference for complex plots, plays which, in the *Examen* (1660) to *Cinna*, he calls *implexes*. *Cinna*, he there says, is light on incidents (that is, episodes) and unencumbered with accounts of events occurring before the start of the action. This emphasis on the present rather than on the past is what the public wants. In the preface (1632) to the tragi-comedy *Clitandre*, however, Corneille wonders whether the audience's memories will not be overwhelmed by the number of plots and encounters to be understood in the play. Those who have only seen the play once, the author states, can be excused for not grasping the storyline clearly. If this early, rather unskilful pseudo-tragedy might seem untypical, Corneille claims fifteen years later, in the *Au Lecteur* (1647) to *Héraclius*, performed that year, that the series of mistaken identities makes the tragedy extremely confused. He perhaps exaggerates the problem slightly, but *Héraclius*, like his younger brother's romanesque 'tragedies' *Timocrate* (1656) and *Bérénice* (1657–8), is a severe test of a spectator's memory. Indeed in 1658 Thomas Corneille goes out of his way in the dedication to *Timocrate* to praise the duc de Guise, who had been one of the few to see through the title-character's disguise long before the dénouement.

So far we have considered the question of the overall quantity of material in a tragedy, and to some extent the way in which it is laid out. But while this amount, great or small, may tell us something about the simplicity or complexity of a play, it is not the only point to examine in a discussion of the unity of action. A large number of characters and happenings can, with skill, be turned into a coherent, well-unified story, whereas rather thin subject-matter may give rise to two or more unconnected plots. We must now turn to what the seventeenth century believed should constitute the action of a tragedy and to the dangers of excess characters or episodes.

If we look at a play which has been identified as more exceptional than typical—Racine's *Bérénice*—it is clear that our interest in that tragedy centres on the three-cornered relationship existing between Titus and Bérénice, who love each other, and Antiochus, who has an unrequited love for the Jewish queen. We may give pride of place to one or other of the first two characters—to Titus, whose decision to reject Bérénice has been taken before the play starts and whose well-nigh impossible task it is to convey this news to his beloved; or to Bérénice, whose progress from naïve confidence through first doubts and growing suspicions to the certainty of bad news and a self-effacing victory over disappointment can be seen as the essential movement of the plot. But there is no doubt in our mind that the action is unified: it starts with Antiochus's decision to speak after five years of silence and ends with the three characters' realisation that for none of them can there be any happiness in marriage.

All but one of Racine's other tragedies can be said to share this triangular disposition, with a legitimate relationship between two (usually young) people being threatened or disturbed by the attentions of a more or less jealous rival. Thus in *Phèdre*—a work which, as we have already seen, Racine built up by amalgamation of various traits from classical and earlier seventeenth-century plays—the love of Hippolyte and Aricie is endangered by the adulterous and (she thinks) incestuous passion of his stepmother. Neither here nor in the other plays can the love of the man and woman stand on its own: it is not sufficient to sustain the core of the play, with its changes of direction and reversals of intention, although it provides the starting-point of the action. The third and subsequent characters (Antiochus in *Bérénice*, Aricie and Thésée in *Phèdre*) have personal goals to realise and are also used by the others to achieve their own ends. They are influenced by the principals but, in turn, exert an influence on the outcome of the initial situation.

A similar pattern can, of course, be found elsewhere in French classical tragedy. Thus in *Cinna* a triangular love-plot unites Cinna and Emilie, with their mutual affection, and the co-conspirator Maxime, whose love is not returned. It is possible that politics plays a greater rôle here than in, say, *Bérénice*, for it is Emilie's desire to avenge her father's death by killing the emperor which lies behind her instigation of the conspiracy; indeed some believe that her hatred of Auguste is always stronger than her affection for Cinna, although the point is a moot one. In *Polyeucte*, despite its essential religious content, the basic framework is built up on three characters: Pauline, her husband Polyeucte and her former lover Sévère.

This scheme, the eternal triangle of love-story writers, is not invariable, although it underlies many apparently more complex plots. But in *Andromaque* Racine, as we have seen, borrows a different arrangement of characters from Corneille and offers us, not a reciprocated love and an unrequited passion but a chain of four characters, none of whom returns the love offered. Thus Oreste loves Hermione, who loves Pyrrhus, who loves Andromaque, who has both unflinching devotion to the memory of her late husband Hector and maternal affection for their young son Astyanax. Although one could (just) imagine one or two more persons being added to this linear pattern, the point is that, however many they be, the action of one starts a chain-reaction which inevitably affects the lives and happiness of the remainder.

In all of these cases, then, the characters mentioned, and others too, such as confidants, are a necessary part of the cast-list. Elsewhere characters can be episodic or simply unnecessary. In 1660, in answer to earlier criticisms by Scudéry and Chapelain during the *Cid* controversy, Corneille admits that the Infante in that play is only loosely attached to the action and that both she and he are therefore open to attack. Although it is possible to justify her rôle as that of a person who provides a contrast to, and thereby enhances the quality of, Chimène's love of Rodrigue, the Infante herself, by her presence and her words, exerts no appreciable influence on the young couple and their dilemma, and can thus be said to break the unity of action.

But not only characters can be superfluous. Writing some twenty years after the first performance of *Horace*, Corneille claims, in the *Examen* (1660), that the action of the play lacks unity

through the second peril into which Horace falls after having escaped from the first. The unity of peril of a hero in tragedy constitutes the unity of action, and when he is rescued from it, the play is ended, unless his very escape from this peril involves him so unavoidably in another that the connection and continuity between the two create a single action.

In the same year as the *Examen* appeared, Corneille had written in his third *Discours* of the 'unité de péril', which he saw as a counterpart to the 'unité d'intrigue' or 'unité d'obstacle' of comedy. Plays could contain more than one peril or obstacle (suitable tragic risks being those of loss of life, loss of States, or of banishment, according to the first *Discours*), provided that one led necessarily into the other.

For Corneille, the action of *Horace*, it seems, should have ended with the young Horace's successful return from the representative combat with Alba: according to the *Examen* he has no need to kill his sister, or even to speak to her. The unmotivated passage from one 'péril' to another is made worse, he claims, in that the first danger Horace faced was a public and glorious one, concerning his duty to the state, whereas the murder of Camille is a private and shameful episode.

Corneille makes similar self-criticisms about a subsequent tragedy of his, the now rarely-read martyr play *Théodore*, in which the virgin princess Théodore, having secretly become a Christian, is sentenced by the Roman governor, not to martyrdom but, if she will not recant, to public prostitution. She escapes this fate but, in a reported scene, is stabbed, along with her converted lover, by the governor's second wife, who then commits suicide. This obvious and bold re-working of the Polyeucte theme was an instant flop on stage but attracted the almost unbounded admiration of a stern critic of Corneille, the abbé d'Aubignac. Although displeased by the improper subject-matter, the author of *La Pratique du théâtre* has nothing but praise for what he believes is Corneille's master-piece, carefully constructed, with well-justified events arising naturally one from the other. The dramatist, on the other hand, points to a possible 'duplication of risk' in his plot, in that once Théodore escapes from the 'infamy' of threatened prostitution, the play does not end, but we are shown the vengeful killings engineered by Marcelle. If these two stages are sufficiently linked, Corneille says in the *Examen*, well and good; if not, he will refrain from appealing against any condemnation from 'les maîtres de l'art'.

Interesting though Corneille's remarks are on the unity of peril, the two cases he brings forward to prove that he himself has failed to observe the rule are not very convincing. In neither *Horace* nor *Théodore* is it necessary, or indeed possible, to detect a meaningful 'duplication of action', an uncalled-for juxtaposition of two major but unrelated risks. The danger which Horace faces in Act V (of being put to death for the murder of Camille) has a close connection with the risk he took in fighting her lover and his two brothers. It is pointless for Corneille to suggest, as he does in the first *Discours*, that the killing of Camille at the end of Act IV is sudden, unprepared, and without that 'juste grandeur' which requires that a tragic action has a beginning, a middle and an end. The play is about the progress of the Horace family, particularly Horace, from before his choice as one of Rome's combatants through the battle with the Curiatii and on to the inevitable consequences: Camille's inability to accept the outcome, Horace's inability to compromise, the spontaneous killing of his sister and the trial in Act V.

Similarly *Théodore* is not just about the title-character. Coming as the play does immediately after *Rodogune*, Corneille chooses to depict a second evil woman in Marcelle, with her implacable hatred, her desire to favour the union of her daughter by a first marriage to her son by her second marriage to the Roman governor of Antioch, and her need to prevent this son's love of Théodore. It is the vengeance of Marcelle rather than the perils facing Théodore which serves to unify this, Corneille's second Christian martyrdom tragedy.

The unity of peril (or, in some instances, perils, and the necessary link between them) can thus be seen as a not altogether helpful addition to discussion of the unity of action. We are taken back to our initial concept, not of unity but of a unification of several strands in a tragedy, in which from early on both the main plot and attendant sub-plots are introduced and where the latter are seen to be indispensable to the furthering of the former. With some exceptions, this practice will be observed, certainly by major writers of tragedy, during the forty-five year period which concerns us in this book. And secondly the material of the play, the scope of which will clearly vary from subject to subject, must be examined thoroughly, so that the action is seen to be complete. As Corneille says, the audience attending a performance of *Cinna* cannot be left wondering what Auguste will do once he has arrested the title-character; the 'end' has not been reached. So the dramatist must take matters further, with the following result, as expressed in the first *Discours*: 'Cinna conspires against Auguste and informs Emilie about his plotting—that is the beginning. Maxime warns Auguste about it—that is the middle. Auguste pardons him [Cinna]—that is the end'.

The problem which faced dramatists—that of attempting to reconcile, on the one hand, the desirability, in theory, of creating an illusion of reality and, on the other, the practical need to provide enough material to interest and surprise the audience, but not so much that it became confused—inevitably gave rise to a discussion of the time which could elapse during the action portrayed on stage. For believers in mimetic art, the logic of the situation requires that fictional time (the duration of the historical or mythological episode chosen and then adapted by the playwright) should coincide with performance time, so creating in the theatre an exact imitation of a part of life outside. The seventeenth-century French convention noted in the previous chapter, that of linking scenes by the physical presence of characters, obviously helps to reduce to a minimum the amount of time covered in the course of the five acts.

But the question of reducing fictional time in drama to a minimum goes back well beyond the seventeenth century. In Chapter 5 of the *Poetics* Aristotle states what was current practice in contemporary or near-contemporary Greece: 'Tragedy endeavours to keep as far as possible within a single circuit of the sun, or something near that.' In his later *Art of poetry* Horace does not mention unity of time, and it was left to Renaissance critics, among them Scaliger, in his *Poeticæ libri septem* (1561) and particularly Castelvetro, with his *Poetica d'Aristotele vulgarizzata e sposta* (1570) in Italy, and Jean de La Taille, in his *Art de la tragédie* of 1572 in France, to examine Aristotle's comments on the 'single circuit of the sun' and their implications for post-medieval European drama. Views then and in seventeenth-century France varied widely. While Scaliger and Castelvetro believed a playwright should, if possible, choose material not lasting longer than the actual performance, Scudéry, Chapelain and d'Aubignac made the same suggestion but realised that twelve hours was probably a more realistic maximum for most dramatists. Chapelain, writing in his *Lettre sur la règle des vingt-quatre heures* (1630), recommends typically that 'the imitation in all plays should be so perfect that no difference should appear between the thing imitated and the imitation'.

Although some late sixteenth-century English critics and playwrights favoured the unity of time (Sir Philip Sidney, for example, or Ben Jonson, who adheres to it in his *Volpone* of 1606, admittedly a comedy), it is a commonplace to say that Elizabethan and Jacobean drama tends to cover a much wider timespan that its equivalent in France. As F. L. Lucas suggests in his book *Tragedy. Serious drama in relation to Aristotle's 'Poetics'* (1927), the typical Shakespearian play is very different from an average Greek tragedy. Sophocles's *Oedipus Rex* starts with the arrival of the oracle concerning the plague in Thebes; by the equivalent of Act IV Jocasta has gone out to kill herself. Oedipus exits in Act V to blind himself, and both acts of self-destruction are recounted in Act VI. A Shakespearian five-act tragedy on the same theme might well have started much earlier, before the birth of Oedipus, with the warning to Laius about what a son might do to him. Acts II and III would then follow Oedipus through manhood, via the oracle at Delphi and the killing of Laius on the road, only reaching in the last two acts the material to which Sophocles devotes the whole of his play.

This general observation holds good for regular French classical tragedy, which is 'crisis' tragedy in that the subject-matter is reduced to the last few hours of the dilemma which is facing the protagonists. Racine and his imitators can be seen to have turned this apparent restriction on time to their own advantage, for, as recent commentators have rightly stressed (J. C. Lapp, for example, in *Aspects of Racinian tragedy* (1955) or Odette de Mourgues, in her *Racine, or The triumph of relevance* (1967)), Racinian characters refer constantly to the imminence of disaster, the pressing nature of decisions, the need for haste. 'Olympias, we must run and stop these brutes': Jocaste's statement in the opening scene of Racine's first tragedy *La Thébaïde* sets the tone for the frantic pace and inexorable pressures which are brought to bear on subsequent characters, from

> For the last time I wish, I order, him
> To leave at once, and not to be found by nightfall
> In Rome or in my court

of Néron in *Britannicus*, through the

> Your murder will suffice to prove my faith.
> Be sure of it, I run to see it done

of Roxane in *Bajazet*, to Phèdre's

> 'O shining Sun . . .
> . . . I see you now
> For the last time

and beyond. Firmly circumscribed present time, allied to a wider panorama of past time, sketched in through narrative flashbacks, and, in some cases, of future time (Bérénice's elegiac 'In a month, in a year . . .'), serves to heighten rather than reduce the sense of tragedy in a play.

It would have been surprising, of course, if, by the mid-1660s, Racine had not accepted the unity of time and found ways to exploit its possibilities. Thirty years earlier, the guidelines were less clearly established, yet even a play as irregular as *Le Cid* observes the twenty-four hour rule: Corneille's critics could not attack him on this score, although among their many points was the comment that Rodrigue had been faced with an improbably strenuous day. Replying more than twenty years later, Corneille admits in the *Examen* that too little time has been allocated to too many events: the King should have granted Rodrigue 'two or three days' rest' between his victory over the Moors and his fight with Don Sanche, while a novel, less bound by 'the inconvenience of the rule', would have allowed perhaps a week between Chimène's requests that Rodrigue be put to death. The third *Discours*, also of 1660, puts the matter in a wider context:

> Many inveigh against this rule, calling it tyrannical, and so it would be if it were founded only on Aristotle's authority; but what ought to persuade us to accept it is natural reason, from which it derives support . . . So let us not stop at twelve or twenty-four hours, but compress the play's action into the shortest possible time, so that its representation may be a closer likeness and thus more perfect. Let us allow the action, if we can, no more than the two hours occupied by the performance . . . If we cannot limit it to these two hours, let us take four, six, ten, but not go much beyond twenty-four, for fear of falling into irregularity and reducing the portrait to so small a scale that it loses all proportion and becomes a mere imperfection. Above all, I would leave this duration to the audience's imagination and never specify the time it uses up.

This final statement, revealing Corneille's view that the power of the imagination is much more important than mere rationalistic cavilling, fits in with the greater freedom of action possessed by characters in tragedy of the 1630s to 1650s: not for them the tyranny of one last chance, of one final day or hour or moment. But it is proof, if proof were needed, that Corneille in particular, while paying lip-service to the imitation theory of art, really believes in theatre as a product of the creative imagination. Out of sight or hearing, out of mind: his readers and audience will not notice the improbably abundant action if their eyes are not constantly being drawn to a clock on the wall.

To soak up excess time, Chapelain among others had suggested, in his 1630 *Lettre*, that action beyond that covered on stage could be relegated to the four intervals of a tragedy. Corneille comes back to this point in 1660: 'When we take a longer time, such as ten hours, I would arrange for the eight which are to be lost to elapse in the intervals between the acts, and for each act separately to cover only the time taken up by the performance.' To these natural breaks can be assigned minor or mundane events, or events which, though important, cannot or need not be shown to the audience.

Naturally, many tragedies from the first half of the seventeenth century (*Cinna* and *Rodogune* are cases in point) have no trouble in observing the convention of limited time, even of identity between fictional and performance time. But in general terms the plays of the Cornelian era are rather less regular in this respect than those of Racine. Taken as a whole, French classical tragedy benefited from the unity of time. Before English-speaking readers reject it as an unnecessary restriction, they would do well to ponder its advantages.

If Aristotle had useful things to say about the unification of action and at least some observations to make on the practice of limiting the timespan of a tragedy's material, the *Poetics* do not discuss the third unity, that of place. As with so many of the Stagirite's comments, this may be because current dramatic practice rendered a specific mention superfluous; the presence, for example, in Greek tragedy of a chorus would naturally reduce the locational changes which a dramatist could introduce into his text. Nor is place brought up by Horace in the first century B.C. or by the Italian theorists of the Renaissance.

Chapter 2 of this book explained how a multiple stage set, inherited and adapted from medieval drama, seems to have lasted in France until around 1640, when it began to be replaced by the single set ultimately known as the *palais à volonté*. The transformation was a major one, yet was accomplished within a generation. Initial discussion of the unity of place round about 1630 coincides with the start of the decline of the *décor multiple* and, of course, with the other rules of drama being brought into force by the *Cid* controversy. The change in stage set may also have indicated, as Jacques Truchet suggests in *La tragédie classique en France*, a more fundamental shift, away from a place or series of adjacent places as experienced by the *actor* to one seen by the *spectators in the auditorium*, their inability to move being translated into the single room or antechamber of a Racinian tragedy.

Be that as it may, the question of the unity or unification of place—an obvious and necessary follow-on from the unity of time—comes to the fore at the very period that Corneille and his contemporaries (Du Ryer, La Calprenède, Mairet, Rotrou, Tristan l'Hermite) are busy with the first wave of regular seventeenth-century tragedies. In an early *Au Lecteur*, that published in front of his comedy *La Veuve* in 1634, Corneille claims to be a keen observer of the unity of place: 'Sometimes I restrict it to the mere extent of the stage, sometimes I extend it to include a whole town, as in this play.' Some twenty-five years later, in his more mature critical writings, the dramatist narrows down the more generous interpretation somewhat: the third *Discours* proposes, not a whole town, but simply two or three specific places set within its walls.

Similar concerns can be seen in the *Examens* to other early comedies and tragedies—*La Galerie du Palais, La Place royale* and *Médée* for example— proving, perhaps, that Corneille has become conscious later of defects in plays written in the 1630s. *Le Cid*, with its multiple set and four locations, had given the author problems, although, as he explains in 1660, the action is at least limited to Seville, a town chosen in preference to the Burgos of Guillén de Castro's play because Seville is on the coast (or near enough, for those who have not been there, Corneille explains disarmingly) and thus lends itself better to a sudden arrival of the Moors than would an inland city. With the audience's or reader's help, a *fiction de théâtre* may allow the action at the end of Act I to be located, partly in the street (while Diègue and the Count quarrel) and partly in front of Diègue's house, into which he would retire on receiving Gomès's blow.

By 1640, a town and its immediate surrounds are seen as the geographical limits of regular tragedy. *Horace* is located in a single room, with reports of the battle being brought back from the ramparts by messengers. *Cinna*, being a conspiracy play, calls for two rooms, although Tristan's *La Mort de Sénèque*, performed soon afterwards in 1643–4, is limited to one— indeed a character says that Néron would hardly expect to overhear discussion of a plot inside his palace, so what better place... In the mid-1640s *Rodogune* moves between Cléopâtre's and the title-character's apartments within the former's palace.

For d'Aubignac, writing in the 1640s, the increasingly applied unity of place fits in perfectly with his illusionist theory of drama. If an actor plays a part, then the character, who must be in some place, can only be where the actor is, 'otherwise the representation would remain incomplete in this respect', for one actor cannot represent two men at once. A revolving stage would help, the author of *La Pratique* adds hopefully. Corneille avoids similar pedantry when commenting on this unity in his third *Discours* of 1660. The damage caused by duplicity of place, where inevitable, can be lessened, he suggests, if specific places are not named but are left undefined within the broader locality: as with time, the average spectator would not notice if his attention is not drawn to the point. And he ends by proposing what he calls a *lieu théâtral*, a theatrical locality, serving as an unallocated antechamber in which it would be conventionally agreed that any character could speak with as much privacy as in his or her own room and to which even major figures would come instead of their being visited in their own apartments by less important characters.

This definition of the all-purpose single room comes from his rival's pen on the eve of Racine's entry into the theatre. Just as Racinian tragedy insists on, and makes active use of, the element of time, so it defines clearly the restricted space within which the characters are allowed to move. Agrippine is to be found in just such a general room, having left her apartments in Néron's palace and been kept waiting outside her son's door as the action starts in Act I of *Britannicus*. A stage-direction in *Bérénice* makes clear that that play takes place in Rome, 'in a room situated between Titus's apartment and that of Bérénice'. *Bajazet*, set in Constantinople, opens with Osmin asking the grand vizier anxiously since when it has been possible to enter a part of the seraglio previously out of bounds, on pain of instant death. *Phèdre* is set in a vaulted room, symbolically—and perhaps literally—positioned between light and darkness. *Athalie*, a final example, takes place in the temple in Jerusalem.

If time pressed in on Racine's victims, so the restricted space is soon found to be claustrophobic. Néron's palace is a death-trap; the room in the imperial palace of *Bérénice* is as much a living hell for its three illustrious occupants as is the one in Sartre's *Huis clos*; the seraglio, with its labyrinthine corridors and unpleasant surprises, is a prison from which few emerge alive; the light into which Phèdre staggers in Act I marks an end to the relative relief from anguish which the previous darkness had afforded her; Athalie finds to her cost that the high priest can turn the temple into a place of ambush from which there is no escape.

At the end of our examination of the unities in French classical tragedy, it can be seen how unity of place is a necessary corollary to unity of time, itself an adaptation of Aristotle's restriction due to the belief in the importance of imitation. Neither of these 'rules', nor the more general guideline concerning the unification of various strands of action, is as unnatural or as irrelevant as English-speaking audiences are sometimes led to believe. The concentration which they together afford goes naturally with the French concept of tragedy, more austere perhaps than much Elizabethan or Jacobean drama but interesting for that reason, different in its effect but leading to the coherence and sense of inevitability which the genre requires.

A final comment may help. Whatever the extent to which different decades of the seventeenth century, or indeed different dramatists, observed the three unities of time, place and action, writers of French tragedy were agreed on what one might term a fourth unity—the unity of tone, what T. S. Eliot has called the 'unity of sentiment'. Not for Racine and his generation, nor Corneille and his, the mixture of fun and seriousness built into Shakespearian tragedy through the grave-diggers or Polonius in *Hamlet*, the porter in *Macbeth*, Lear's fool in *King Lear*, Cleopatra's clown in *Antony and Cleopatra*. The French of the day could laugh: indeed, the seventeenth century produced France's greatest-ever comic playwright in Molière. But they seem to have preferred to laugh and cry in separate theatres or over separate texts.

8 Action and plot

The last two chapters have attempted to show some of the conventional constraints which seventeenth-century France placed upon the outward shape of its tragedies and the material incorporated into them. Other restrictions which dramatists had to cope with or get round will be mentioned later—the choice of language, the call for verisimilitude (probability, more or less), observance of the proprieties. And while it is the aim of this book to point out not just the facts and their drawbacks but also the advantages to be gained, it may seem that the writer of French classical tragedy was faced with considerable obstacles in putting his play together. At least, you will say, he must have had free rein when it came to injecting activity and movement into his plot. Yet what strikes the modern English-speaking reader of Corneille, Racine and their contemporaries perhaps most is the apparent absence—or the whittling down to an absolute minimum—of physical movement in tragedy, the priority which seems to be given to words over deeds, and the suspicion grows that *Cinna* and *Rodogune*, *Andromaque* and *Mithridate* are more concerned with psychology than the portrayal of events, with characterisation rather than action.

Now the earliest major dramatic theorist, Aristotle, had insisted on the primacy of action in tragedy. In the standard specification of the genre which he provides in Chapter 6 of the *Poetics*, as we have seen, is defined as 'the imitation of an action ... in a dramatic, not in a narrative form'. Later in the same chapter Aristotle continues:

> The action (that which was done) is represented in the play by the Fable or Plot. The Fable, in our present sense of the term, is simply this, the combination of the incidents, or things done in the story ... Tragedy is

essentially an imitation not of persons but of action and life, of happiness and misery. All human happiness or misery takes the form of action; the end for which we live is a certain kind of activity, not a quality. Character gives us qualities, but it is in our actions—what we do—that we are happy or the reverse. In a play accordingly they do not act in order to portray the Characters; they include the Characters for the sake of the action. So that it is the action in it, i.e. its Fable or Plot, that is the end and purpose of tragedy; and the end is everywhere the chief thing. Besides this, a tragedy is impossible without action, but there may be one without Character.

By 'character' Aristotle does not here mean 'dramatic personage'. What he does mean is difficult to define, but corresponds approximately to an ethical nature, not existing in man at birth, like sight or hearing, but only revealed in action or in act, in the desiring of an end and in the choosing of the means towards it. Humphry House, whose little book *Aristotle's Poetics* (1956) provides the elements of this explanation, says further:

> We learn to become good or bad by acting well or ill just as a builder learns to build by building. By repeated acts of a certain kind we acquire a habit or bent of character. In this way qualities of character are legacies of past acts . . . In real life, quite apart from drama, character is subordinate to action because it is a product of action.

So Aristotle is saying not that you can have a tragedy without dramatic persons, but rather that one is impossible without such persons possessing character-in-action, in the ethical sense described above.

This confusion between 'character' and 'a (dramatic) character' is partly due to Greek and English having only the one word to cover both. French can differentiate between *caractère*, the eventual 'characteristics' and hence nature of a person, and *personnage*, a member of the dramatis personae. But Aristotle's comments are distinguished not just by our need to clarify 'character': he moves at will between this term and 'characters' in the sense of personages, and between 'action' and 'plot'. Thus further on in Chapter 6 the statement 'the first essential, the life and soul, so to speak, of Tragedy is the Plot; and . . . the Characters come second' appears to be, but is not, a re-phrasing of 'a tragedy is impossible without action, but there may be one without Character'. Character, that is, character-in-action, is different from a character-personage. Equally action is not quite the same thing as plot.

Some definitions may help. For Edwin Muir, talking about prose fiction in his *Structure of the novel* (1928), plot is 'the chain of events in a story and the principle which knits it together'. Moving specifically to the theatre, we find Eric Bentley, in his seminal book *The life of the drama* (1965), defining plot as 'narrative with something "done to it"', something added. The something done to it is a rearrangement of the incidents in the order most calculated to have the right effect. The something added is a principle in terms of which the incidents take on meaning.' S. W. Dawson writes in *Drama and the dramatic* (1970) that plot is 'a consecutive account of the events of the play which is abstracted as far as possible from the significance of those events', whereas action in drama is 'the gradual unfolding of the meaning of the initial situation', making explicit what was already implicit. H. T. Barnwell expresses this distinction in *The tragic in French tragedy* (1966) when he says that 'plot is the means whereby the inner or mental action in the mind of the playwright is conveyed to us. I can make it no clearer and no more explicit than this, for here we touch levels of consciousness where all is mysterious.'

The *plot* (what the French call *intrigue*) is thus the bringing on to the stage, in an arranged form, and the public expression, through actors and their acting out, of events which until then, as *action*, had existed only in the dramatist's mind. The inadequacy which critics feel in pushing this distinction further is underlined by the confusion between the terms even in semi-technical discussion. What, for example, following the convention, we called in the last chapter 'unity of action' should, strictly speaking, be re-named unity of plot, i.e. unification of the strands in the account of the events of the play. Again, action, in the rather abstract sense defined in the last paragraph, is something quite distinct from action as activity/activeness, although the difference is often not made or not clearly made. The difficulty lies in the overlap of ideas: just as a character-personage includes elements of 'character', so action-as-activity is not divorced from the inner or mental action and certainly not from its outward manifestation, plot.

Happily, for the purposes of the present chapter, we can perhaps leave such thorny problems there. But they needed to be aired at least, since Aristotle's critical statement about the pride of place to be accorded to action is echoed in seventeenth-century France by both the great practitioners of tragedy. In the preface to *Bérénice*—a text as distinctive as the play itself—Racine says that blood and deaths are not necessary in *every* play and adds, 'It is enough if the action is great, the characters are heroic, the passions are aroused, and all is imbued with that majestic sadness which constitutes the whole pleasure of tragedy.' Action comes before characters (personages) and both of these precede the creation, through them, of the tragic emotions of pity and fear.

Corneille does not offer us such a conveniently concise summary of his priorities, but the importance he attaches to activeness in tragedy comes through vividly in two passages from his second *Discours* of 1660, the *Discours de la tragédie*. He is talking about the effects of various types of tragic situations and relationships, and is unwilling to accept Aristotle's condemnation of a character who (in the words of the *Poetics*, Chapter 14) 'is with full knowledge on the point of doing the deed, and leaves it undone'. For rejection of such a situation would condemn his own *Le Cid*, *Cinna*, *Rodogune* and other tragedies. A mere change of heart on the character's part would indeed be open to criticism. 'But when for their part they do all that they can and are prevented from carrying it out by some superior force, or by some change of fortune which causes them to perish or places them in the power of those they sought to destroy', a form of tragedy more sublime than any known to Aristotle has been achieved. When, he adds in the same *Discours*, a character acts *à visage découvert*, that is, openly and also with others, in full knowledge of his own identity and that of his opponent, then the resultant conflicts form the major part of the play and stimulate pity, fear or wonder in the audience.

The comments and the practice of Corneille and Racine appear to coincide not just with the recommendations of the *Poetics*; they are in line with sixteenth and seventeenth-century dramatic theory as well. The playwright Jean de La Taille states in his *Art de la tragédie* (1572) that the main point of a tragedy is to know how properly to set it out, to build and develop it in such a way that it can reach and change the minds of those who listen to it. This emotional diversity comes partly from the disposition of the plot but also from the developments in that very plot, a movement all too often lacking in French Renaissance tragedy, the essentially static quality of which is amply summed up in this definition from Julius Caesar Scaliger's influential *Poetices libri septem*, published in Lyon in 1561:

> Tragic matter is lofty, terrible, concerning the edicts of kings, deaths, despair, hangings, exiles, bereavements, parricides, incests, conflagrations, fights, blindings, weepings, wailings, lamentations, burials, funeral orations and dirges.

Almost a century after Scaliger and La Taille, the abbé d'Aubignac writes in *La Pratique du théâtre* that tragedy

> is called *Drama*, that is to say, *Action* and not *Narration*; those who

perform it are called *Actors*, and not *Orators*; those who are present at it are called *Spectators* or *Watchers*, and not *Listeners*; finally the place used for these performances is called a *Theatre* and not an *Auditorium*, that is to say, *a place where one watches what is happening* and not where *one listens to what is said*.

With these varied testimonies to support us, we can turn to look at how 'action' is translated into 'plot' and how the latter is injected with action/ activity, despite first impressions to the contrary. In Chapter 10 of the *Poetics*, Aristotle makes a distinction between what he calls simple plots and complex ones: the former exist 'when the change in the hero's fortunes takes place without Peripety or Discovery', the latter when either one or other is involved, or both. A peripety, he adds in Chapter 11, is 'the change from one state of things within the play to its opposite of the kind described ... in the probable or necessary sequence of events'.

Now all drama requires a progression, indeed a change, in the hero's circumstances, whether temporary, as in comedy, or permanent, as tends to be the case with tragedy. Rather than being simply a change of fortune, Aristotelian *peripeteia* can be defined as a reversal of intention, human effort which, due to blindness, has as its ironical effect the exact opposite of what was intended—a reversal as seen by the character concerned and brought about by circumstances or other characters' actions. Thus the messenger who informs Oedipus about his mother and seeks to allay his fear of marrying her ends up sending him to the very fate he is trying to avoid.

Humphry House, in his *Aristotle's Poetics*, adds that from the point of view of the spectator or reader peripety 'is, in the plot of the play, as a whole, a reversal of the direction of the action'. The perspective is thus a double one. For the stage character, House continues, 'in the word peripety is contained the idea of the boomerang or recoil effect of one's own actions, of being hoist with one's own petard, falling into the pit that one has dug for someone else'. The audience has a different view of events: for it and the actors together 'the action is complex because it moves on two levels, as it appears to the doer and as it really is, and because the cause of the disaster is woven in with the good intentions and right means to achieve them'.

Discovery, defined by Aristotle as 'a change from ignorance to knowledge', covers both material recognition, discovery of physical identities, and—much more importantly—the self-discovery that a tragic character like Shakespeare's Othello, Auguste in *Cinna* or Thésée in *Phèdre* comes to, the realisation of past error, the awareness of present despair and the ac-

ceptance of the new situation and its implications. Both these notions—
peripety as a reversal leading to unconscious self-destruction, and
discovery as recognition of guilt—will be examined more fully when we
look, in Chapter 12, at the essence of tragedy. For our present purposes it
is enough to say that French classical tragedy follows Aristotle's preference and invariably offers plays involving one or other or both; the
'simple' plot was unknown among major seventeenth-century French
dramatists.

It is no contradiction, then, to claim that Racine, whose belief in simplicity we looked at in the last chapter, can be among the most 'complex'
tragedians of our period, for by the 1660s and 1670s the pared-down
outward structure of tragedy drew attention all the more forcibly to
characters, the analysis of whose nature ensured the incorporation into
plots of peripety and discovery. As Saint-Evremond said in his *Défense de
quelques pièces de M. Corneille* (1677), the days when fine subjects had to be
chosen and when audiences were primarily interested in that aspect were
now past. 'Racine is preferred to Corneille and characterisation prevails
over subject-matter.' But the *beau sujet*, so typical of the 1630 generation,
as we have seen, and its treatment differed only in detail and not in nature
from the later variety. There is much more that unites *Horace* or *Rodogune*
and *Iphigénie* or *Athalie* than separates them.

Corneille may have said it, but Racine and the two dramatists' respective contemporaries would agree that choosing the right event to put on
stage is to win half the battle of adapting a piece of history, myth or legend
to the live stage. If the unity of time calls for a compressed event or series of
events, then the playwright would do well to select a long-awaited and significant day. All four plays mentioned in the previous paragraph could be
said to fit this prescription. The two by Corneille are mentioned in his
third *Discours* as examples of subjects based on the choice of an illustrious
and eagerly-awaited event, *Horace* dealing with the day chosen for the
battle between Rome and Alba, *Rodogune* setting out, as the opening lines
tell us, to solve several problems at once. Will Cléopâtre, the Syrian
queen, speak out at last? If so, which of her twin sons will prove to be the
elder? Will the Parthian princess Rodogune agree to marry him? Will she
thus be freed, and will Parthia and Syria be at peace again?

Corneille's one-time admirer and subsequent critic, the abbé d'Aubignac, likewise recommends in *La Pratique du théâtre* (1657) that playwrights
choose 'the finest event in history' as the subject-matter of tragedy and, if
circumstances permit, the day which most conveniently allows 'tous les
Incidents du Theatre' to be brought together. Should this compression
not be possible naturally, a little tinkering with events is quite permis-

sible, as long as it does not show . . .

In Racine's *Iphigénie*, Agamemnon's dilemma is heightened by the remarks of his servant in Scene 1, recalling the countless ships which have waited three months for the wind to blow and allow them to set sail for the attack on Troy. Compared with this long and literally calm period, the leader of the Greek fleet is faced with the imminent arrival at Aulis of his daughter Iphigénie, whom an oracle is apparently requiring him to sacrifice. Almost seventeen years later, Abner opens the Biblical tragedy *Athalie* by explaining to the High Priest Joad that his presence in the temple is due to a desire to celebrate Pentecost, the Jewish feast of Shabuoth, commemorating the giving of the Ten Commandments by God to Moses on Mount Sinai. The different events associated with this festival, Racine claims in the preface, provided varied material to be used by the chorus.

This last point reminds us that one structural difference between Renaissance and French classical tragedy is the absence from the latter of the chorus, still to be found in Jean de La Taille, Montchrestien and Robert Garnier, but dropped in the main by Alexandre Hardy from his surviving plays, performed and published at the watershed between sixteenth-century tragedy, with its static and largely literary qualities, and the seventeenth-century variety, which had to appeal to a wider, theatregoing public. While the chorus was useful, not just for its moralising comments but for its ability to recount previous events, its recurring presence inevitably reduced the pace of a play at a time when movement in the plot was coming to be appreciated.

As we noted earlier, the France of Louis XIII and Louis XIV preferred non-didactic tragedy, where the audience was allowed to draw its own conclusions. But the other function of the dramatic chorus, the conveying of information through narration, has to be retained throughout the seventeenth century and is allocated to characters in the main plot. The *récit* meets several requirements in different ways. It can appear towards the start of a tragedy, when the story-so-far element which the audience needs in order to situate the present action is recounted, either by a major character or by a minor one such as a confidant, messenger or soldier. Or *récits* can come later in the play, even at several points in the plot, conveying information, perhaps, or at other times atmosphere (rarely local colour, more an evocation of past circumstances which justify current attitudes). Again, such accounts can refer to the present action of the plot, relating incidents which cannot or need not be shown on stage. Both playwrights and critics are insistent that events should always be acted out wherever possible, but pressure from the unities or, as we shall see,

restraints imposed by moral considerations, as well as mundane organis-
ational difficulties in the theatre company, could make a narrated
account necessary.

How far were such *récits* able to avoid the obvious danger of being seen
as artificial, static embellishments, intrusions into a moving plot? Some
are undoubtedly there for effect and will be looked at later. But the vast
majority aim to help the action along; indeed, they constitute the action at
that point. Accounts coming early in a play, as part of the exposition, were
particularly vulnerable: at this stage, background information has to be
conveyed, yet any audience can take in only a certain amount of information at once, especially if the action involves little-known persons. In
the first half of the century, some dramatists, having put together fairly
complex plots with a large number of characters, added an *Argument* to the
play when printed, a simple summary of the action which readers could
master before turning to the text. No such help was given to theatregoers,
and although some plays got off the ground with a series of realistic dialogues, the risk of the slab-effect narration remained.

Rodogune is a good example of how difficult it sometimes is to present
basic information quickly, concisely and naturally. In the opening scene
Timagène, tutor to the two princes Séleucus and Antiochus, is being
addressed by his sister, confidante to their mother, Cléopâtre. After
twenty-two lines of an account which forms the basis of the subsequent
action, Timagène adds twenty of his own, to explain part of the more
distant historical background and how he has been away from court for
some time, protecting his charges from the unstable political situation.
This is a cue to Laonice to continue her account, which lasts a further
twenty-seven lines before Antiochus turns up, whereupon the queen's
confidante says that she will complete her story 'another time'. She in
fact stays for the next two scenes but says nothing while Antiochus, then
Antiochus and Séleucus together discuss their plight. Once they have left,
Timagène presses Laonice to finish her account, which she does in an un-
broken speech of seventy-three lines.

Thirteen years after the play's first performance, the abbé d'Aubignac
underlined a basic defect in Corneille's method. 'Timagène pretends to
only know a part of this princess's [Rodogune's] story', says *La Pratique du
théâtre*.

Everything which he has briefly repeated to him and which is told to
him is afterwards explained fairly clearly by the various attitudes of the
characters, so much so that this narration was not even necessary. In
addition it is not credible that this Timagène, who had been at the King

of Egypt's court with the two Syrian princes, should have been unaware
of what he is being told . . .

In his reply to d'Aubignac's objections, Corneille admits in the *Examen*
(1660) that he must bow to some of the criticisms but believes that the *récit*
still serves some purpose. Cléopâtre's disclosures in Act II, for example,
as well as her self-portrait in a soliloquy in that same act and Rodogune's
attitude at the close of Act I, would be meaningless to the audience
without the information conveyed earlier. Yet it is unskilful and recounted to a minor character who plays virtually no further part in the action
and who could easily have come by the same information in nearby Egypt
before his return to Syria. Moreover he had been back a while, yet waited
for this important day before getting the picture clear in his mind. As he
had pointed out in the *Examen* (1660) to *Médée*, discord between two
countries or other public matters made it almost impossible to introduce
characters who can easily claim to be unaware of what is going on.

At least the account of the background to the little-known subject of
Rodogune was split into two sections, if rather clumsily, separated by the
lively self-presentations by Antiochus and Séleucus. This technique is
seen in more refined form and at a later point in the five-act structure in
another Corneille tragedy, *Horace*. Halfway through the action news is
brought to le vieil Horace that Rome has apparently been defeated by
Alba. Julie, standing on the ramparts, had seen the last surviving Horace
son flee from the battlefield. An interval follows the father's statements of
indignation and shame, and it is only two scenes later (IV.2) that a different character arrives to put the record straight. Horace had only fled in
order to isolate and then kill his three opponents in turn. This misunderstanding based on false information and creating dramatic suspense
makes good use of a fundamental limitation—Corneille's inability to
show on stage even the representative combat, involving only six men in
all.

A second example of a mid-action *récit* proves the range of effects which
can be drawn upon by dramatists to advance the plot even when physical
action is ruled out. In *Andromaque* (1667) Racine gives each of the four
main characters an opportunity to evoke, in similar yet different terms,
the sacking of Troy. For Oreste and Pyrrhus in Act I, for Hermione in Act
IV, the memories are haunting but are briefly described. Andromaque's
own recollection, however, conveyed to her confidante in the closing
scene of Act III, can be termed a *récit*, an emotion-charged, vivid yet infinitely poignant evocation of the death of her husband Hector and the circumstances which justify her present attitude of passive resistance to her

captor, Pyrrhus. The account is not pure embellishment. It reflects the weight of the past pressing on the character, marking her present but also helping to shape the future. As such, what appears to be mere lyricism is an active constituent of the plot and a major contribution to the characterisation. One more example of this important form must suffice. The well-known *récit de Théramène* in Act V Scene 6 of *Phèdre* has been much criticised. It is long, almost one hundred lines, and appears to delay intolerably the dénouement of the play. Yet its artificiality is reduced in various ways. Théramène follows a practice established in Renaissance tragedy by announcing the essential part of his message straightaway: 'O tardy and superfluous cares!/Vain love! Hippolytus is no more'. (The same procedure can be found in earlier long seventeenth-century narrations, for example Achorée's account to Cléopâtre of the death of Pompée in Act II of Corneille's *Pompée*). Then, before launching into his vivid account, Hippolyte's tutor makes clear to Thésée that his son was innocent.

The *récit* provides the audience with necessary information about the fate of Hippolyte and Aricie and includes, with a passing reference to a divinity, a fairly restrained description of the sea monster which causes the son's chariot to crash on the rocks. It thereby carries the plot forward, completing the description of the young couple which a classical tragedy calls for and doing so in a reasonably compact and interesting way. Its length and form can also be justified if we remember that Théramène has just returned from witnessing the scene and has had no time or inclination to edit his impressions. But above all the account, during which Thésée speaks just six lines, allows the father to come to a discovery (Aristotle's *anagnorisis*), his recognition that he has misunderstood the situation and condemned Hippolyte to an unwarranted death: 'My son! dear hope that I have taken from me!'

As long as it is necessary, told by an appropriate character at an appropriate place in the plot and, if possible, broken up naturally by questions or comments from the person or persons listening, the *récit* is an unavoidable feature of French classical drama which talented playwrights could put to good advantage. Regular monologues, too, can be used to advance the action of a play. The soliloquy has a long tradition in the theatre, going back to both Greek and Roman drama, with their restricted number of characters and long declamatory speeches. It had a further lease of life in the sixteenth century, when humanist tragedy indulged in plots in which the catastrophe came early on and where much of the play was given over, not to the resolution of a dilemma, but to the passive acceptance by characters of their fate and to a lamenting of it.

By our period, the balance within tragic plots had changed radically. Certainly from the 1630s onwards, during the time of Corneille and his contemporaries, the play, unified as we have seen in the previous chapter, works towards, rather than starts from, a crisis; there is a proper issue at the beginning, a complication of this during the *nœud*, a climax point and then a resolution. Although, as Jacques Scherer points out in *La dramaturgie classique en France*, the monologue was still much in favour in the first forty years of the seventeenth century, in comedy as well as in tragedy, and retained its lyrical qualities, giving actors an ideal chance to show off their declamatory talents, the excessive reliance which dramatists placed on this device (Corneille, for instance, introduced up to eighteen monologues into his comedies of the early 1630s) gave way to a more selective use just at the time when tragedy in particular started to provide characters with the possibility of making genuine and important decisions.

The monologue is a time for self-analysis, a chance for the character to weigh up alternatives, free from the constraints imposed by other persons, even largely silent ones such as confidants. For the audience, similarly, it provides an opportunity to see the character as he or she really is—or as near to this as any play allows. Naturally, the monologue will be used particularly at moments of despair or times of difficult decision; a character who is having success or who has made up his mind and is prepared to continue the struggle is unlikely to withdraw and soliloquise. Consequently the content varies between soliloquies where a dispassionate or emotional review of the situation leaves the character still undecided and those where, often with great difficulty, the speaker manages to make up his mind.

Not all the latter are to be found in the plays of Corneille, commonly believed to present us with forceful, clear-sighted characters, nor does Racine have a monopoly of inconclusive monologues. The anguished emperor Titus in *Bérénice*, having 'decided' before the play begins that political reasons force him to renounce his love for the Jewish queen, has still not, by Act IV, summoned up the courage to tell her this to her face. His fifty-three-line soliloquy ranges widely over the possibilities, past and present, full of self-questioning and self-answering, yet in the last two lines he resolves to delay no longer and to obey what duty (he calls it honour) requires, a promise he keeps seconds later when he tells Bérénice that they must separate. Similar decisiveness is shown in Racine's later tragedy *Mithridate* (1673), when the title-character, on learning that not just Pharnace but his other son, Xipharès, too is in love with Monime, the person he wants to marry, resolves, after a short soliloquy full of question marks, to trick Monime into confessing her love for Xipharès. Yet in the following act the same Mithridate finds that confirmation of this love has not solved his own dilemma. What can he do: kill Monime? kill his favourite son? From the typical Racinian question 'Who am I?', the old warrior takes one step forward and two steps back in his arguments, but ends by admitting that he can see no solution.

Nor can the emperor in Corneille's *Cinna*, aware of his own criminality as well as of the conspiracy now being formed against him. Like most characters driven to soliloquise, because torn between two or more courses of action, Auguste can see advantages and disadvantages in every idea that occurs to him. His wife, who turns up in the next scene, will give him a suggestion which eventually leads to the resolution of his dilemma, but his self-analysis had ended literally on his being unable to decide whether to live or to die. Five years earlier, the famous monologue in Act I of *Le Cid* had provided Rodrigue with the chance to weigh up the agonisingly equal alternatives of duty to his father and duty to Chimène, allowing him to move from the stalemate of 'I owe my beloved as much as I owe my father' at the halfway point to 'I owe everything to my father rather than to my beloved' in the closing lines.

This last soliloquy is different from the other three just mentioned, in that it is in the form of *stances*, a lyrical monologue divided into stanzas, with lines of less than twelve syllables as well as alexandrines and a break from the rhyming couplets used invariably in normal scenes in French classical tragedy. These poetic interludes, particularly appropriate at times of decision-making or despair, serve the same purpose as the regular monologue and contribute equally to the development of the plot through the characterisation. But their heyday lasts a mere generation, from the early 1630s. Just as the monologue proper declines from mid century or even earlier, so *stances*, commonly found in major dramatists like Corneille and Rotrou, have died away before the pedantic abbé d'Aubignac suggests, in *La Pratique du théâtre*, that, while rhyming couplets are just tolerable as a conventional substitute for prose, characters wishing to indulge in lyrical drama must be given at least an interval during the play in which to 'work on' the polished, varied verse that *stances* require.

Apart from 'normal' scenes where two or more characters, major or minor, converse, plan, conspire and thereby move the plot of the play forward, we have seen, then, that even such apparently unpromising devices as *récits* and regular or lyrical monologues can, in skilled hands, contribute to the advance of a tragedy's action. Many narrations and soliloquies, of course, do not rise above the mediocre, but we are not concerned with unsuccessful dramatists in this study. Yet talented writers such as Corneille and Racine are not concerned just with these additions to the standard mix of dialogue scenes. They and their principal contemporaries see that if stage conditions and restraints like verisimilitude and propriety require drama to give pride of place to words rather than to actions, the text itself, through careful arrangement of its parts, can create as much interest and suspense as more obviously eventful drama.

Although Georges May is wrong to suggest in his book *Tragédie cornélienne, tragédie racinienne* (1948) that Corneille's principal, indeed almost sole, interest is the creation of surprise, the author of *Le Cid* does attach great importance to surprise and suspense in his tragedies, even though he rejects plots where discovery of physical identity plays a part (and which Aristotle favoured, since they 'will serve to astound us', as Chapter 14 of the *Poetics* puts it). Plays where characters act with full knowledge of whom it is they are attacking might seem less suited to surprise, yet, as we have seen, the resolute Cornelian hero, unswayed by events, is largely a myth put about by late nineteenth-century critics. The last act of *Cinna* and the effect of Auguste's decision on all three conspirators—and indeed on the emperor himself—is a good example of the unexpected exerting a considerable influence on his character and on the plot of the play. Corneille's previous tragedy *Horace* introduces different changes of direction, as when the mistaken news of Horace's defeat, followed shortly afterwards by the correct version, is seen to affect le vieil Horace and the two women, especially Camille, in a way which is far from gratuitous.

It would be wrong to think that Racine is above using such methods. Indeed he goes further in a sense, for in two of his best-known tragedies he takes over a device used frequently by his contemporaries Thomas Corneille and Quinault, but gives it greater force by integrating it into the heart of his plot. This is the unexpected return of a character believed dead. Lesser dramatists made use of this *truc*, but once used and having caused a momentary diversion it was discarded and further devices were introduced. In *Mithridate*, however, it is only the report of Mithridate's death that allows first Xipharès, then Pharnace to declare their love to Monime publicly. Their joy is shortlived, for in the very next scene the king of Pontus is declared to be alive and on the point of return. With four acts of his tragedy to run, it is clear that Racine is interested not in the surprise as such, but in the long-term effects which the declarations of the first act will have on the two sons and the woman they love. Similarly in *Phèdre* it is only the rumour that Thésée is dead (I.4) that allows Phèdre, despite her weakness, to declare her love to her stepson (II.5). The husband's return to Troezen in Act III ends Phèdre's brief, if tormented happiness; she has to face greatly increased feelings of guilt in the second half of the play.

As the late Geoffrey Brereton points out in his chapter on Racine in *French tragic drama in the sixteenth and seventeenth centuries* (1973), the author of *Bérénice* uses many devices and stage effects, borrowed from romanesque tragedy, to engender suspense in his plots. False reports are one thing; but *Iphigénie* contains a case of concealed identity (Eriphile), and the same play, like his first, *La Thébaïde*, introduces an oracle with a less than clear message. Elsewhere, too, faced with doubts about several characters' emotional preferences and with other ambiguities, the audience is as confused as some of the cast, although the confusion is never gratuitous but, rather, productive of dramatic tension. The latter can also be achieved by well-engineered *coups de théâtre*, for example, by the timely appearance of a messenger to prevent the death of one of the main characters. Corneille's *Rodogune* and Racine's *Mithridate* both contain fortuitous arrivals of this kind in their fifth act. But while the entry of Timagène forestalls Cléopâtre's plan by stopping Antiochus and Rodogune from drinking the cup which they are unaware is poisoned, the arrival of Arbate in *Mithridate*, although equally dramatic and necessary, is rather less melodramatic: Monime is aware that she is drinking poison, but Mithridate has changed his command at the last moment and the cup is dashed from her hands in order that she may witness his arrival and death and be united with the man she loves.

A similar concern is evident in Racine's use of physical objects—the sword that Hippolyte inadvertently leaves behind him in Act II after Phèdre's confession of love and which is later used by Thésée to incriminate his son, or the letters which Bérénice writes to Titus (*Bérénice*, V.5) and which Bajazet writes to Atalide—a letter confirming his love and Roxane's suspicions, part of the text of which is read in Act IV of that play.

A further procedure used to increase tension in both audience and characters is the eavesdropping scene, more common in comedy. The often-quoted example here is the moment in Act II of *Britannicus* where Junie is forced by her captor Néron to appear to reject the advances of Britannicus, while the emperor overhears the conversation from nearby. As he tells her beforehand, he will be able to understand and to 'hear' (a play on the two senses of *entendre*) even the silent glances she may give her lover, who is understandably distraught when she refuses to look him straight in the eye.

Surprise, then, *coups de théâtre*, and their effect on the stage character are a legitimate concern of even the greatest dramatist, provided they are put to use in the plot and are not merely designed to amuse the audience briefly. Of course, the audience in its turn may be surprised by events in a play which are not surprising to the participants. D'Aubignac comments in his discussion on deliberation scenes that the position of Cinna and Maxime in the consultation with Auguste in Act II of *Cinna* is very puzzling to the audience. How will the conspirators react to the emperor's sudden desire to sound them out? And when the audience has heard the advice they give him, it may be led to think that 'the treason will not take place', especially as Cinna and Maxime appear to waver. But when the latter decide to go ahead, the spectators no longer know what to expect, says d'Aubignac.

Our discussion is already touching on the second of the two terms introduced earlier, suspense. Again, this affects the characters in a tragedy's plot but perhaps even more this time the members of the audience. We have seen how a strict division of plays into five acts, with four intervals, was counteracted to some extent by the necessary linking of scenes within each act. It would be fair to say that French classical playwrights also paid attention to the linking of each act to the following one. Like present-day television or magazine serial writers, they saw the drawbacks of the clearly-defined one-act slot but also the possibilities for dramatic tension created by ends of acts, intervals and the next instalment of the story to come in the following act.

Corneille remarks in his third *Discours* on the desire for continuity through a play, with incomplete sub-plots serving to carry forward the main action and keep the spectator in a pleasant state of suspense, 'une agréable suspension', especially at the close of an act. Earlier, in the first *Discours*, he advises delaying the dénouement of a tragedy as long as possible in Act V, the better to maintain tension in the minds of the audience. The critic is himself a master of suspense. The closing scene of Act I of *Cinna*, with its sudden summons to Cinna and its effect on Emilie, is a prime example, but each of the three following acts also ends on a question mark or series of them. The same is true of *Rodogune*: the first four acts end with us asking in turn, 'Which of the two princes does Rodogune love? How can Séleucus and Antiochus cope with Cléopâtre's demand that Rodogune be put to death? How can Rodogune's parallel request to the princes be met? Will Cléopâtre succeed in killing her two sons?'

In Racinian tragedy, as critics have pointed out, acts tend to end with statements or decisions rather than questions, with problems temporarily solved rather than urgently posed. Thus in *Bérénice* Act I closes with Bérénice confident of Titus's love, Act II with her belief that he may be jealous but that that is proof of his affection. In Act III scene 4 Antiochus has decided to leave Rome, snubbed by the Jewish queen, while Act IV ends with Titus's momentous decision to obey the Senate's call rather than succumb to the temptation of visiting Bérénice again. But this decisiveness is largely illusion. Given the characters' nature, we know that they are easily swayed and that nothing is permanent, no final solution has been or can be reached. Thus our expectations are kept alive, the gap necessarily created by the interval is in part bridged, and the plot is given further unity and momentum.

The modern reader may have no series of intervals to hold him up, but he or she is thus deprived of some of the movement and gesture a live performance of a French classical tragedy, then or now, is able to provide. The text of the play in these two settings, on stage and in study, has different conditions to cope with each time. But either way it can perhaps now be seen that a general absence of physical action does not result in mere elegiac tragedy.

9 Characters

'The first essential,' Aristotle said, 'the life and soul, so to speak, of Tragedy is the Plot; and ... the Characters come second.' Modern interest in stage characters, and in the 'tragic hero' in particular, is not something which seventeenth-century French dramatists or critics appear to have shared; action and its problems came before the psychological study of persons in crisis. But the framework of the plot has to be clothed in some way, and, as we have seen, writers of French classical tragedy followed their predecessors in choosing as protagonists the kings, queens, emperors and other persons in authority who had been deemed suitable from Aeschylus onwards.

True, Corneille in 1650 published a romantic tragi-comedy called *Don Sanche* (which he labelled a 'heroic comedy') in which the widowed queen of Castile falls in love with a mere warrior of unknown origin, who secretly believes he is a fisherman's son but who turns out, to everyone's satisfaction, to be heir to the throne of Aragon. Although the apparently bourgeois, indeed plebeian hero is proved to have royal blood, Corneille argues in the dedication prefacing the play that Aristotle does not prescribe noble birth but only noble behaviour, so tragedy could justifiably 'go lower' in choosing its protagonists. Indeed, since the *Poetics* believes that the tragic emotions are best aroused in the audience by the sight of suffering characters who are 'like ourselves', what better source of pity and fear than characters 'whom we resemble perfectly'?

Ten years later, in the second *Discours*, he can claim that as long as the action in tragedy is suitably distinguished, the status of the characters is of secondary importance. The misfortunes of people other than kings and princes could be shown if they were afflicted by sufficiently illustrious and extraordinary ones and if history took the trouble to tell us about them.

But since the critics have attacked a previous tragedy of his, *Théodore* (1645), for its lack of propriety, subjects with characters from the Third Estate might run into similar problems. Seventeenth-century France, perhaps remembering Aristotle's requirement that a character should 'fall', draws the same conclusion as England, where under rather different conditions Elizabethan tragedy, too, had avoided bourgeois themes except in a few instances (*Arden of Feversham, A Yorkshire Tragedy*). It would be wrong to think, though, that French tragedy in our period dealt in only well-known names. Jacques Truchet usefully reminds us in *La tragédie classique en France* that the seventeenth-century repertoire is not limited to variations on the Oedipus and Phaedra stories. Of course, as has been pointed out, duplication of subjects was common, rival dramatists vying to be first to bring out a tragedy on a particular theme in a particular year. But common though this practice was, it related to only a small proportion of the total production of plays; and simultaneous tragedies often proved what varied results could emerge from the same starting point—an examination of Racine's *Bérénice* and Corneille's *Tite et Bérénice* will confirm this. Further diversity, even with well-known characters, comes from their re-appearing in different guises, at different points in their careers, like the recurring characters in Balzac's *Comédie humaine*. But the great majority of plays, while having a background into which famous persons intrude, are essentially focused on minor or even unknown historical or legendary characters. This is particularly true of secondary dramatists of both the 1630 and 1660 generations, but it also applies to Corneille: the *beau sujet* he favoured is easier to tackle if it has not been treated before on the stage. Only Racine falls back almost invariably on familiar topics and figures, and these he changes, often radically.

Characters, then, were of royal or imperial rank, and often chosen from among the less well-known. A third general point worth remembering is that in any tragedy the number of characters that can be shown is strictly limited, not so much for theoretical reasons (although there were suggestions about the optimum number) but for practical purposes. While Shakespeare, benefiting from a large and versatile company of actors, could introduce on average thirty-nine characters into each of his historical plays and twenty-eight into each tragedy, Corneille, Racine and their contemporaries were faced with far smaller companies at the Théâtre du Marais and the Hôtel de Bourgogne in Paris—perhaps no more than ten or twelve actors at any one time. Consequently the cast-lists had to be much shorter than in Elizabethan England. Sometimes there could be a small amount of doubling-up; occasionally minor parts might be taken by players from outside the resident troupe; and, as we shall see, not all characters in a tragedy even need to appear on stage. But these procedures did not alter the situation radically.

One advantage of a restricted cast-list is that unity of action and unity of tone are easier to maintain, while playwrights, knowing the personalities of a theatre troupe during a particular season, could compose their material accordingly, bearing in mind the strengths and weaknesses of individuals, the overall balance of the company, even a basic matter like the proportion of men to women. In Cornelian tragedy there are invariably more male than female parts (often the proportion is two or even three to one), whereas by Racine's time the composition of the Bourgogne troupe is slightly different: *Bajazet* and *Phèdre* both require more actresses than actors. At least, even by Corneille's time, both sexes were available—Shakespeare's tragedies and others in England before the Restoration are based very largely on male characters, since any women's parts had to be played by young men before their voices changed.

Comedy, it is generally believed, shows us 'types', while tragedy deals with individuals. In fact, the distinction is not quite so clear, as the plays of Molière prove in respect of the first category. Nor are all the cast in French classical tragedies given enough separate traits to be called individuals, 'rounded' characters. But within a number of fairly clear categories the principal figures in Pierre Corneille or Racine, Rotrou or Thomas Corneille, do stand out, differentiated from each other. Since tragedy depends for its effect on the interplay of closely related persons, 'when murder or the like is done or meditated by brother on brother, by son on father, by mother on son, or son on mother', as Aristotle puts it in Chapter 14 of the *Poetics*, it is natural to expect characters to be separated into two generations, parents and children.

What do we find? If we invert our normal order and take Racine as our first example, we discover that almost all his tragedies introduce at least two generations of characters. What is more, many do not survive the play and very few of those who do could be said to survive happily. In *La Thébaïde*, his first completed play, the enemy brothers plus their mother Jocaste, sister Antigone and cousin Hémon all die, while their uncle Créon, the sole survivor, sums up his position by calling it a living death. In *Alexandre*, Porus, the local Indian king, who is defying the conquering Alexander the Great, is defeated but forgiven, while his jealous neighbour, Taxile, dies. *Andromaque* contains the deaths of two of the four principal characters, Pyrrhus and Hermione, and the (no doubt temporary) madness of a third, Oreste; only Andromaque is left intact, but in far from happy circumstances. In *Britannicus*, the youthful tyrant Néron has Britannicus poisoned, the girl he loves must seek refuge with the Vestal Virgins, and the emperor's mother is left to live in constant fear of her son.

After *Bérénice*, a play with no physical deaths, as the author boasts, but the much more significant decision of the characters to part for ever, and *Bajazet*, where the helplessness and eventual deaths of Bajazet and his cousin Atalide are more important than any age difference between them and the Sultan and Sultana, the distinction between young and old returns: *Mithridate* shows the ageing king committing suicide to avoid defeat by the Romans, *Iphigénie* the saving of the title-character from the sacrifice apparenty demanded of her, while Eriphile is made a victim in her place. Racine's last and perhaps best-known tragedy, *Phèdre*, culminates in the death of stepmother and stepson and Thésée's loss of wife and son.

Leaving aside the two late, Biblically-inspired plays *Esther* and *Athalie*, where the Jews represented by Esther and her uncle, and then the young king of Judah and the High Priest Joad repel all attacks while the Persian king's adviser and then Athalie and her evil adviser Mathan perish, the message is clear. Apart perhaps from *Alexandre*, with its heroic title-character, and *Mithridate*, where the father's death is counteracted by his Cornelian strength of purpose and the survival of the younger generation, majestic sadness such as Racine talks about in the preface to *Bérénice*, or something worse—the deaths, frequently violent deaths, which he there says are not necessary in every tragedy—is what predominates. Most often the blame must be laid on the self-gratification or desire for self-preservation of the older generation, who operate in a world from which most explicit moral values seem noticeably absent.

The main characters shown by Corneille have many similarities with those of Racine, but also some differences. Here, the younger people are seen to be excessively victorious or else victims, while their parents or rulers, those who govern in theory, are shown in practice to be either weak or tyrannical. The titles of many of his best-known tragedies—and we can only examine a selection—take the names of mere youngsters, in some cases not yet out of their teens. Rodrigue (called 'Le Cid'), Horace, Cinna, Nicomède or Suréna, to cite some examples from Corneille's production between 1637 and 1674, are each seen as stronger than the fathers and/or monarchs who should normally control them: Don Diègue and King Fernand in *Le Cid*; the old Horace and King Tulle in *Horace*; the emperor Auguste in *Cinna*; Prusias in *Nicomède*; Orode, the king in *Suréna*. Diègue is aged and without the physical strength to avenge the personal insult he receives from Don Gomès, Comte de Gormas, early in the action, while the king, saved from a Moorish invasion thanks to Rodrigue, who has also killed the Count and defeated a challenger in a duel, comes to realise that Diègue's son is indispensable to the State and puts him in charge of the army after only a hectic twenty-four hours of valorous combat.

In *Horace*, the father sees his three sons as defenders of Rome and his successors in battle and speaks up strongly for the title-character against the charge that he has murdered his sister Camille. Tulle cannot ignore that crime but admits that Horace's services to the State make it impossible to punish him. Similarly, Auguste, though conscious of Cinna's treachery, is even more aware of his own past criminality and in the end (if one interprets the surprise outcome correctly) finds it prudent to forgive and forget, while at the same time consolidating his own position and establishing a new identity for himself.

The weak Bithynian king Prusias, dominated by his scheming wife Arsinoé, is defied by Nicomède, his son by a first marriage, who, helped by a popular revolt, is freed from imprisonment to find himself in command. Suréna, a victorious Parthian general in love with a captive Armenian princess, is judged by the king of Parthia to have become too powerful. The play ends with his death, presumably at Orode's instigation, but the tyrant ruler has won a Pyrrhic victory.

Other inadequate rulers from Corneille's early period include Félix, governor of Armenia, eventually dominated by the conversions of both his son-in-law Polyeucte and his daughter Pauline and brought, by their example, to embrace Christianity himself, and Ptolomée, the Egyptian king in *Pompée*, ruled, as we shall see, not by one of his children but by an evil adviser. All the male characters named are a prey to weakness, inflexibility, political expediency or self-preservation, and often to two or more of these at the same time. Although their motives are often not of the purest, they are human in their obvious failings. Writing in 1660 about one of his early 'tragedies' *Clitandre*, published as a tragi-comedy in 1632, Corneille comments on the difficulty of staging a king, provincial governor or equivalent person. He may be shown, the author suggests, either as a king or as a man or as a judge, or else with two or even all of these attributes. His Auguste, he claims, is depicted as a mere king-figure, concerned not with any personal passion but only with preserving his position in the state, which is being undermined.

Characters in the heroic comedy *Don Sanche* (1650) and tragedy *Pertharite* (1651) are shown as private human beings, since they are beset by private passions which do not affect the state. The third category is represented by King Fernand in *Le Cid*, who acts as a judge when, independently of any interest in the state or in personal advancement, he intervenes to solve another person's problems. This rôle is really unworthy of a king's status, Corneille adds, and cannot be given to first-rank actors. But some of his protagonists combine different functions: Antiochus in *Rodogune*, Nicomède in the play of that name and, we would add, the Auguste of *Cinna*, are both kingly and human, while Félix in *Polyeucte* and Valens, the Roman governor of Antioch in *Théodore*, exercise authority and also act as judges.

Inadequate though this analysis is, it shows that Corneille was aware of the problems of depicting male characters whose age or political or social status might suggest that they would be little troubled by feelings of inadequacy. Contrasted with them he has set a group of children or subjects (the difference is not great) who appear more successful, but at times betray signs of extremism or obstinacy. After Rodrigue, the perfect young hero, following his duty without relinquishing any of his passion, as Corneille says in the *Examen* to *Le Cid*, we find the resolute, successful but idealistic figure of Horace; then Cinna, whose love of Emilie overcomes his feelings of guilt and his respect for Auguste; Polyeucte, whose neophyte's fervour enables him to surmount his mere human ideal; Nicomède, a man who, as Geoffrey Brereton puts it, 'combines the stiff upper lip with a capacity for bitter sarcasm'; and finally Suréna, who, like Rodrigue and Chimène and Nicomède and Laodice, has an unblemished love for Eurydice but also an obstinate unwillingness to heed the tyrant Orode's ultimatum. Of these male characters, only Suréna dies unnecessarily; Polyeucte's martyrdom is 'successful' in that both his wife and father-in-law are converted by it, while Rodrigue, Horace, Cinna and Nicomède live to fight another day.

Alongside these two generations of men Corneille places an extensive range of women characters. Some are eminently human, concerned above all with their passion, although they may have other ideals as well. Chimène and the Infante in *Le Cid*, Camille and Sabine in *Horace*, Pauline in *Polyeucte* are all inspired by love, while even Emilie, the instigator of the conspiracy in *Cinna*, can claim that she loves Cinna even more than she hates Auguste. But other of Corneille's female characters are of a different nature. Médée, heroine of his first tragedy, Cléopâtre in *Rodogune*, Marcelle in *Théodore* and to some extent Arsinoé in *Nicomède* are shown as inherently evil, willing to stop at nothing to further their own ambitions. In his dedicatory epistle of 1639, Corneille describes Médée as completely evil and does not attempt to excuse her crimes, which include the killing of her young children. But in the lengthy *Examen* some twenty years later he suggests that Créuse and her father Créon, who both die from contact with a dress poisoned by the title-character, deserve their fate because of what they have done to Médée. The enchantress thus combines supernatural power and self-sufficient human egoism with a certain justification, for she has been badly treated by Créon and her faithless husband Jason.

The power-hungry Cléopâtre, 'this second Médée', as Corneille calls her in the *Avertissement*, schemes to avoid having to pass the power she wields in Syria to one of her twin sons, kills the younger of them and all but succeeds in murdering the other and Rodogune, the captive princess he might marry. The queen's forceful exit, drinking the poison she destined for the young people, makes her an archetypal 'Cornelian heroine', a source of awe or astonishment in an audience which could never begin to give moral approval to her actions. Marcelle, too, has ambitions for her daughter by a previous marriage and requires first to humiliate, then to exterminate the Christian Théodore. The killing she undertakes in person, stabbing Théodore's lover and then herself at the same time. In comparison with this 'unnatural mother' and her two predecessors, Arsinoé in *Nicomède* is mildness itself. As the author remarks in both *Au Lecteur* and *Examen*, she, like other second wives, has complete control over her elderly husband, but is frustrated from securing power for a son by her first marriage by a popular uprising and this very son's magnanimity.

This large gallery of Cornelian and Racinian principals, old and young, rulers and ruled, successful and unsuccessful, ruthless or faint-hearted, is served by two main categories of persons: advisers and confidants. Like Shakespeare with Edmund in *King Lear* and Iago in *Othello*, Corneille and particularly Racine present us with advisers who are at worst wicked, at best misguided. Among examples are Photin in Corneille's *Pompée*, Narcisse in *Britannicus*, Oenone in *Phèdre* and Mathan in *Athalie*. All four exert influence, but all die in the end—an outcome which has no direct bearing on the dénouement of the main action but can perhaps best be seen as natural justice, the victory of good over evil, to the greater satisfaction of audience or reader. Photin, the most Machiavellian of the weak Ptolomée's three henchmen, a self-assured minister but an unprincipled opportunist and poor judge of the Romans, ends up being put to death by César. Narcisse, tutor to Britannicus and at the same time adviser to Néron, is needed by the young emperor to establish his dominance over his mother Agrippine. While Néron survives, Narcisse the traitor is lynched by the crowd. In Racine's last play, Mathan, the priest of Baal, who gives counsel to, and acts as messenger for, Athalie in her attempt to silence the last member of the royal line of David, ends up being butchered.

The Machiavellian rôle of many *mauvais conseillers* in French classical tragedy is summed up by the arguments put forward in the early 1640s by

Photin to Ptolomée in the opening scene of *Pompée*. The King should kill the refugee Pompée in order to save his own (Ptolomée's) head. Nor should his master share power with his sister, Cléopâtre. Justice is not a virtue of State, Photin maintains; monarchs should spare no-one, for the art of kingship is destroyed by fearfulness and a sense of fairness.

But there are other and more subtle functions which advisers carry out. Oenone, for instance, Phèdre's nurse in Racine's tragedy, is basically well-intentioned, with her mistress's best interests at heart. She has her own prejudices about Hippolyte, but believes that, with Thésée reported dead, Phèdre's passion for her stepson becomes 'an ordinary love'. Hence her encouragement of Phèdre and her accusation against Hippolyte after his father returns home. The 'execrable monster', abandoned by her mistress once the latter learns of Hippolyte's love for Aricie, commits suicide by drowning—a saddening end to a difficult part which, as we shall see in Chapter 11, is designed by Racine largely in order to reduce the criminality of Phèdre, helping to make the title-character 'neither entirely guilty nor entirely innocent'.

The other category of main characters referred to—confidants— is much larger, appearing in virtually all French classical tragedies. Going by various names—for example, *dame d'honneur, suivante, gouvernante* or *nourrice* in the case of women, *gouverneur, écuyer* or *affranchi* in the case of men, or simply *confidente* and *confident*—these persons can be misunderstood by English-speaking audiences. Derived from Latin and indeed Greek tragedy, they fulfil an often vital rôle as consciences to the main characters, providing them with an opportunity to speak in circumstances not too far removed from the natural ones which imitative drama might require. They are essentially listeners, allowing the protagonists to unburden themselves in scenes which, but for the presence of the confidant, would be monologues. Their questions and interjections help to break up lengthy *récits*, especially exposition narratives, and move the action in a new direction. They also act as message-bearers and are often entrusted by dramatists with an account in Act V containing important information about off-stage action which affects the dénouement.

Their existence is sometimes derided by modern critics or audiences, who see them as the equivalent of photographic negatives, as lamp-posts or crutches on whom the principal characters can lean in times of stress, or as human sponges who merely soak up the outpourings of their master's or mistress's fevered minds. By their largely self-effacing presence, they are not unimportant, however, adding both to the relative realism of the situations in the plot and to the cross-section of the population represented in any tragedy.

A final group of characters must be mentioned, if only because they are absent from the cast-list and the staged performances. Very occasionally a quite important figure with a major part in the action does not appear at all duringthe five acts. The title-character of one of the plays discussed above, Corneille's *Pompée*, falls into this category. Pompey, defeated by Julius Caesar at Pharsalus, is put to death by Ptolemy as soon as he arrives in Egypt seeking refuge. This act defies the wishes of Caesar and of the woman Caesar loves, Ptolemy's sister Cleopatra, and leads eventually to the killing of the Egyptian king in battle. In the 1660 *Examen* of the play, Corneille states that, although there is 'something extraordinary' in Pompée's absence, he still remains, in some respects, the main actor, since his death is the sole cause of all that happens.

Thirty years after *Pompée*, Racine also writes a tragedy—*Bajazet*—from which a character strongly influencing the action is physically absent. The sultan Amurat, waging war round Babylon, never appears at Constantinople in the course of the five acts. But he is ever present in people's minds, through his order that his younger brother Bajazet, a possible rival in the power struggle, be put to death and a subsequent message, recounted in Act IV, in which he announces his imminent arrival and expresses the hope that his brother is by now dead. Amurat's final influence is exercised through his messenger Orcan (another non-appearing character), who fulfils his master's command and kills Roxane with his own hands before being put to death by onlookers.

In both these well-known tragedies it could be argued that much more tragic pressure is built up by the absence of principal characters than could be created, had they been present. Dead or distant men cannot speak but exercise continuing influence through the doubts, fears and mistaken opinions of those they leave behind. A not dissimilar effect is achieved, as we have noted in passing, by protagonists who are rumoured dead but who then are found to be still alive: Mithridate, for instance, or Thésée in *Phèdre*.

Lastly, we must remember the pressure exerted on stage characters, not by absent individuals but by bodies or forces less easy to circumscribe who, while not appearing in front of us, often have as important an influence as a single character. In *Bérénice*, for example, a play which proceeds with only three, indeed perhaps only two main characters, the new emperor Titus is brought to realise that Rome is now as necessary a consideration in his life as Bérénice, his personal love. The opinion of the people will determine his future happiness or unhappiness, and the Senate, anxious to know of his intentions, is set in direct opposition to the

Jewish queen when, at the end of Act IV, Titus is forced to decide between one and the other. 'Rome', 'the Senate' and 'the Roman people' thus become unseen but important protagonists in the play, and similar additions to the official cast-list can be found in other seventeenth-century tragedies.

On a more general level, it is worthwhile considering the whole question of the amount of exposure a dramatist should give to characters in tragedy. Much can be gained by keeping appearances down, by ensuring, for instance, that major figures need not be called upon in every act. As Jacques Scherer reminds us, Phèdre appears in only 40 per cent of the scenes of the 1677 tragedy—even Thésée, absent until over halfway through the third act, is seen by the audience just as much. Ten years earlier, Racine had pulled off an even greater coup in centring all the action and atmosphere of *Andromaque* on an eponymous heroine who is present in only a quarter of the scenes.

Corneille, of the previous generation, does likewise, going against a trend in the first half of the century which is summed up in 1657 by the abbé d'Aubignac. His *Pratique du théâtre* insists that the heroes or main characters should be introduced early on in a play: the audience is keen to see them, and if a principal character's entry is delayed, spectators become confused, having taken those who did appear at the beginning to be more important than they later turn out to be. Moreover, main characters should then appear as often as possible; their parts are normally taken by the best actors, the costumes they wear are more luxurious, and this all contributes to greater customer satisfaction.

Unfortunately, d'Aubignac's arguments only prove how out of touch this often interesting theoretician but unsuccessful dramatist is with the practical problems of staging plays. Leading actors and actresses, then as now, wanted a chance to be seen, and to be seen to *briller*, so playwrights had to orchestrate their presence on stage accordingly. The very timing of their entrances was important: plots and hence characterisation had often to be structured so as to allow the principals to come on for the first time in the opening scene of Act II, achieving maximum effect from the interest stirred up in them by minor characters in Act I. Horace, Auguste, Cléopâtre and Prusias in Corneille, Néron, Titus and Bajazet in Racine are among well-known examples of figures whose entry is heightened in this way.

In a short chapter like this it has been possible only to scratch the surface of the problem posed by dramatic characters. Until we have a typology of characters such as that called for by Jacques Truchet, the full importance to be attached to each category of person in French classical tragedy will remain partly hidden by the diversity of plays and plots. Insofar as the theory of art imitating nature has any meaning at all, we can at least say that writers of tragedy between 1630 and 1680 range widely over that segment of mankind which tradition allows tragedy to depict. Both Corneille and Racine and their respective contemporaries limit themselves to characters united by blood kinship or close friendship, who nominally wield considerable political power, but who do so in very divergent ways, from the ambitious, self-assured, largely unprincipled Médée and Cléopâtre through the guilt-ridden, remorseful Phèdre to the cringingly indecisive king Ptolomée.

The word 'hero' which this chapter has tried to avoid using is as difficult to apply with confidence to the characters named above as it would be in the case of, say, Marlowe's Tamburlaine or Shakespeare's Macbeth. In particular, what is one to make of unmitigated criminals like Cléopâtre in *Rodogune* or Richard III, 'subtle, false, and treacherous', as Shakespeare has him describe himself in the opening scene of that play? The evil virtuosity of such characters, their ruthless singleness of purpose and fundamental amorality often appear to us to be compensated for by a fund of will-power and an all-pervading energy which are not unattractive ('A horse! a horse! my kingdom for a horse!', shouts Richard III defiantly at the moment of death). Indeed, a form of inverted morality may make us wish to empathise more readily with these supercharged monsters than with their weak-willed opposites.

Some characters develop and change much more than others during the five acts—in particular, the more forceful criminals may hold to their beliefs and ambitions from the beginning to the usually bitter end. But if it is perhaps unhelpful to give priority to characters over action, it is certainly wrong to identify an isolated character as the sole centre of interest in a play. The Médées and Nérons of French classical tragedy are surrounded by more obviously 'human' figures of similar rank and position, just as Prusias and Phèdre are counterbalanced by active persons. Together, these grouped characters battle their way through the difficulties raised by their very position in society, the dilemma caused by the inevitable clash of public duty or political ambition and private issues, in particular personal love.

The range of characters in tragedy is both wide and limited: wide, in that history and legend offer many potentially tragic themes; limited, in that various conventions, from the selection and adaptation of source-material to the traditional structure of plays and grouping of characters and the practical restrictions of staging, impose restraints on a dramatist's freedom. In the end, though, the writer of tragedy has perhaps a fractionally easier task than the comic dramatist. A spokesman for Molière in *La Critique de l'Ecole des femmes* (1663) affirms that 'it is much easier to indulge in high-flown sentiments, to defy Fortune in verse, to accuse Destiny and hurl insults at the gods than to get underneath the skin of men from their ridiculous side, and to make everyone's defects seem pleasing on the stage'. The contrast is over-simplified but not invalid.

10 Language

We have seen in previous chapters how the conventions dictated both the outward form and the inner coherence of a seventeenth-century French tragedy, while unavoidable restrictions (put to good use by the best dramatists) affected the amount of physical action depicted on stage and hence the contemporary audience's understanding of the terms plot and action. Now in the *Poetics* Aristotle is careful to suggest that language is secondary to plot and hence to action. In Chapter 9 he says that 'the poet [i.e. the playwright] must be more the poet of his stories or Plots than of his verses, inasmuch as he is a poet by virtue of the imitative element in his work, and it is actions that he imitates'; and the list of constituent parts of tragedy in Chapter 6 places Diction after Plot, Characters and Thought but before Melody and Spectacle.

'To speak is to act', d'Aubignac writes in Chapter 2 of Book IV of his *Pratique du théâtre*. His emphasis, like that of Aristotle, is on action, for he argues that tragedy is drama and not narration. But turning the phrase round it is also true to say that, given the absence of much real movement, action is often conveyed through the medium of speeches couched in appropriate language. Who the characters are, where they come from, what they do, why, and with what consequences is all transmitted to reader or audience through the words they are given to speak. Language is thus a means of expression by which dramatic personages identify and define themselves for us who are outside the play. It is also the instrument which they use to converse with other characters inside the play, to influence and persuade them.

Of course, just as it is dangerous to take one character and study him or her in isolation, so it is in the end unwise to try to separate language from content, medium from message. But there are several aspects of seventeenth-century French and its use in tragedy which are not immediately apparent to the twentieth-century English-speaking reader. (Many of the same problems arise for that reader if he is approaching Corneille or Racine through English translation.) Individual items of vocabulary need careful scrutiny, for the French language developed rapidly during the half-century covered by classical tragedy, and usage has altered considerably again in the three hundred years since then. Then if we extend the notion of language, the question arises: what effect does drama written in verse have on the words it contains? Thirdly, passing from the single word or line, we need to consider the elements of language and style contained in, say, a single speech and eventually the different levels of language used by one character in an act or whole play, or by the various characters presented in any one tragedy. Finally, have we any information at all about how the finished product was put over to the contemporary audience? What about language in performance?

It will hardly come as a surprise if we note that the overall effect which Corneille seems to have wanted to create through his alexandrines is rather different from Racine's. In his various prefaces the author of *Phèdre* concentrates on discussing his sources, the amount of material he has chosen to incorporate, and changes he has made to the characterisation. There are few remarks about the construction of his plays, and fewer still about his language and style. Perhaps in both cases his mastery made it superfluous for him to comment. Only the preface to *Bérénice* reminds us that, in addition to the violence of the passions, the tragic writer should aim to portray the beauty of the feelings and the elegance of the language. The language will thus be a suitable vehicle for action aimed at Racinian majestic sadness.

Corneille, on the other hand, includes comments on style and language in a number of his critical writings. His aim, in subjects drawn more from Roman history than Greek legend, is perhaps appropriately to achieve a strong, rocky style (he lists *la force des vers* among aspects he approves of in one of his favourite plays, *Rodogune*), to play the language up rather than down. In a 1644 prefatory epistle he claims that *Pompée* was written to satisfy those who found the verse of his previous tragedy, *Polyeucte*, less powerful than that of the one before it, *Cinna*, and to prove that he could revert to a grandiose style when the subject merited it. *Pompée*, he says in the 1660 *Examen*, is blessed with the most elevated style of any play of his written until then; it contains the most majestic lines he has yet composed, thanks largely to ideas he has borrowed from Lucan's *Pharsalia*. He had managed not just to take over characters but to fall into the epic poet's style—an advantage he had not had when writing *Médée*, where his additions to passages from Seneca had been of much poorer quality. The key word in Corneille, then, is not elegance, an unobtrusive style, but pomp—majestic, grandiose verse, matching his often larger-than-life characters.

But before we come to look at language in the context of the speech, scene or act and the effect on that of the rhetorical tradition, what of individual lexical items? The most recent research suggests that neither Corneille nor more particularly Racine kept to quite the restricted vocabularies which previous commentators on classicism believed they did. Racine's range of language is rather more extensive than the 1200 to 1500-word version of basic French sometimes ascribed to him. In an article in the review *Le français moderne* published in 1978, Charles Bernet shows that in his nine secular tragedies from *La Thébaïde* to *Phèdre* the dramatist uses 2867 different *vocables* or terms in a total of over 132,000 words. His two sacred tragedies *Esther* and *Athalie* require 2163 terms, giving for all eleven tragedies a vocabulary of 3263 different items among almost 159,000 words used.

Corneille's production is much larger, of course, but leaving aside his machine plays, heroic comedies and the tragi-comedy-cum-tragedy *Clitandre* (despite their serious elements), and including *Le Cid*, his eighteen tragedies, with over 303,000 words, call on 4019 separate lexical items. After standardisation of length (for Racine, as we have seen, wrote shorter plays than dramatists of the 1630 generation), it would appear that Corneille's vocabulary is richer overall than Racine's and also more extensive even in his later period, which coincides with Racine's career. But Corneille reduces his range as he gets older (possibly in an attempt to follow the precepts of Racinian restraint), while with time his younger rival tends, paradoxically, to use rather more words, introducing a little more local colour and following his ancient sources more closely.

A statistical count like this is not all, of course. If ten per cent or so of the vocabulary is taken up by proper nouns, much of the rest will cover nouns, verbs, adjectives and adverbs where the dramatist is able, or forced, to select from a wide range of possible terms. As the next chapter will show, observance of the proprieties, attention to decorum in line with the requirements (or supposed requirements) of polite society, exerted a strong influence on the content of French tragedies within our period. Prior to it, under Hardy at the beginning of the century, crude language mirrored scenes of violence, rape and unbridled love. There was no attempt at a specific (some might say artificial) stage language; explicit everyday, indeed obscene, terms were included where the plot called for them. By the 1630s, social patterns and needs having changed, all this had been swept away, and language, while far from being homogenised, was at least restricted to words in keeping with the generally elevated subject-matter of tragedy. To good effect on the whole, for the occasional less than lofty term which it is necessary to introduce stands out all the more clearly.

As today, seventeenth-century French varied from one area of the country to the other and, in general, from one part of the century to another. The youthful Racine, spending a period with an uncle in Provence while in his early twenties, writes from Uzès that, as a northerner, he has difficulty in understanding what the locals are saying. In a letter to La Fontaine in November 1661 he says that he is in as much need of an interpreter as a Muscovite would be in Paris. He has realised that the locals speak a tongue incorporating words from Spanish and Italian—languages he knows and sometimes uses when he replies to them—yet he still ends up being largely misunderstood.

But more important than this problem of dialects, which did not arise in tragedy, was the evolution of the literary language during the century. When founded in 1635 the Académie-Française set itself the task of compiling a dictionary and a grammar. The latter did not appear until the 1930s, and even the first edition of the dictionary was only published in 1694, after the pioneering dictionaries of Richelet (1680) and Furetière (1690) had brought together the vocabulary used in classical literature. However, despite its excesses, the *préciosité* movement, whose aim was the pursuit of delicacy of taste, manners and language, had at least helped to draw attention earlier to the value of language and the need for precision, for shades of meaning. And thanks to the efforts of, among others, Malherbe, the official poet of the Courts of Henri IV and Louis XIII, and Vaugelas, whose *Remarques sur la langue française* were published in 1647, successful attempts were made by authors from the first half of the century to clarify the language and update vocabulary, word-order and constructions. The extensive revisions which Corneille made to his early plays, culminating in the collected edition of 1660, are a witness to the changes which these rather unsystematic grammatical observations, based on usage and Court usage at that, were bringing to the literary language.

Finally, in this first section on individual words, we need to consider the changes between seventeenth-century French and present-day French, differences of which not only modern readers of plays in the original language but to some extent those approaching Corneille or Racine through translation must be aware. Footnotes to the many excellent editions produced by British and American scholars draw attention to the main pitfalls, and arid and inconvenient though such notes may be, they can make all the difference between the understanding and the misunderstanding of key terms in a play. For while many words had the same range of connotations as today, some were more restricted, while others had extra meanings they have since lost, or different emphases. Thus *ennui*, which now means 'boredom', had as its main sense the much stronger '*tristesse, déplaisir*' quoted in Richelet's dictionary; the same goes for the verb form, *ennuyer*.

In particular, the vocabulary of the passions, so important in French classical literature, has to be studied carefully and the nuances noted. One soon becomes accustomed to contemporary jargon, for example the convention of *feux* or *flammes* for *amour-passion*, often worked into not very happy extended metaphors which sound more like firemen's than lovers' talk. Again, *amant* is not 'lover' in the modern sense (a man having sexual relations with a woman to whom he is not married), but indicates rather a man who has declared his (genuine or insincere) feelings of love to a woman and who is usually loved in return. *Amitié* can be stronger than 'friendship' and mean 'love', or it can refer to pleasure taken in a non-human object. And what about *estime, tendresse, passion, respect, obéissance, bonté* and the other affective layers discovered and discussed by salon society and worked into contemporary writing, including tragedy?

Outside the realm of the passions, there are several key concepts which underlie the behaviour of many characters, particularly those in Cornelian tragedy and other literature of the first half of the century. Some of these are especially deceptive. *Vertu*, for instance, can mean 'virtue' in the modern sense, but in Corneille often denotes courage, strength of mind, decisiveness, a firm resolve to remain independent and self-controlled (nuances derived from the Latin source, *virtus*). Thus Corneille can call some of his evil queens *vertueuses* without our needing to believe that he has lost his sense of moral values. *Générosité* and the adjective *généreux* refer usually to noble birth (source in the Latin noun *gens*). *Gloire* and *glorieux* can denote the product of brave actions, akin to the modern English 'glory', but as Octave Nadal, in his book *Le sentiment de l'amour dans l'oeuvre de Pierre Corneille* (1948), and subsequent critics have remarked, the term is often applied, not to an outward public celebration but on the contrary to an intimate, personal and hence often indefinable satisfaction, a state of mind achieved by a tragic character such as Corneille's emperor Auguste, against all odds.

These few remarks on items of vocabulary are mere indications of the delicate task facing modern readers or spectators of seventeenth-century French tragedy. For clearly the main impression conveyed by drama, in print or on stage, is not transmitted by the single word but by more substantial groupings: the speech, the dialogue contained in a scene, a short series of linked scenes, and so on. Within single speeches the use of figures of speech to extend and adorn individual nouns, for example, means that we must now examine the influence of rhetoric and rhetorical devices on the presentation of French classical tragedy—an influence which will be modified, for better or for worse, by the verse form of seventeenth-century plays, which we shall discuss later.

The rhetorical influence on drama in our period is due in part to the concept of tragedy in the sixteenth century, where the crisis is reached early in the course of the action (if indeed it has not preceded the first act) and the characters therefore devote their time, not to solving a dilemma but to commenting on or bewailing their fate. The declamation of long, static speeches naturally called for a plentiful supply of devices of formal rhetoric. Then again, to some extent, the smallness of the acting area and the less than ideal shape of the theatre building, encouraging as they did a lack of extensive movement of characters on stage, led to the development—or the retention, at least in the first half of the seventeenth century—of an oratorical, inflated style rather than a more natural one.

But perhaps above all writers of French classical tragedy found themselves remembering the significant part which rhetoric had played in their secondary schooling, particularly if, like Corneille and many of his contemporaries, they had been brought up by the Jesuits. Jesuit colleges, more so than, for example, the Jansenist establishment at Port-Royal where Racine was educated, laid considerable stress on the acquisition and practice of eloquence. It was included in the trivium, the lower division of the seven liberal arts, comprising grammar, rhetoric and logic; the teaching of rhetoric, based essentially on Aristotle, Cicero and Quintilian, included training in declamation and, in Jesuit schools, participation in the Latin tragedies specially written by teachers for public performance by pupils at the annual summer prize-giving ceremony. With or without the benefit of this practice to add to the theory and book learning, Corneille, Racine and many of their generations (including the comic dramatist Molière, a former pupil of the Jesuit Collège de Clermont in Paris) had been carefully instructed in how to persuade their hearers, how to construct an argument, and what style to choose in order to put it over. In turn, teachers of rhetoric in the second half of the century chose extracts from secular tragedy as examples in their lessons—a 1666 course in rhetoric at the Jesuit college in Limoges, for instance, pointed to the closing scene of Corneille's *Cinna* as an example of love, to Camille's monologue in *Horace* (IV.5) for its treatment of hatred and to the *stances* of Polyeucte in Act IV of that play—all good models of different kinds of persuasion.

Formal rhetoric was split up into a number of aspects, covering the various stages of production. The writer as such was concerned with three main concepts: *inventio*, the finding of ideas or arguments to put into a speech, in other words discovering what to say; *dispositio*, finding the best sequence for these ideas or arguments, deciding in what order to put them; and *elocutio*, the shaping of what has been found by *inventio* and arranged through *dispositio*, that is, the use of language or 'how to say it'. A further stage concerned the speaker or, in our case, actor: *pronunciatio*, the delivery of the material, by the use of memory, voice, gesture and so on. We have dealt elsewhere with *inventio* and *dispositio* and will return later in this chapter to the matter of declamation. Much of the playwright's effort has to be devoted to *elocutio*, the fundamental stage at which his ideas and basic material are put into the words which are all that remain for us of seventeenth-century drama. What do we find?

The point is often made that, given the nature of seventeenth-century France, the position of its writers and in particular the concept of tragedy they had inherited from previous periods, the language—restricted in its range as we have seen—tends to be general rather than particular, abstract rather than concrete. The grandiloquence of Corneille, the majesty ('majestic sadness') combined with elegance of Racine, are indeed perhaps best expressed in these ways, conveying the aim of universality. But of course there is much in both writers that is intimate and personal, or at least embellishing as well as utilitarian. This decorative function, extending the basic vocabulary, counts on a number of rhetorical devices. Among several referring to single words or small groups is metaphor, by which one object or concept is compared with another. As Peter France points out in his suggestive book *Racine's rhetoric* (1965), the suitability of metaphors was largely a convention in seventeenth-century France: some were acceptable, others less easily tolerated. If we return to the realm of the passions mentioned earlier in this chapter, we find that love (*amour* or cognate terms) is frequently compared to war (*vaincre*), sacrifice (*sacrifier*) and particularly captivity (*fers, chaînes, noeuds, liens, tourments, esclave*). Other metaphors common in this area of tragedy introduce light and darkness, sight and blindness, heat and cold.

Already in the seventeenth century some of these metaphors could be classed as 'dead'. But others were very much alive. Light and dark play a crucial part in our understanding of *Phèdre* and the feelings of its title-character; captivity and the seraglio as a prison are at the heart of *Bajazet*. Even the fires and flames could be put to good use in skilful hands, as the well-known conceit in *Andromaque* shows. 'Brûlé de plus de feux que je n'en allumai' ('Burned with more fires than I myself have kindled') describes at once the fires of love and their violence, the obstacle which Troy represents, separating Andromaque from Pyrrhus, and the latter's distorted judgement—can any single passion hurt more than the whole Trojan war? While some metaphorical expressions reassured the audience, distancing them slightly from the action, allowing them to watch rather than become involved in the plot, others contributed to the drama of a play, heightening the emotion or creating shades of character or atmosphere by comparison with unmetaphorical statements.

Further extension of a limited vocabulary in the cause of establishing a suitably elevated tone can be found in other devices of decorative rhetoric as described by Professor France. Metonymy (substitution of one word for another when the objects or concepts each refers to are normally related) is a commonplace of French classical tragedy. Thus the family can be described as *sang* or *maison*, royal power as *trône, sceptre* or *couronne* and so on. Much effect can be gained in particular when these terms are used in both their literal and figurative meanings: *sang* as family or heredity, for instance, together with *sang* referring to blood or bloodshed, as in some of the many seventeenth-century tragedies in which deaths do occur.

Periphrasis, euphemism and epithet, too, serve to add either variety or dignity to a play, as required. The last of these, the addition of a descriptive adjective to a noun, can turn a general, abstract word into a much more particular expression or give life to a weak, dead noun. Euphemism removes what could be unpleasant or unseemly, such as direct references to death, while periphrasis helps to avoid the constant repetition of, for instance, proper names by replacing them with (inevitably slightly longer) descriptions of a character's function (king of X) or relationship to others (husband of Y, daughter of Z). Such circumlocution has incidental advantages: it reminds the reader (and indeed the characters) from time to time of what these rôles and relationships are, who Cinna or Rodogune or Iphigénie actually are; it enables characters to be presented from various standpoints by other members of the cast; it serves to transmit a hint (no more) of local colour through the genealogical references, which situate the action in a specific place and at a specific time in history or legend; and it can serve to lower tension by contrast with direct statement.

Needless to say, some commentators would argue that much of what rhetoric is discernible in tragedy is there for even more mundane reasons. If we can believe a text quoted in the *Mémoires* of Racine's younger son Louis, who was only six when his father died, the author of *Andromaque* used to draft his plays in prose, scene by scene, before turning them into verse. Corneille, according to a late seventeenth-century report by

Bordelon in his *Diversités curieuses*, needed three attempts at writing the fifth act of *Othon*, performed in 1664, composing more than 1200 lines of verse before he felt satisfied. And the hoary legend persists that Pierre Corneille was constantly lifting a trapdoor in his house in the rue de la Pie in Rouen to ask his obliging dramatist brother Thomas for a rhyme.

Despite remarks in 1630 in which he condemned the French, 'the last of the barbarians', for using verse, especially rhymed verse, in the theatre, Chapelain was right to add that he could not see how the 'abuse' would ever be stopped. Verse was looked on as prose and, as we have seen, illusionists like d'Aubignac believed that characters uttering *stances*, 'real poetry', needed time to prepare their lines and rhymes. A critic distant in time and outlook from the learned abbé, Eric Bentley, has offered a more enlightened defence of verse-plays:

> There is much evidence for the proposition that the natural medium of drama is verse: prose dramatists seem desperately to need rhetorical substitutes for meter. Meter brings an element of the expected, whatever may be its surprises in rhythm and content, and this makes for solidity. While the man in the street will think of prose as gloriously free, the prose artist will know that this freedom constitutes precisely the difficulty in making prose effective. (*The life of the drama*, 1965)

As noted earlier, irregular verse forms as represented by *stances* (lyrical monologues) were a feature of certain tragedies from the 1630s but had died out by 1660, while Corneille's isolated attempt at writing mixed verse in *Agésilas* (1666)—a combination of eight and twelve-syllable lines, with a variety of rhyme schemes—only resulted in the well-known comment by Boileau: 'After *Agésilas*, alas . . .' The normal line of French classical tragedy is the twelve-syllable alexandrine, grouped into series of rhyming couplets. Indeed, the basic unit is usually not two but four lines: both Corneille and Racine follow this pattern, in which most often one couplet is linked to a second by 'and' to form a quatrain. This was to be the standard formation within which dramatists sought to achieve a pleasing variety of effects. The danger is that series of blocks of four lines become too regularly designed, with clauses coinciding in length with each alexandrine, producing at best a monotonous, sing-song pattern, at worst the gobbledygook of second-rank dramatists determined to give their readers value for money with well-padded but not always comprehensible couplets of quatrains.

Rhythm and rhyme were additional factors constraining the writer of French classical tragedy. In the seventeenth century the alexandrine was divided into two six-syllable sections, with a main break or caesura in the middle and the possibility of secondary stresses elsewhere. Although this seemingly rigid pattern could be infinitely varied in skilled hands, a balance between the two so-called hemistiches was usually inevitable, and playwrights often required fillers to complete a six-syllable unit. Whence the exclamations 'O!', 'Ah!', 'Ciel!' and 'Hélas!' which can be a necessary part of the expression of emotion, or simply redundant.

Rhyme, too, could be a limitation as well as an opportunity, with one word conjuring up a rhyming companion. Among examples chosen at random are *mort* and *sort*, *amoureux* and *rigoureux*, *rang* and *sang*, *gloire* and *victoire* or *mémoire*, *pleurs* and *malheurs*, *Romain* and *inhumain*, *noeuds* and *feux*. The dramatist's task, then, is to combine the basic vocabulary, necessary for the creation of an appropriate tragic atmosphere, with less predictable words, thus avoiding—or at least partially disguising—the sequence of cliché expressions which could so easily result.

These and other rules of versification all play their part in shaping the component elements of a seventeenth-century French tragedy. Of course, there have been attempts to see the genre, especially Racine's plays, as poetry rather than drama, indeed as examples of 'pure poetry'. The abbé Henri Bremond was the best-known exponent of this interpretation. In his book *Racine et Valéry* (1930), he writes of the former author:

Being at once a poet and a dramatist, two claims, the pure and the impure, dispute his allegiance; onward! cry the rules of drama, *semper ad eventum festina*; while poetry would have him hover in all but motionless flight. Martha and Mary, action and contemplation, discourse and melody. Should he let himself become absorbed by the progress of the plot, his inner lyrical gift will soon fail; but this lyricism will keep the action from advancing. He must then satisfy each of the two claims—advance and hover at the same time, bustle with Martha, and yet not interrupt the contemplation of Mary. A programme impossible, if not absurd. Yet Racine has carried it out, and seemingly without trying.

The 'hovering' poetic mystery, where melody is divorced from structure and other elements, is far from being all that interests us—or playwrights, as we saw even in the preface to *Bérénice*, a tragedy which has been described as a mere series of madrigals and elegies. The late Eugène Vinaver, in his Zaharoff Lecture for 1960—*L'action poétique dans le théâtre de Racine*—reminds us that discourse and the prerogative of the speaking character are all-important in drama of our period:

If, in tragedy as comedy, each speaker has the floor until the end of his argument, it is because the aim is to give every play the character of a rhetorical contest, the rhythm of a duel. In tragedy this rhythm spreads to dominate every phase of the action . . . Everywhere the struggle is without breathing-space, unless to lay out arguments in preparation for a new encounter, without respite, unless to give greater force and brilliance to the speech. At the decisive moment, the carefully whetted blade, always poised over the action, descends victoriously to hasten its advance.

This discourse takes a variety of forms, as previous chapters have shown, and provides various opportunities for formal rhetoric to be deployed. The construction and embellishment of a monologue, with its to-and-fro series of questions and answers, its *péripéties* or changes of direction and its transitions, is the ideal vehicle for oratorical devices similar to those used in a non-theatrical context. Likewise the *récit* or narrative account, often anchored in physical events, including deaths off-stage, and descriptions of places and people, combining a semblance of naturalness and chronology with the artificiality and advance preparation needed to enhance the account and give it the aura necessary in tragedy. The *récit de Théramène* at the end of *Phèdre* is a good example of this amalgam of breathless normality and structured formality.

As the 1660 *Examen* to Corneille's *Clitandre*, performed almost thirty years before, makes clear, monologues were becoming unfashionable as early as the same author's *Pompée*, in the mid to late 1640s. Of the generation of 1660, only Racine, significantly, makes consistent use of this device. His characters, less grandiose and confident than Corneille's perhaps, and his gift for elegant, poetic expression cannot disguise the continuing rhetorical tradition of the soliloquy. The *récit* was seen to combine several functions, including the conveying of information, and it is noticeable that, particularly with lengthy accounts, the essential news is given to the listener in the opening lines. Thus Achorée begins his 104-line account of the death of Pompée in Corneille's play with a four-line summary, enough to give Cléopâtre rapid confirmation of what she had feared—a procedure which, as we have seen, is followed by Théramène in *Phèdre*.

Corneille, in an interesting comment in 1660, justifies the lengthy account Cinna gives Emilie in Act I of the 1642 tragedy by pointing out that both characters have 'all the patience necessary'—and the opportunity—to deliver or listen to it, for Cinna is delighted that he is carrying out his instructions and Emilie is filled with joy at her lover's apparent determination. Despite its 104 uninterrupted lines, the rhetorical ornaments which enrich it, Corneille claims, prevent the narration from seeming too artificial, and the variety of figures used justifies the time spent on it. Médée, he says in the *Examen* to his earlier tragedy, is in a different position. She has no time for the minute details of Jason's success with Créuse and the imprisoning of Egée, so when Nérine eagerly adds 'But learn how . . .', her mistress stems the flow of words with a curt 'Say no more.'

To break up the soliloquy or narration or, indeed, the standard dialogue speech, other devices borrowed from rhetoric could be called upon. Variety and movement can be injected by the occasional use of *sententiæ*, single-line moral aphorisms of a general nature woven into the fabric of a speech, when the speaker justifies his own conduct or argument by setting the personal concerns he is discussing in a wider context. Another figure, like the *sententia* much used in the first half of the century, is antithesis, the expression (usually contained within a single alexandrine) of the irreconcilable opposites facing the character.

Corneille's tragedies are commonly—and rightly—seen to depend for much of their effect on such stark alternatives: the so-called 'Cornelian' choice, as between love and duty or love and honour, is frequently summed up in this figure. But it is not limited to the 1630 generation. Racine's Titus, for example, having deluded himself that he could become emperor and still reconcile his public duties with his personal desires, is forced to recognise that he can no longer live as a private citizen but must reign: 'But it is no more a question of living. I must reign.' This antithesis, which the Swiss critic Theophil Spoerri sees as the key to Racine, contains the implication that wielding power leads not even to a life in public, but to death itself.

Given voluble characters who, convention dictates, do not dry up in mid-flow (*Waiting for Godot* is still three hundred years off) and whose appropriately framed speeches are listened to with respect, how does the dramatist vary the sequence which, like the individual speech or even alexandrine, could otherwise become unnatural and monotonous? Questions and exclamations serve to break up a series of replies and often occupy less than the twelve syllables of a line. A more extended contrast to the symmetrical blocks of alexandrines comes with stichomythia, the exchange of short phrases in which one character takes up the construction and at least some of the words used by his interlocutor and replies at similar length. Corneille and his generation are particularly fond of this rapid repartee, suited to moments of vigorous argument and intended, not always successfully, to appear natural, but similar persuasive dia-

logue can be found in the second half of the century, too. Finally, the confidant, as we have noted, can have a functional rôle in providing an
alternative voice in the course of a conversation.

Not just another voice but (in the best plays at least) a different *kind* of
voice. For despite the generally elevated tone of tragedy, attempts were
made to fit words to characters and indeed to show different levels of
language within a single character at successive moments in the action. A
nurse or other confidant will normally be given rather simpler vocabulary
and perhaps less involved syntax than the protagonists, although there is
certainly not the difference in tone to be found between servants and
masters in a Molière comedy. More importantly no doubt, the 'voice' of
the main characters will change according to the context. As Boileau says
in the third canto of his *Art poétique* (1674), 'each passion speaks a different
language', anger being proud and calling for lofty terms, while dejection is
expressed in less haughty words. This choice of appropriate language in
keeping with a person's changing moods and fortunes extends to the use of
a device like irony, which can be open and impassioned, or more subtle,
hidden in the language of the character but just as telling and provoking
for his or her opponent.

Figures of rhetoric, then, play a considerable part in the shaping by the
playwright of what he has found to say in his tragedy. They serve two main
purposes: self-conscious embellishment or ostentation for the creation of
pomp, and the introduction of a dramatic element. But there is a final
stage the author must consider, that of *pronunciatio*, the public delivery or
declamation of the material. Once again, the evidence available to us is of
the slimmest. What would a modern scholar not give for a seventeenth-
century recording of *Horace* or *Andromaque!* Alas, all he has to work with are
much less reliable tools. It is sometimes said that the punctuation and
capitalisation of seventeenth-century editions, usually much heavier
than modern practice requires, give us a clue to the way in which plays
were performed, by indicating the original word-groupings and stresses.
There may be something in this argument, although it is possible that
punctuation was one chore sometimes undertaken by the printer and not
the author. In any case, a fully punctuated text does not really tell us
whether delivery was akin to that of, say, opera or in a more natural mode.

Our main sources of information are comments by Molière, in two of
his comedies, on the declamatory style of the Hôtel de Bourgogne, where
all of Racine's tragedies from *Andromaque* to *Phèdre* were first staged, and a
number of reports on the training Racine gave one of the leading actresses,
Mlle Champmeslé, his mistress, who joined the Bourgogne company in
1670 after two years with Molière's troupe and created the rôles of

Monime (in *Mithridate*) and Phèdre among others. Both sources can only
be treated with extreme caution. In Scene 9 of the one-act comedy *Les Pré-
cieuses ridicules* (1659), Mascarille says he will give a play he has composed
to the Grands Comédiens, the Hôtel de Bourgogne actors:

Only they are capable of showing things off to best advantage. The
others are ignorant people who recite as one speaks. They do not know
how to rant the lines or how to stop at the finest points. And how can one
know where the finest lines are, if the actor does not pause there, indicating in this way that it is time for noisy applause!

Four years later, in the opening scene of *L'Impromptu de Versailles*, Molière
launches a wry, lampooning attack on their pompous style of acting, in
particular that of the veteran and extremely obese Bourgogne actor Montfleury. A dramatist with a play to perform objects to a recently arrived
company of players, who want to give the rôle of king to an actor of normal
proportions and not to a man 'as fat as four', as the playwright would wish,
and who propose to deliver their lines naturally rather than bombasti-
cally, with frequent emphases—the last being the only way, the dramatist
says, to gain approval and noisy applause.

Each of these short Molière plays precedes the earliest Racine tragedy
(1664). Although the Hôtel de Bourgogne style here being derided will
not have changed in the interval, the testimony of even a highly accomplished comic actor like Molière should not be exaggerated. It is known
that he believed himself competent to play tragedy and his company put
on many contemporary tragedies before and after his return to Paris from
the provinces in 1658. But the young Racine, who had given his first play,
La Thébaïde, to Molière's troupe at the Palais-Royal (it was performed
without success in early summer) appeared dissatisfied with their playing
of his second tragedy *Alexandre le Grand*, staged in 1665 during a much
more appropriate month, December, and in a discreditable move he
allowed the rival Bourgogne theatre to act it simultaneously.

In 1747 were published the *Mémoires* of Racine's younger son, Louis,
who was only six when his father died in 1699. Looking back across this
long gap, Louis tells us that 'everyone knows the talent my father had for
declamation, and he managed to communicate the real flavour of it to
those actors capable of acquiring it. Those who believe that the declamation he introduced to the stage was bombastic and sing-song are, I
think, mistaken.' Racine had trained La Champmeslé to deliver her lines
just as he wished. 'He got her first to understand the lines which she had to
speak, showed her the gestures, and prescribed the tones, which he even

noted down.' And although Mlle Champmeslé, Louis remarks, had beauty, a voice and a memory, she was not a born actress and had to be shown exactly what to do. Yet his father's tuition made her appear to be 'inspired by nature'.

An earlier testimony to Racine's training of the actors comes in a work published in 1719 by the abbé Jean-Baptiste Dubos, of the Académie-Française, *Réflexions sur la poésie et sur la peinture*. He comments on the difference in pitch during performance of a seventeenth-century tragedy: a passage delivered 'lower than the meaning seemed to require' was done in this way so that the higher pitch which the actor had to reach two lines further on would strike all the more forcibly. This technique was that of Mlle Champmeslé in the part of Monime, instructed by the author to lower her voice unnaturally when declaring her love of Xipharès to his father (*Mithridate*, III.5, lines 1109–12) in order to jump an octave higher between the first part of line 1112 ('We loved each other') and the second ('You grow pale, my Lord'). 'This portamento, extraordinary in declamation', the critic adds, 'was excellent for showing the mental turmoil into which Monime had been thrown on realising that Mithridate's trick had made her reveal information which could now endanger both her and her lover. The same care went into Racine's training of La Champmeslé for the rôle of Phèdre, allowing Dubos to conclude that a tragedy whose delivery was transcribed into musical notation would allow indifferent actors to perform it moderately well.

In the end it is difficult to judge how artificial these performances may have been. By modern standards they were certainly nearer to song than to conversation, bombastic and stilted rather than natural. But a final comment on the Hôtel de Bourgogne style stresses the latter quality. In the seventh of a series of *Entretiens galans* published in 1681—only four years after *Phèdre*—the anonymous author writes that an actor's declamation is 'a sort of song, and you would certainly agree with me that La Champmeslé would not please so much, had she a less agreeable voice. But she is able to control it with such skill and give it such appropriately natural modulations, that she appears to really have in her heart a passion which is only in her mouth.'

Did tragedy in performance set out, then, to lead its audience to an understanding of the text, to listen to its meaning, or was it largely a musical event, a recital of pure poetry through which the emotional content of the lines was ultimately conveyed to the reader? The distinction between drama as *chant* and drama as *discours* may not have been the problem in the seventeenth century which it can be for certain directors or actors today. Other elements too—gestures, facial expressions, stage-movements,

silences—must all be borne in mind when we consider public performance of a French classical tragedy, under stage conditions which we have
seen were far from ideal. It is little wonder that a declamatory style
appears to have been necessary, in the absence of the respectful hush that
accompanies a modern performance.

Yet, as Corneille notes in the first *Discours*, the dramatist is not like a
public orator: he must carefully disguise his art, since it is not he who is
speaking, and those who are are not orators. What remains, if we examine
the tragedies written in the fifty central years of the century, is the astonishing range of tones and styles, high-flown and intimate, passionate and
reasonable, brash and subtle, general and particular, decorated and
plain, reflecting the evolution of the French language itself within this
period and the change of emotional and ethical emphasis between Corneille and Racine. It is hard to believe that only Mlle Champmeslé and a
few other actors and actresses like her were able to transmit such varied
music in all its splendour to the large audience, few of whom had bought or
would buy the scores.

11 Proprieties

Underlying many of the ideas examined in earlier chapters of this book is a concept dear to the hearts of most writers in seventeenth-century France, that of what they called *la vraisemblance* (or *le vraisemblable*) and which is usually translated into English as 'verisimilitude'. This desire to avoid showing what was, or might be judged, improbable and to insist on probability can be seen to fit in with several aims—with the 'moral purpose' which many dramatists said they gave to their plays (even if such didacticism was often far from clear), with the unification of the action and observance of the unities of time and place, and in general terms with the universality rather than the particular nature of classical literature as a whole. And while verisimilitude might seem to contrast with the theory of imitation contained in *ut pictura poesis*, it has its part to play in illusionism.

The notion of *vraisemblance*, going back at least to Castelvetro in 1570, is of crucial importance for our understanding of French tragedy and of the perspective which seventeenth-century playwrights had on their craft. What both critics and practising dramatists rejected almost unanimously, from before *Le Cid* to the time of Racine's last secular tragedy and beyond, was the possibility of choosing material which might be *true* (historically true, or attested in legend) but which did not have the stamp of probability *as well*. Matters came to a head in 1637, during the quarrel about Corneille's revolutionary tragi-comedy. Among the many attacking points made by Scudéry in his *Observations sur le Cid* was one concerning the projected marriage of Chimène to her father's murderer. This, while true (*vrai*), claimed Scudéry, was improbable and hence of historical but not literary interest. Chapelain, whose *Lettre sur la règle des vingt-quatre heures* (1630) had re-launched the debate on *la vraisemblance*, repeated in the *Sentiments de l'Académie Française sur le Cid* later in 1637 that verisimilitude was the 'immutable aim of poetry'. These views were echoed in 1639 by La Mesnardière, whose *Poétique* took up a phrase used by Aristotle in Chapter 24 of the *Poetics* ('A likely impossibility is always preferable to an unconvincing possibility') and stated that what is false but verisimilar is preferable to what is true but 'strange, monstrous and incredible'.

D'Aubignac, summing up the criticism of the previous twenty to twenty-five years in his *Pratique du théâtre* (1657), devotes much time to the question. His views are clear and uncompromising. The stage is not concerned with things as they have been but as they might have been. So *le vrai* by itself (and what is merely possible, too) are banished from the theatre, since 'there are many true things which must not be seen there'. Only *le vraisemblable* can 'reasonably' provide the beginning, middle and end of a play; verisimilitude is 'the essence of drama'. What is historically true can be included, but only if, in addition, these events or characters are sanctioned by *vraisemblance*. Writers of the next generation follow the abbé's guidelines. Thus Racine can write in the 1671 preface to *Bérénice* that 'only what is verisimilar touches us in tragedy', while three years later Boileau's *Art poétique* lays down that an audience must never be offered anything improbable, since the mind is not moved by what it does not believe in.

Taking his cue from Aristotle, a commentator like Scudéry could distinguish two kinds of verisimilitude, ordinary and extraordinary. The first would cover the case of a child making mistakes, the second that of a tyrant being overcome. The possible is something different again, for example that a good man commits a crime. If the aim of poetry is what is useful, then verisimilitude can be more helpful in reaching that goal than what is factually true. For the purposes of this chapter, we need not worry about the sub-divisions of *vraisemblance*. What the examples quoted from the *Observations* show, however, is that critics and playwrights had to reach a compromise on the question.

Chapelain remarks in the *Lettre sur la règle des vingt-quatre heures* that, although it is intrinsically true that what is shown is a simulation, nonetheless the spectator should look on it as genuine. If he is unable during the performance to believe this, to enter into all the feelings of the characters and to imagine them as actually occurring, he will be deprived of the main gift that drama can offer him. Such a recognition of the need for authenticity had to contend with an inevitable lack of total verisimilitude. Strict *vraisemblance* regarding unity of place clashed with the needs of the action and the physical limitations of the stage. Similarly with time: even if this is kept to the two or three hours of the performance and the number of incidents restricted accordingly, much that is essential is still omitted. Convention allows this to happen, as it does the existence of a fair number of improbabilities in the plot, be it Cornelian or Racinian: the ever-so-convenient arrangement of certain events and arrival of characters, the lack of awareness of confidants, allowing protagonists to recount to them information essential to the audience, and so on.

A concern for verisimilitude dominated seventeenth-century French literature, including non-dramatic texts. One of the few authors with an alternative viewpoint was Pierre Corneille, whose tragedies remain so different and controversial over three hundred years later largely because he wished to substitute belief in *le vrai* for subservience to *le vraisemblable*. Two documents from 1647 give a clear idea of his opinions. In the *Avertissement* to *Rodogune*, performed two years earlier at the Hôtel de Bourgogne, he states that his main source has been *The Syrian Wars*, from Appian's *Roman History*, but with many changes and additions. The latter include the uncertainty about the order in which Antiochus and Séleucus were born, the imprisonment of Rodogune, Cléopâtre's hatred of her, the queen's suggestion to her sons that Rodogune be killed and the princess's parallel proposal, Rodogune's love of Antiochus, Cléopâtre's jealousy. All these 'embellishments of invention', Corneille claims, are but credible means of reaching the outcome recorded in history, the death of the Syrian queen. The 'laws of drama' (and, of course, the public's prior knowledge of the story) did not allow him to alter the ending—although he has turned Appian's account of Antiochus forcing his mother to drink poison into Cléopâtre's defiant suicide—but he reserves the right to alter and indeed invent the means used to reach the end, the route taken to the agreed destination. As long as the historical outcome is preserved, all of what he calls the circumstances or intermediate steps is within the dramatist's discretion. 'At least', Corneille adds, 'I do not believe I have seen a rule which restricts this freedom which I have given myself.'

The position is re-stated in the *Au Lecteur* to *Héraclius*, a complex tragedy of the same year. 'All truths' are acceptable in drama, Corneille writes, although it is not obliged to follow them. The freedom drama has to diverge from such truths is not a requirement, but verisimilitude is a necessary condition only in 'la disposition', that is, the organisation of the plot, and not in the subject chosen nor in incidents which are authenticated by history. Everything included in a play must be credible, and it can be, according to Aristotle, by one of three means: truth (*la vérité*), verisimilitude (*la vraisemblance*) or public opinion (*l'opinion commune*). He concludes, indeed, by proposing that the subject of a fine tragedy ought not to be verisimilar.

Thirteen years later, Corneille returns to the question. The subject, he says in the first *Discours*, need not be *vraisemblable* (the requirement of 1647 is now an option); 'the great subjects which stir the passions deeply, and provoke impetuous clashes with the laws of duty or the ties of blood, must always go beyond the probable'. According to the second *Discours*, also of 1660, 'the obedience which we owe to the rules of unity of time and place exempts us therefore from verisimilitude, although it does not allow us the impossible'. Historical truth is all that is required; there is no need to add 'the ornaments of verisimilitude', for 'public opinion is sufficient to justify us when we do not have truth on our side'.

These quotations sum up Corneille's important and maverick position. For him, all that is attested in history books or legendary accounts is material for tragedy. The subject, that is, the subject-matter or initial situation selected is therefore 'true'; it may also be credible but need not be. What he agrees must be *vraisemblable* is the conduct of the plot: the *beaux sujets*, the extraordinary actions he chooses to dramatise, may strain our belief, even though they be historical, but the subsequent treatment must be believable, the play must be organised in a coherent, consistent fashion. Of course, the divergence between Corneille and most other dramatists and critics was not always unbridgeably wide: much in the former complies with the requirements of verisimilitude, and not all the latter spend their whole time carefully avoiding what is true but improbable. The author of *Le Cid* is unique, however, in according equal importance to historical truth and *vraisemblance*, indeed to these two and to public opinion as well.

This preliminary discussion about truth and verisimilitude, relevant as it is to aspects of French classical tragedy discussed in earlier chapters, provides a natural lead-in to an examination of *les bienséances*, the proprieties. We have seen that the improbable, however dramatic, is not generally considered sufficient, by itself, to guarantee acceptability. Concern about this coincided in France with greater attention being paid, not just to the plot and its progress, but to the characters and their behaviour. Now an element of violence is basic to all tragedy, indeed to most drama. As Eric Bentley writes in *The life of the drama* (1965), 'if you wish to attract the audience's attention, be violent; if you wish to hold it, be violent again'. But while what can be called humanist tragedy in France—from around 1550 to the death of the playwright Robert Garnier in 1590—included deaths but only off-stage, with a later *récit*, French drama in the years from 1580 to 1620 or so depicted much more violence or cruelty on stage and descended into greater sexual explicitness. 'The more tragedies are cruel', Laudun d'Aigaliers wrote in his *Art poétique français* of 1598, 'the more excellent they are'.

Alexandre Hardy's surviving output, written in the early years of the seventeenth century but only published in the mid to late 1620s, includes much brutal physical violence. In *Scédase*, both the title-character's daughters are raped, killed and their bodies thrown down a well. In another of his tragedies, *Timoclée ou la juste vengeance*, Timoclée, a Theban woman, is raped by an invading army captain. She manages to lure him into a well, pushes him down and drowns him. According to the texts, the rape in *Scédase* is carried out on stage or is represented in some way other than in a narrated account, while that in *Timoclée* is at least started before the chorus intervenes at the end of Act IV. These and similar scenes could be seen as dramatically exaggerated versions of certain social behaviour at the time, at least in the capital. The immorality of Paris in the years of Henri IV and, after his death in 1610, during the regency of Marie de Médicis is frequently mentioned in fairly trustworthy accounts. The *Journal du règne d'Henri IV* by Pierre de L'Estoile, for example, comments that 'the reputation of Paris is today so bad that one has strong doubts about the chastity of any woman or girl who has spent any length of time there'.

The 1630s still saw produced a quantity of tragedies with horrific elements in them. Corneille's *Clitandre*, printed in 1632 and probably performed the previous year, depicts Dorise, pestered by Pymante, for whom she has no love, stabbing him in the eye with her pin and leaving him to soliloquise (IV.2) as blood flows from the eye-socket (replacing tears, as he still manages to say, preciously). The dramatist Monléon in 1637 has a play staged on the Atreus and Thyestes story. Atrée poisons his brother Thyeste's sons and serves some of their flesh up to their father. He then carries in their heads, arms and legs in a basin, together with the body of their mother who has committed suicide. Two years before, a much better-known dramatist, Rotrou, brings out *Crisante*, in which Cassie, a Roman centurion, rapes Crisante, the captive queen of Corinth (the attack is here recounted, not shown), before killing himself. Crisante then cuts off Cassie's head and throws it at her husband's feet to prove her innocence. Since the husband still doubts, she commits suicide, as does he.

Other tragedies of the same period, while avoiding the inclusion of severed human heads, arms and legs, revel in dead bodies. La Calprenède's *La Mort de Mithridate*, also played in 1635, is a good, if often-quoted example of the deadening and eventually untragic effect which multiple deaths can have. In this siege-play, Mithridate, his wife, his two daughters and his daughter-in-law, facing an imminent Roman invasion, decide that suicide is the only solution. All drink poison and when the collaborator son arrives, he finds the corpses of his father and mother propped up on thrones and his wife and sisters dead at their feet. 'Ye Gods, what a spec-

tacle!' Indeed. Horror, as here or in *Thyeste*, for example, is proof of a continuing Senecan influence on Parisian drama in the first third of the
century. Corneille's *Médée* (1635) has as one of its sources Seneca's *Medea*
and includes in Act V a lengthy depiction on stage of the death-agonies of
Créon and Créuse, although Médée's children are killed off-stage. Horror
was to be maintained for some time yet among provincial writers and to
some extent in school tragedies such as the Jesuits put on in their colleges.

But the mood was changing fast, and we are left to marvel that a play as
baroque as *Crisante* or others on the Lucretia theme coincide with Mairet's
regular *Sophonisbe* and the early masterpieces of Corneille. Perhaps helped
by the rise of the literary *salons* and even the establishment in 1634 of a
second permanent theatre in Paris—the Marais—women, whom plots
such as those described had kept away from the theatre, now started to
attend in much greater numbers. As noted elsewhere, their importance is
stressed in the preface (1636) to a contemporary play, Mairet's licentious
comedy *Les Galanteries du duc d'Ossonne*, performed in 1633, as well as by
other dramatists of the time: by Rotrou in the *Avertissement* to *Cléagénor et
Doristée* (played and published in 1634) and the dedication (1635) to *La
Bague de l'oubli* (1629), and by Corneille in 1635–6 when Alcandre, in Act
V of *L'Illusion comique*, talks of 'un peuple tout entier' attending the theatre
in Paris. To accompany women's arrival, or perhaps preceding it—there
is a chicken-and-egg situation here—dramatists, encouraged also by the
influence of Richelieu and Louis XIII, paid increased attention to
matters of decorum. A royal declaration in April 1641, supporting the
theatrical profession, made it illegal for actors 'to represent any dishonest
episode or to use lascivious words, or phrases *à double entendre*, liable to
offend public decency'. Not only the more macabre elements began to be
excised, such as the dismembering of bodies, the eating of human flesh
while under siege, or jumping off towers and landing head first; references
to beds, snoring, making love and even kissing started to be banished from
the stage.

In-between these extremes, other elements are also avoided. The sight
of blood being shed becomes rarer. In *Horace*, for example, the title-
character, according to stage directions in the first edition, should kill his
sister in the wings and then come back on stage. But it appears that, at
early performances at least, Camille was stabbed in full sight of the audience, for in the *Examen* twenty years later Corneille says that Camille's
death on stage 'would be the fault of the actress rather than mine, for when
she sees her brother put his sword in his hand, the fear which is to be expected in a woman should make her take to her heels and receive the blow
off-stage, as I indicate in this printing.' (Corneille indeed clarified the

stage directions in 1660 by adding 'putting his hand to his sword and pursuing his sister, who runs off').

The 'fear' which, together with pity, constituted the tragic emotions, according to Aristotle, had become cruelty or horror. But between 1630 and 1640, both in plays themselves and more explicitly in critics' writings, horror had given way to terror or fear again (*terreur* or *crainte*). Indeed, this begins to be played down altogether, for we find La Mesnardière, in his *Poétique* at the end of the decade, saying that 'the poet should try to ensure ... that terror is much less than feelings of pity', even that terror is dispensable, since it is 'unpleasant' (*désagréable*). Yet virtually all tragedies continue to include deaths, but happening off-stage and recounted. This is in part a question of propriety, but it can be argued that it allows the audience to imagine more horror than a staged display could ever show.

Unlike verisimilitude, the proprieties (*les bienséances*) are not discussed in great detail in seventeenth-century France, perhaps because they concern not what should be included but rather what should be left out of tragedy. There is an obvious overlap between the two concepts, but Jacques Scherer, in an attempt to distinguish them, suggests that *vraisemblance* is essentially an intellectual requirement, calling for cohesion, rejection of what is absurd or arbitrary, while *bienséance* is a moral imperative, ensuring that a play does not shock the tastes, moral ideas or prejudices of its audience. Decorum requires that nothing violent or indecent be shown, but it also demands that what is unfamiliar, alien to seventeenth-century French customs, be left out as well. We shall return to this point specifically later in the chapter, when looking at how pagan material is transposed for a Christian audience.

Borrowing an idea contained in Pierre Nicole's *Traité de la vraie et de la fausse beauté*, the Latin original of which appeared in 1659, René Bray divides the proprieties into two kinds, internal and external. *Bienséances internes* relate to the connection between 'an object and its own nature', while *bienséances externes* govern the relationship between the object and the public, reader or audience. By the first category the author of *La formation de la doctrine classique en France* (1927) suggests, in effect, that elements of a play, including the dramatic persons, should be consistent with themselves, 'the same throughout'—a requirement laid down in Chapter 15 of Aristotle's *Poetics*. Thus Antiochus, the surviving son in *Rodogune*, is too much of an *honnête homme* to make his ruthless mother poison herself; this characteristic has been established early in the play, and any later change would seem out of place and could shock the audience. But in discussing character, that is, character-in-action in the ethical sense described earlier—as we have seen, not a personage but what Corneille correctly translates as *moeurs*—Aristotle said that a person's character should be not just consistent but also 'like reality', by which he probably means 'in accordance with the traditional picture of it as seen in history or legend'. Thirdly, and still within the field of Bray's *bienséances internes*, character should be appropriate.

The fourth quality of character mentioned in the *Poetics*—that it should be good—falls into the domain of *bienséance externe*, which we shall look at shortly. But 'appropriate' character (Corneille's *moeurs convenables*) needs some explanation. In the first *Discours*, Corneille suggests that appropriateness can be distinguished from realism since 'appropriate' refers not to historical or legendary figures but to purely invented ones, *personnes imaginées* created in the mind of the dramatist. Maybe: it is by no means clear from the *Poetics* what reality is being spoken about or what the character is to be appropriate or fitting *to*. Aristotle's example is that 'the Character before us may be, say, manly; but it is not appropriate in a female Character to be manly, or clever'. By this we are perhaps to understand that there should be harmony not so much between the character of the person and the situation in which that person finds himself but rather between a character and his behaviour.

After these necessarily difficult and tentative comments on *bienséances internes*—for Aristotle is far from clear on the matter and his cryptic notes caused much subsequent confusion—we can pass to the more tranquil or at least better-charted waters of 'external' propriety. Apart from the early seventeenth-century Grand Guignol elements described earlier, matters that were taboo in tragedy of Corneille's and Racine's time included prostitution, incest and bigamy. *Théodore, vierge et martyre*, to give it its full title, had a remarkably mild reception from d'Aubignac in 1657. The *Pratique*, as we have seen, initially praised the play's structure highly, saying that events were carefully prepared, so much so that the abbé thought it Corneille's masterpiece to date, with the audience being left with mere 'mauvaises imaginations'. But in preparing for a second edition which was never published, d'Aubignac carefully removed all these compliments, leaving only an earlier passage where he had commented that the subject 'could not please' and that, despite its tactful descriptions, some 'disgust' was inevitable. Corneille himself, three years later, has no illusions. He accepts that the play flopped because of the threat of public prostitution it contained and not because of its structure or the lack of verisimilitude in its incidents.

Incest—a potential hazard in tragedy, since the latter usually deals with characters closely linked by family ties—is usually legitimised, when a couple who believed themselves related are found not to be, or else prevented by *la voix du sang*, the call of blood or instinct which warns a person in due course that the girl or young man found attractive is not an appropriate marriage partner. The case of bigamy is an interesting one, for two well-known tragedies from within our period provide contrasting evidence about its acceptability. In Mairet's *Sophonisbe* (1634), the author has ensured that the Numidian queen's ageing husband Syphax has been killed (Act II) before she marries Massinisse (third interval), to whom she had previously been betrothed. In Corneille's tragedy of the same name almost thirty years later, Syphax is only taken prisoner by the Romans and their ally Massinisse; the latter marries Sophonisbe bigamously during her husband's captivity. Sophonisbe's argument is that Syphax should have committed suicide in true African fashion in order to avoid humiliation by his foreign captors. In any case, Corneille adds in the *Examen*, in Roman law captivity ended a marriage, and presumably Carthaginian law was as stern, if not more so. Mairet, says Corneille, had changed history and invented Syphax's death; he, Corneille, could not copy that, as it would have been an 'attack on his glory'. And if two husbands are to be criticised, why did nobody object to Pompée having two wives in his previous play, *Sertorius*? There is point in some of what the author says, but d'Aubignac was predictably scandalised. Although the 1663 *Sophonisbe* may be rather out on a limb, Jacques Truchet is right to suggest, in *La tragédie classique en France*, that in the general field of propriety, particularly the *bienséances externes*, minor dramatists are perhaps more conservative than major authors.

The one form of death which could be openly staged was suicide. As we have just seen, it was regarded as a true Roman's means of ending a desperate or humiliating situation, and it is natural to find such forceful exits in Corneille's tragedies, at least in those where a 'happy ending' does not rule them out. In *Médée*, Créon, being consumed by the enchantress's poison after touching Créuse's dress, decides to hasten his end and stabs himself, leaving his daughter to die a more agonising death. In *Rodogune*, too, Cléopâtre, suspected of killing one son and wanting to kill the other, seizes the cup of poison and drinks from it herself. While Créon expires in full view of the audience, Cléopâtre's last moments are off-stage: as signs of her imminent death are described (wild eyes, sweaty face, swollen neck), she is helped away by her confidante, either to reduce the impropriety of the scene or (as she herself claims) to save her personal pride from the 'affront' of collapsing at her intended victims' feet.

The convention that in the theatre taking one's own life did not contravene Christian teaching was accepted not just by the generation of 1630 but by the next one, too. Where necessary, Racine does not hesitate to have his characters kill themselves. Sometimes, as in Corneille and else-where, their deaths are merely recounted; but others die on stage. Atalide commits suicide in front of her slavegirl in the closing scene of *Bajazet*, Mithridate stabs himself off-stage in Racine's next tragedy but comes in to die in front of Xipharès and Monime, while Phèdre adopts a similar procedure with Thésée and Théramène, using poison rather than a dagger.

Proof that, in certain critics' eyes at least, suicide was acceptable while the killing of another was not can be found in d'Aubignac's comments on the death of Camille in *Horace*. Writing in the *Pratique* that drama should show things not as they are but as they ought to be, and that the playwright is entitled to touch up his subject to make it conform to the rules of the game, just as a painter improves an imperfect model, d'Aubignac suggests that although the story is a true one, history and propriety could be satisfied if, instead of being stabbed by her brother, the desperate Camille, seeing Horace with a drawn sword, had fallen on to it. 'Thus she would have died at his hand', the abbé remarks, 'and he would have been worthy of compassion.' Corneille's *Examen* puts paid to this prim re-arrangement. Even if she were to stab herself in despair at seeing her brother with a sword in his hand, the author writes, the brother would still have committed a crime in drawing it against her, since there was no third party on stage at the time for whom he might have destined the blow.

This example from *Horace* leads us, finally, to see how our two major writers, Corneille and Racine, dealt with the often unspoken need not to shock the audience's sensibilities. In 1644 Corneille depicted in the Cléo-pâtre of *Rodogune* a character who would seem to contravene in most respects Aristotle's first requirement, that of goodness. But 'such good-ness is possible in every type of personage', Chapter 15 of the *Poetics* runs, and the first *Discours* makes Corneille's position clear. As he writes, it is dif-ficult to relate goodness to the need for error or wickedness in a tragic character. Cléopâtre is evil but determined and accomplished, arousing astonishment as well as disgust in the audience. So, he concludes (prob-ably correctly), the term 'goodness' must be relative, applicable to both virtue and vice, depending on the person concerned. The Syrian queen's character, then, is good of its kind. But what of Rodogune, her captive, loved by the queen's two sons and in love with one of them? The 1647 *Aver-tissement* notes that, unlike Appian's character, Rodogune has not yet married Nicanor, 'so that his two sons could feel love for her without shocking the spectators, who would have found their passion for their father's widow strange if I had followed history'.

Other elements of unseemliness are omitted elsewhere. In *Nicomède*,

Corneille rejects details from his source, Justin, who depicted Prusias planning to kill his son Nicomède in order to favour his children by another marriage and then being put to death by Nicomède, who had just got wind of his intentions. Such a dénouement, the dramatist writes, would be quite barbaric: far from giving the son such a criminal nature, he makes him fall in love with Laodice, queen of neighbouring Armenia, the better to arouse the wrath of the Romans. Injection of a love-element is even more necessary in his next play but one, *Oedipe*. While Sophocles and Seneca could depict Oedipus with gouged-out eyes, a civilised 1659 Paris audience would not expect such horror. In Corneille's words:

> I realised that what had seemed miraculous in those distant centuries might seem horrifying to ours, and that the eloquent and elaborate description of the way in which the unhappy king puts his eyes out, and the sight of those selfsame empty sockets still dripping blood down his face, which fills the whole fifth act in those incomparable sources, would revolt the refined feelings of our ladies, who make up the most important part of our audiences and whose distaste quickly inspires the censure of their escorts.

The audience is thus spared 'this dangerous spectacle', recounted in a mere couple of lines in the closing moments of the play, and to compensate for the absence from the source of both a love interest and female rôles, Corneille has grafted on a sub-plot, the love of Thésée for Dircé.

Even Attila the Hun is subject to French influence. When depicted by Corneille in 1667, the year of *Andromaque*, the Scourge of God is no longer polygamous, a point noted in the *Au Lecteur*, though only in passing. Indeed he has plenty of time to devote to deciding whom he should marry, the sister of the Roman emperor or that of the Frankish king.

But the play of Corneille which had to fight hardest to overcome the charge of impropriety was, of course, *Le Cid*, thirty years earlier. It was not so much Chimène's love of Rodrigue which the Académie criticised through Chapelain (for she had loved him before her father's murder), but rather that her love subsequently has priority over her duty, her 'natural obligations'. At the very least Chimène's two interests should have been kept in balance.

If treatment of the subject could not have been avoided altogether, at least Corneille could have thought of more seemly outcomes. The *Sentiments de l'Académie Française* offered three solutions 'against the [historical] truth': that the Count should be discovered not to be the father of Chimène; that he be found not to have died of his wound; or that, if the projected union of the young couple is to go ahead despite the killing of Chimène's father, it be made clear that 'the safety of king and kingdom depends absolutely on such an inappropriate marriage'. Fortunately Corneille resisted these suggestions, even the third one, and his revisions of the text in 1660 do not (I would argue) alter in any way the likelihood that Chimène will in due course wed Rodrigue.

Like his predecessor, Racine is alive to the need to modify many of his characters and situations so that they conform more closely to public opinion in the 1660s and 70s. In *Andromaque*, for instance, the title-character is not Pyrrhus's concubine, and the child she had by him in Euripides's play, Molossus, is here Astyanax, her son by Hector. Additionally, he has altered the character of Pyrrhus compared with that in Seneca and Virgil. The task was a delicate one: how to soften a brutal warrior (Racine talks in the first preface of his 'ferocity'), while still retaining the powerful position which allows Pyrrhus to effectively control the destinies of Andromaque, her son and Hermione. It is his prisoner who describes him in Act IV as 'violent' (as well as sincere), and a previous chapter has shown how his bloodthirstiness at Troy a year earlier is still present in every memory, including his own. 'Pyrrhus had not read our novels' is Racine's answer to those who criticised his cruelty. Thus the need to observe the *bienséances externes* clashes with the *bienséances internes* of appropriateness and consistency which dictate that Pyrrhus must remain, at least to some extent, violent.

Writing in the journal *Le Mercure galant* in January 1672, Donneau de Visé says that having seen *Bajazet* at the Hôtel he cannot agree with those who say that the play is not Turkish enough. Not all Turks are impervious to love, and it takes no more effort to invent people of taste and feeling than to show barbarians who would not be acceptable to today's ladies, whom it is important to please above all. The criticisms against Racine mentioned by de Visé are taken up in the author's second preface, where the point is made that women can have had little else to do in the seraglio than to learn to please and be loved.

A final example from Racine could well be *Phèdre*. Just as Corneille had refused to kill off Syphax before Massinisse's arrival to tempt Sophonisbe, so Racine goes further than some of his minor predecessors seventeenth-century France who had treated the theme and had shown Phèdre as only the fiancée of Thésée—rather like Monime with Mithridate in the 1673 tragedy. In our play Phèdre is shown to have a husband, albeit one who is temporarily believed dead. In Athenian law at least this 'death' removes any hint of adultery— she could now legitimately marry her stepson Hippolyte. Nor, being merely a stepmother, is she incestuous.

But she has to cope with the knowledge that she loved Hippolyte before Thésée's departure and still does after her husband's return, and with the personal conviction that, adultery aside, her relationship with Hippolyte is unnaturally close. Thésée, Hippolyte and Phèdre herself all talk of incest: it is what the characters believe, not what the facts, when closely examined, suggest, that is important. This crushing awareness of guilt, and the audience's consequent sympathy for Phèdre, help to reduce the feelings of impropriety we may experience.

As for Hippolyte and his father, Racine's comment in the preface to the play is apposite: 'Hippolyte is accused, in Euripides and in Seneca, of having actually violated his stepmother: *vim corpus tulit*. But here he is accused of no more than the intention. I wished to spare Theseus from feeling shame, which might have made him less acceptable to the audience.'

Mention of Racine's last secular tragedy leads us to consider a final category of plays where *bienséances* played an important part: tragedies containing supernatural elements, Christian or pagan. In the Middle Ages drama readily contained a mixture of the sacred and the profane, but this combination could hardly expect to succeed or even survive in the seventeenth century, especially as the professional theatre was coming to believe in the separation of genres. What we find, until the 1640s, are a number of religious tragedies with non-sacred elements: *Polyeucte* and *Théodore*, Rotrou's *Saint-Genest* (1645) and so on. Corneille claims in the *Examen* to the first of these that his play is an amalgam of human love and divine interest, enough to satisfy both society people and the devout.

But this is precisely the point on which he is attacked, by d'Aubignac for example, in a manuscript chapter prepared for the revised version of *La Pratique du théâtre* which never came. Even the treatment of religion alone is beyond most dramatists, the abbé believes. They have to avoid the temptation of simply preaching to their audiences, who do not come to the theatre for that, yet playwrights are not sufficiently trained to explain divine mysteries and resolve problems raised by their depiction on stage, or to counter the views expressed by unbelievers. For these reasons, religion is best left to the drama presented, for instance, in the Jesuit colleges. It is the latter, and the general Jesuit influence on France, which allows a play like *Polyeucte* to succeed, with its mixture of human passions and religious fervour and its no less ambiguous portrait of a Christian martyr impelled by seemingly very human will-power. By the middle of the seventeenth century, perhaps coinciding, as Jacques Truchet suggests, with the rise of Jansenism, such plays, contravening the beliefs or sensibilities of many potential readers or spectators, had all but died out.

The pagan supernatural had a longer career in French classical tragedy and, like the Christian, may be thought to contravene not just the proprieties but verisimilitude. The magic chariot in which Médée escapes in the penultimate scene of Corneille's 1635 play is drawn by two dragons. This detail, the author maintains in his third *Discours*, is not beyond belief, at least no more so than some of the evil queen's other actions, such as the invisible flames which consume Créuse and Créon (these had to be invisible, Corneille adds carefully, because he needed to bring both characters on stage towards the end of the play, as otherwise his last act would not have reached the required length). Some forty years later, Racine is unable to accept the substitution of a hind as sacrificial victim for Iphigénie, as in Euripides's *Iphigenia at Aulis*. Instead he makes the unknown captive princess Eriphile, a character he has invented, turn out to be a daughter of Helen of Troy. Her suicide placates the gods, the winds blow and the Greek fleet can sail to attack Troy. Because of the audience's inability to countenance strange pagan happenings, the hind is replaced by something less unfamiliar, although (one might think) hardly more *vraisemblable*.

There remains the question of the gods and fate. The former are absent from Corneille's theatre, while the latter plays only a minor part. Even his last play *Suréna*, contemporary with *Iphigénie*, shows us two victims, Suréna and Eurydice, caught up in the political power-game that fascinated Corneille in the 1660s and early 70s but condemned to be losers not by any force from outside but by their own human obstinacy. The author's treatment of *Oedipe* fifteen years earlier is a good indication of his attitude. 'I have taken a different road from theirs', he says in the *Au Lecteur*, and his play is indeed very different from those of Sophocles or Seneca on the same theme. In Corneille, Thésée, the prince of Athens who is in love with the daughter of Jocaste by her first marriage, denies the all-powerfulness of the gods, who are said to act on man's behalf, removing the opportunity of independent human action. He wishes to be freed from what he terms 'such blindness' (IV.1), adding that

> The heavens, fair in punishment as in recompense,
> To give to deeds their penalty or reward
> Must offer us their aid, then let us act.

In Racine things seem rather different. *Iphigénie* and *Phèdre* both contain references to gods in action. Yet an examination of the passages (Act V Scene 6 in each play) shows how careful Racine has been in his watering-down of the two stories. In the earlier play an incredulous soldier tells how Diana came down on to the pyre in a cloud, but his account is given just four lines in a long *récit* and is heavily qualified. The same thing happens in the *récit de Théramène* in *Phèdre*. A vivid description is provided of the sea-monster emerging to attack Hippolyte, then in two lines and no more Racine adds

> It is said that there was even seen, amid the frightening disorder
> A God who was spurring on Hippolyte's dusty horses.

This concession to the legend is paralleled by another explanation: as Théramène says sadly to his charge in Act I, Hippolyte has stopped training his horses of late. Can he have other things on his mind, such as love? It is, the text in Act V suggests, because the horses are deaf to a voice they have become unfamiliar with that their master's body is broken on the rocks. Even when the supernatural is retained, Racine provides his audience with an alternative, possibly more acceptable reading.

It is true, of course, that certain characters in Racinian tragedy are related to the gods by blood. Clytemnestre is a daughter of Jupiter, Iphigénie being his grand-daughter. In *Phèdre*, the title-character, a victim of Venus, is daughter of Minos and Pasiphaë and hence connected both with the Sun and the underworld, while Thésée has struck up a friendship and a tragic bargain with Neptune. But while the semi-divinity of persons in this last play contributes to our understanding of them, this is not a feature which is as widespread in Racine as many people think. Even when characters refer to their unhappiness and attribute it to the gods or fate (the terms seem often interchangeable), it is rarely that we find named divinities, or indeed any force beyond the characters themselves, guiding their destinies. When Oreste in *Andromaque* announces in the opening scene 'I follow blindly my impelling fate', is he not led rather by his passion, the noun which Racine only replaced with *destin* in late editions? And in *Phèdre*, when the title-character appears for the first time, confessing her love for Hippolyte, it is significant how easily she slips from calling Venus a goddess into calling her stepson a god:

> In vain upon the altars I burned incense;
> My lips in vain implored the goddess, but I worshipped
> Only Hippolytus; and seeing him
> Each day even at the altar's foot
> I offered all to the god I dared not name.

Certainly in *Iphigénie* and *Phèdre* the gods intervene directly. The plot of the former play depends on their having becalmed the Greek fleet at Aulis, and the death of Eriphile unleashes a host of events (thunder, winds, flame, lightning) which, as Raymond Picard has aptly said, restores to the play 'a sort of mythological orthodoxy'. Racine tells us in the preface to *Phèdre* that it is her destiny and the wrath of the gods which give rise to the illegitimate passion which she is the first to abhor; Phèdre's crime is a punishment from the gods rather than a willed act of her own. But many modern critics would say that, with the exception of these two plays, references to fate or divine intervention are an admission of characters' ineffectualness and frustration, an attempt by them to transfer the blame for their own actions, rather than proof of supernatural influence. Even in *Phèdre*, the heroine remains full of human dignity, weak but lucid, passionate yet guilt-ridden, able—from her own resources, it would seem—to come in Act IV to confess all to her distraught husband, then, prevented from doing so by Thésée's chance revelation of Hippolyte's love for Aricie, capable of returning in Act V to confess and absolve her stepson from guilt. This possibility of initiative surely proves that even Phèdre is not just a puppet in 'a sort of theological pantomime', to use Professor Picard's words.

One of the latest commentators, Philip Yarrow, sums the matter up in his book *Racine* (1978) when he writes, specifically of *Esther* and *Athalie*: 'Divine providence is at work, but, whatever Racine himself may have believed, it is open to the spectator to explain everything in terms of human psychology.' External forces can be mere projections of characters' consciences; even a god like Neptune in *Phèdre* 'accomplishes nothing that could not have happened otherwise. Thésée could have punished his son by other, less picturesque, less poetically satisfying, means.'

Having said that, it is only fair to make two points in support of the supernatural in Racine. It can be argued that the result of the divine intervention in *Phèdre* is infinitely more significant than the mere brief description of the god, and that the author is rightly concerned only with that effect. More generally, the dramatist is at pains to stress, in his preface to the play, the need to 'retain the verisimilitude of history, and yet lose none of the embellishments of fable, so rich in the stuff of poetry'. The supernatural, in other words, is important well beyond the mere level of the plot.

Whereas the claims of verisimilitude, and the difference between it and historical truth, are relatively easy to codify and understand, the proprieties and the constraints which their observance placed on dramatists would seem more difficult to define. All we can do is examine the texts of plays and note what is tolerated, what in the source-material is not accepted and what is altered, slightly or greatly, to conform with public taste. Every period has its standards and its taboos, which are a reflection of many different pressures at work within society. As with the more formally expressed rules we have looked at in earlier chapters, the notions of *vraisemblance* and *bienséance* are not proof that Frenchmen between 1630 or so and the end of Racine's career were puritanical killjoys. Corneille and Racine can be muted and restrained, but Eric Bentley is surely right to point out that the latter's drama (and he might have included Corneille's as well) 'ranges from the peaks of the human spirit to the depths of animalism. If it is ultra-civilised, it is also ultrabarbaric'. English-speaking audiences should not need to be reminded of the many virtues of understatement.

12 Tragic element

Tragedy is undoubtedly the main glory of seventeenth-century French literature, immensely rich though that literary period is. Yet one astonishing fact stands out as we look back three hundred years later: no writer or critic of the time seems to have felt the need, or else had the ability, to give a clear and comprehensive definition of what the tragic element in contemporary plays was. Of course there are several treatises which take up and develop earlier ideas—those of Greek and Latin writers and of Renaissance Europe—and various *Poetics* and writings on the theatre appear, dealing not just with tragedy but with tragi–comedy and comedy too. Vauquelin de la Fresnaye's *Art poétique* (1601), Chapelain's various writings, the *Cid* quarrel documents of 1637, La Mesnardière's *Poétique* (1639), d'Aubignac's *Pratique du théâtre* (1657) and comments on some of Corneille's later tragedies, to say nothing of the latter's own writings about drama: these are merely the more important critical works during the period in which regular tragedy is seeking to establish itself.

Then again, as we have seen in earlier chapters of this book, much writing and theorising about tragedy is contained in the prefaces provided by the dramatists. Even here, however, definitions of the tragic are usually implicit rather than explicit; they have to be pieced together from remarks on the handling of source-materials, the dramatic structure of the play, the balance of characters and so on. Perhaps we should not expect what is often a mere covering note to delve into the heart of the matter, but the absence of any regular or systematic attempt to relate the content of serious plays to a theory of tragedy is, at first sight, rather baffling.

We are forced back, then (if that is the right expression), to the plays themselves. As elsewhere in this study, remarks will be confined in the

155

main to the two major dramatists, Corneille and Racine. They it is whom modern readers approaching classical tragedy come into most contact with, and what they have to say about the effect of the plays they write is probably as near as one can get to a seventeenth-century playwright's view of the tragic. Of course, we must not forget that they are exceptions in their respective periods: the average dramatists who were their contemporaries are more 'typical' and often more popular, because less intellectually demanding, than the geniuses whom they both imitated and inspired. Yet the difference between the great and the less great is seen more in the areas of dramatic technique, language and to some extent characterisation than in the theory of tragedy.

A second consideration is that drama has two kinds of audience—the live one in the theatre, many of whom have little, if any, prior knowledge of the play's content; and the reading-public, which can study the text at leisure, looking ahead, as with a thriller, to see how the plot is resolved and, more importantly, able to look back, to go over scenes and acts and ponder them at length. Many of these readers will not have seen the play staged and may never do so. Novelists and even to some extent poets are not faced with this double audience; the dramatist always is, and his need to arouse the emotions of at least the live theatre audience must mean that there can be no absolute criterion by which one can judge tragedy. As Geoffrey Brereton points out in his *Principles of tragedy* (1968),

> in looking for 'tragedy' in a play or a situation, we are thus obliged to take account of the existence of non-participants. This apparently unexceptionable principle has far-reaching consequences. It must eventually lead to the conclusion that the significance of a work of art is dependent on the emotions which it generates.

Let us begin with the impact of tragedy on the all-important *stage-character*, before considering later its influence on the *audience or reader*. In Chapter 13 of his *Poetics*, Aristotle discusses the aim and effect of tragedy as he saw it in Greece in the fourth century B.C. Drawing on his knowledge of the fairly recent plays of Aeschylus, Sophocles and Euripides, he rejects three different possible situations in which the tragic protagonist can find himself. Firstly, a character who is enjoying a normal, happy life must not fall into great misfortune as a result of events in the play. Secondly, the opposite must not occur either: a villain should not be shown turning into a happy, successful person. Finally, says Aristotle, the situation should be avoided in which an extreme villain passes from happiness into misfortune.

What is wrong with these three specimen plots? The first, according to the *Poetics*, would be a case of the perfect hero coming to grief; it goes against all common sense of justice and for that reason excites the spectator's or reader's distaste, not his sympathy. The second situation 'is the most untragic that may be', since the rule of fair play is manifestly being broken. Lastly, in the case of the moral villain who ends up in misfortune, the public considers his downfall to be totally deserved; he gets what he asked for. We cannot therefore pity him, yet we do not experience fear either, for he is on a quite different level from us; we have no contact, no point of comparison; he is not 'one like ourselves'.

So what is left? In Aristotle's terms, translated by Ingram Bywater,

> the intermediate kind of personage, a man not pre-eminently virtuous and just, whose misfortune, however, is brought upon him not by vice and depravity but by some error of judgement, of the number of those in the enjoyment of great reputation and prosperity ... the change in the hero's fortunes must be not from misery to happiness, but on the contrary from happiness to misery; and the cause of it must lie not in any depravity, but in some great error on his part; the man himself being either such as we have described, or better, not worse, than that.

This is a vital statement. The key word in the Greek is *hamartia*, and Bywater, in the preface to his Clarendon Press translation of the *Poetics*, has this to say about it:

> *Hamartia* means originally *a bad shot* or *error*, but is currently used for *offence* or *sin*. Aristotle clearly means that the typical hero is a great man with 'something wrong' in his life or character; but I think it is a mistake of method to argue whether he means 'an intellectual error' or 'a moral flaw'.

Maybe: the point is that the term covers both areas, depravity (i.e. some innate failing) *and* a simple error of judgement or a mistake based on ignorance. The latter is in every way the equal of the former. By no means is tragedy simply the punishment of sin.

Other commentators conclude that *hamartia*, in the context of Aristotle and Greek tragedy, means a mistake only. Thus D. W. Lucas, in his 1968 commentary on the *Poetics*:

> The essence of *hamartia* is ignorance combined with the absence of wicked intent ... *Hamartia* is lack of the knowledge which is needed if

right decisions are to be taken . . . not frailty as opposed to badness, but error as opposed to evil intent.

Now in 1660, in the second of the three *Discours* on tragedy which he published to accompany a revised edition of his dramatic works, Corneille quotes Aristotle's first three examples, paraphrasing the Stagirite's preference for 'un homme qui ne soit ni tout à fait bon, ni tout à fait méchant, et qui, par une faute, ou faiblesse humaine, tombe dans un malheur qu'il ne mérite pas'. The middling character can arrive at his undeserved misfortune either through 'human weakness' or because of a *faute*, the equivalent of the error or mistaken judgement which the *Poetics* talks about.

Rodrigue and Chimène in *Le Cid* might be said to fit this category, if their mutual love is looked on as a weakness. Other central Corneille characters suffer from flaws rather than errors. The title-character in *Horace* exhibits extreme, perhaps excessive patriotism and overweening pride (*hubris*) alongside what some critics, at least, believe to be a sensitive nature, while *Cinna*'s Emilie has desire for revenge allied to an innate goodness. A number of the dramatist's most memorable protagonists, though, appear to step beyond the bounds even of a 'flaw' and wallow in crime; we must return to them and the emotions they arouse later in this chapter.

Just a few years afterwards Racine has similar comments to make about certain of the characters in his own tragedies. Néron, the emperor Nero in *Britannicus*, he says in the first preface to that play (1670), has been criticised for excessive cruelty, while others claim he is painted in too favourable a light. The dramatist's own view would be that the historical Nero was more than cruel; he was a monster. But as it happens, the episode depicted in *Britannicus* shows, not the adult emperor, but Nero in his early years, as just a fledgling tyrant, a *monstre naissant*. His most wicked deeds— the killing of his mother, his wife and so on—are still to come, so that the character, although already seen to be criminal, is relatively middling. Five years later, in the preface to *Iphigénie*, Racine reviews his various sources and predecessors and concludes that the title-character, as he has finally depicted her, 'deserves to some extent to be punished, although without being entirely unworthy of compassion'.

But the best-known, certainly the most often discussed example of a morally average Racinian character is Phèdre, heroine of his 1677 tragedy. Now as we saw previously, the Phaedra of Euripides had remained a background figure, refusing to declare her love directly to her stepson and hanging herself in shame well before the death of Hippolytus.

The play dealt essentially with the rivalry between the goddesses Artemis and Aphrodite. In his preface to *Phèdre* Racine mentions both Euripides's protagonist and his own rather different creation, in such a way that it is difficult to know whether his remarks relate to the figure of antiquity and Phèdre or just the latter. Certainly they *include* Phèdre, whose characteristics, the author boasts, have all the qualities that Aristotle requires of a tragic hero or heroine. She is neither entirely guilty nor completely innocent. Her destiny and the wrath of the gods have drawn her into an unlawful passion which she is the first to abhor. Frantic attempts are made to overcome it and she would rather die than disclose it to anyone. When forced to do so, it is abundantly clear, Racine says, that her crime is a form of punishment from the gods rather than an impulse of her own will. As for her stepson Hippolyte, the paragon of virtue depicted by Euripides has had to be replaced by a more middle-of-the-road person. 'I felt I should give him a failing that might render him somewhat guilty towards his father, without detracting in any way from the magnanimity which makes him spare Phèdre's honour and go to his death without accusing her.'

At first sight, then, it would seem that both major dramatists follow the Aristotelian line, advocating human characters, neither all black nor all white but an acceptable shade of mid-grey. Such is not quite the case, though, at least with Corneille. As we shall see, the latter in his theorising appears to envisage tragic characters who arouse pity but no—or very little—fear in the audience. We sympathise with their plight but do not often experience the personal fear of committing the same sort of error as the stage character.

Closely linked to this view will be his belief in a third tragic emotion, *admiration*, in the original Latin sense of 'astonishment' or 'wonder'. The martyrdom of Polyeucte and the magnanimity of Nicomède, in the plays bearing their names, are proof, he would claim, that tragedy can occur with completely 'good' characters. This is his theoretical position. Perhaps it is fairer to suggest that in practice their great qualities, which the dramatist mentions (the word *vertu* conveniently meaning both 'virtue' and 'strength of will or purpose' in seventeenth-century French, as we have noted), only serve to mask defects which do exist: Polyeucte's pride, Nicomède's inability to act, at least in the situation in which he finds himself. Similarly with his moral villains—Médée in 1635 and Cléopâtre in *Rodogune* (1644), for example, are each described by their creator as very wicked, yet in a passage of his *Discours du poème dramatique* he specifically qualifies his criticism of Cléopâtre (and implicitly that of Médée, too), suggesting that her criminal acts are offset by an element of magnanimity, *grandeur d'âme*, which produces a feeling of amazement in the reader or audience. In short, while it would be wrong to see Cornelian tragedy embracing entirely good or bad protagonists, the proportion of badness in the first set of characters mentioned and of goodness in the second is remarkably small, probably more so than in any play by Racine.

In the last chapter we noticed the rôle played by such outside forces as fate and the pagan gods and the measure of responsibility which characters themselves—protagonists and confidants—are willing to accept. What is easy to forget is the point mentioned by Aristotle and taken up by both Corneille and Racine in their critical writings, that the heroes of tragedy undergo their ordeal for one of two main reasons, neither of which will, in all likelihood, result from a deliberate decision on their part to do evil. The inborn character defect and the accidental wrong choice are alike no fault of the person who has or makes them—which is not to say that he or she will not feel a guilt which contributes to the tragic effect of the play.

But often the characters in tragedy are influenced, not by forces beyond their control such as the gods or innate flaws nor even by wrong decisions, but rather by elements of which they are totally unaware. This is where a distinction must be drawn between audience or reader and stage character. A character in drama is never present all the time; many important figures appear in remarkably few scenes. This physical absence from the stage only serves to underline the lack of knowledge which afflicts most protagonists in tragedy and the dramatic—or 'tragic'—irony which results from misunderstandings. The audience, on the other hand, is privileged: it has a fuller, though still incomplete view of events and can frequently foresee the outcome of wrong decisions or of decisions which are deliberately being postponed.

The self-destructiveness which is the hallmark of so many characters in French classical tragedy is often not willed by the person concerned. Supremely unconscious of the gap between reality and what they, in ignorance, plan to do or wish to happen, they only realise the depth of the abyss when it is too late. In *Andromaque*, Hermione asks for Pyrrhus's death, but when this occurs she turns on Oreste with the words 'Who told you to?' The realisation that she loves the man who spurns her more than she hates him has come too late. In other Racinian plays lack of knowledge affects the course of events in equally important ways. The Roman emperor Titus, believing he cannot marry Bérénice, asks prince Antiochus to take her away, not realising that Antiochus has been, and still is, in love with the Jewish queen. In *Phèdre*, too, the queen pours out her love to her stepson, unaware until the last moment that she has a rival in the person of Aricie, Hippolyte's beloved.

But insight or the ability to discriminate are not guarantees of success and survival. In *Bajazet* Atalide believes she can distinguish between her cousin the title-character and his brother, the sultan Amurat. Yet this gets her nowhere, for Amurat has decided to rid himself of a possible rival, especially as his sultana Roxane has fallen in love with Bajazet. The latter's death is matched by that of the protagonist in *Mithridate* who, confident that he knows the difference between his two sons, his favourite Xipharès and Pharnace, soon learns that Xipharès is a rival in love for the hand of Monime. Despite (or is it because of?) the tightly-knit family groups which feature in tragedy, communications are poor: the relative omniscience of the audience contrasts strikingly with the isolation of the character who, through ignorance, can literally create his own tragedy.

Linked to this discussion of the stage character's tragic error is the question of recognition. Aristotle talks about it in two sections of the *Poetics*, with a different meaning in each place. In Chapter 16, he deals with recognition or discovery on the basic, material level, 'discovery by signs or marks'. This is the sort of event that occurs more often in tragi–comedies than in regular tragedies in seventeenth-century France, where an infant, for one reason or another, is brought up by someone else, then late in life, at some crucial moment, it is discovered that he is, perhaps, a king or emperor. Yet physical recognition also plays a part even in Racine, with the discovery *in extremis* of Eriphile's parentage (*Iphigénie*) or the concealed identity of Joas—known to the High Priest and his wife, and to us—being revealed in the course of the action to the young boy's tormentor, the Queen in *Athalie*.

But the more important sense of recognition comes in Chapter 11 of the *Poetics*. As so often, Aristotle, in the fragmentary lecture-notes that make up his work, is allusive rather than explicit, describing recognition here as 'a change from ignorance to knowledge and thus to either love or hate'. Discovery or recognition in this sense is not material but mental or psychological; it no longer has to do with outward physical identity but relates to a character's coming to terms with a new situation and with himself, realising that he has done wrong or been blind or deserved what has come to him and perhaps resolving to make amends for his mistakes.

The indirect hints that Aristotle drops about really meaningful recognition seem disappointing. Corneille, if anything, appears even less aware in his critical writings of the importance of inner rather than outer discovery. This may be because, as we shall see, he rejects mistaken identity as unsuitable for tragedy and simply never gets round to probing the other kind of discovery. Yet both Greek and Cornelian tragedy provide examples of characters arriving at the moment of truth: Jocasta and Oedipus (where physical identity and realisation of guilt are masterfully fused), Auguste in *Cinna*, Pompée in *Sertorius*. In Racine, Agrippine comes to realise that she has misjudged her son Néron (*Britannicus*); Bérénice finds out that she, too, has misunderstood the emperor Titus, and so on. Now a play's tragic value does not seem inevitably linked to recognition by characters; it can be the audience rather than the protagonists who 'discover' the truth. But in those cases where the character is enlightened, he or she may, in the process of making this discovery, experience peripety, that is, a reversal not so much of fortune as of intention. Thus Agrippine finds that the person she has put on the imperial throne descends to killing his step-brother Britannicus, while Bérénice's arrival in Rome, far from hastening her union with Titus, only serves to underline how impossible the marriage would be. The actions of Mithridate and Phèdre recoil on those characters in a similar fashion. This self-destruction due to blindness, or destruction of someone one loves rather than hates, is another example of tragic irony, of irony of circumstances.

We have seen in previous chapters how, when choosing the plots and characters for their plays, Corneille and Racine had very different, at times almost diametrically opposed ideas; the same is generally true of their respective contemporaries. For Corneille and other writers of tragedy in the 1630s, 40s and early 50s, the main character or potential hero (often but by no means always the title-character) will, when committing the deed or deeds which result in tragedy, be fully aware of whom he is attacking and largely conscious, even, of what he is doing. Corneille's second *Discours* advocates characters who act openly, aware of the material identity of the opposition. Thus Rodrigue faces the Count and ultimately his daughter Chimène; Horace knows all too well that he is fighting his brother-in-law-to-be Curiace and ultimately his own sister Camille; Cinna, Emilie and the other conspirators plot to kill Auguste, and so on. And yet, even in these cases, there remains a significant gap between what the character believes the situation to be and the reality. The Racinian hero, on the other hand, and those of Thomas Corneille, Quinault and others in the 1660s and 70s, will tend more to follow the precepts in Chapter 14 of the *Poetics*, where Aristotle prefers situations in which the deed is done, but in ignorance, or else the doer, again in ignorance, steps back from the action at the last minute.

Given this general difference, it is perhaps only fair to point out that both the major dramatists we are discussing would advocate depicting characters who are eventually brought to 'see the light'. Tillyard's famous classification of tragedies in his book *Shakespeare's problem plays* (1950) listed three kinds: plays dealing with destruction and renewal; sacrifice and expiation; suffering and endurance. The last category may well include an element of self-awareness, and in any case provides a minimal definition of tragedy. But the first two, which cover all the main tragedies of Corneille and Racine, imply that characters transcend suffering in a much more meaningful way. Thus in *Phèdre* Racine shows how the step-mother, racked by guilt at the thought of the love she feels for Hippolyte, comes to terms with herself and commits suicide in the belief that this will expiate what she, at least, sees as a monstrous crime. Similarly Hippolyte's father, having in a paroxysm of rage condemned his son to death, gradually realises his mistake and in the end makes amends, not by killing himself, but by accepting into his family Aricie, who was a mortal enemy. Some thirty-five years earlier, in Corneille's *Cinna*, the emperor Auguste realises, in the course of the play, that he has been as guilty as the conspirators now plotting to overthrow him. He redeems himself and his criminal past by pardoning them in a fairly disinterested way, and they respond to this gesture by accepting his clemency.

Thus it is that error is compensated for by an admission of error or guilt. Often, of course, the character finds that the burden of guilt can only be relieved through suicide, the physical death that one instinctively expects at the end of a tragedy. In other cases, for example when the criminal deed is not accomplished, the reaction can be different. In his partial gloss of the *Poetics*, Racine describes the character 'meditating some deadly injury to another, in ignorance of his relationship' (to use Bywater's terms) and discovering in sufficient time, not the physical identity of the victim, which Aristotle implies, but the horror of the act about to be perpetrated ('l'horreur de son action'). Often, though, discovery of self means something more positive or extensive than this: self-realisation and, in the end, self-acceptance due to a new awareness of the limitations of our human condition, of the need to live with the situation we find ourselves in and thereby achieve dignity as human beings. For Auguste, Cinna, Emilie, Bérénice and others this can be a true measure of a hero's tragic stature.

In this respect it might be useful to look at an example of a seventeenth-century play with a different flavour, where such self-knowledge or awareness is not attained by the final curtain. Corneille's *Horace*, which preceded *Cinna* by only two years, is the story of how Horace and his two brothers, in a representative battle, defend Rome against the enemy Alba, represented by an equally valorous trio. Horace wins, as he alone is left alive; but he then kills his sister Camille (engaged to one of the three Albans), faces trial for his crime and is acquitted for reasons of state. The tragedy is in many ways enigmatic and has given rise to numerous interpretations. Horace does not refuse to discuss his guilt or innocence at their simplest, most obvious level. But what seems beyond doubt is that he never penetrates—or lets his colleagues, the other characters, penetrate—into the recesses of his mind where, presumably, he is having to come to terms with his various deeds.

Horace lives on to fight another day, to 'serve the State'. So do the conspirators Cinna and Emilie, pardoned by Auguste in a gesture which, incidentally, guarantees his own survival, too. But it would be wrong to think that it is only Corneille who lets some of his tragic characters survive. Although Phèdre and her stepson both die, the three central figures in Racine's *Bérénice* conclude that, despite their ordeal, life is still worth something and that their experience can indeed act as an example to others of the value of noble resignation and self-sacrifice in the cause of love. In the preface, the author points out that blood and corpses are not a prerequisite of tragedy. Rather, as we have noted elsewhere, it is enough if 'the action is great, the actors are heroic, the passions are aroused, and all is imbued with that majestic sadness which constitutes the whole pleasure of tragedy'. We shall return to some of these terms shortly, when considering the spectator's or reader's reaction. But what Racine is in part saying is that the nature of the ordeal which the protagonist has to face, the quality of the struggle which he puts up, is an essential, perhaps *the* essential, part of the tragic element. Corneille's view is different in many respects, but he foreshadows Racine when he says in 1660 that characters are tragic who act and resist to the best of their ability, only to be prevented 'by some superior force, or by some change of fortune which causes them to perish or places them in the power of those they sought to destroy'.

The so-called 'happy ending' of bloodless tragedy is perhaps not so happy after all, certainly less carefree than the dénouements of many of the tragi-comedies with which it is often inevitably compared. What distinguishes true tragedy, whether ending with deaths or not, from the lesser genres is that the main characters in it—with some notable exceptions—are brought to reassess their attitudes to life, to assimilate, if possible, the changes to them which the action of the play has caused to occur. Things will never be the same again. This, indeed, is one of the features distinguishing tragedy in general from comedy. In comedy the characters have an experience, but it rarely changes them radically—they are the same at the end as they were at the beginning, and the situation could be, and probably will be, repeated. Orgon will fall for the next Tartuffe he meets, Alceste will soon leave his 'little dark corner' and mix with the society he professes to hate, Harpagon's experience with his money-box will not alter his *avarice*. But tragic figures, through the singular ordeal they undergo, often discover for themselves, or have revealed to them, the mistakes and circumstances that have caused their dilemma and they generally learn from them. As we saw when discussing the aims of tragedy, seventeenth-century dramatists in France did not on the whole write didactic plays, with one and only one clear message. A tragedy without deaths does not necessarily indicate the triumph of virtue, any more than the destruction of one or a number of characters may be sufficient to suggest that vice reigns supreme. The serious issues at stake cannot be resolved into right or wrong, or if so, only rarely.

Turning from the characters to the audience or reader, we find that Aristotle again provides a useful starting-point. In a brief definition in Chapter 6 of the *Poetics*, he says that tragedy is

> the imitation of an action that is serious and also, as having magnitude, complete in itself; in language with pleasurable accessories, each kind brought in separately in the parts of the work; in a dramatic, not in a narrative form; with incidents arousing pity and fear, wherewith to accomplish its catharsis of such emotions.

We must return to the idea of catharsis shortly. But for the moment it is useful to consider Chapter 14 of the *Poetics*, where Aristotle defines two ways of arousing the emotions of pity and fear in the audience—by the spectacle, that is, by the mere sight of disaster, or by the very structure or incidents of the play, where the same emotions would be produced even if there were no scenery or even staging and the play were simply read as a text.

To stimulate pity and fear in the audience, the stage-characters have to be related, known to each other. The close-knit family circle creates the inevitability, the chain reaction that is part and parcel of tragedy, and its disintegration leads to the necessary isolation of the tragic character, Aristotle distinguishes four situations involving characters of the type just mentioned, a couple of close friends or members of a family. In the first case A knows who B is, he goes ahead and, say, kills him. In the second example A is unaware of B's identity, he kills him and then finds out. Thirdly A does not know who B is, but he finds out in time to draw back and refrain from killing. Lastly, A knows B's identity, but he has second thoughts about his proposed action and does not kill him. Now of these four situations, Aristotle says, the least tragic is the last, where the criminal, in full knowledge of the relationship/identity, draws back at the last minute; there is no suffering, therefore no real tragedy. Next comes the first example, in which the character again has knowledge, but this time carries out the deed. What the author of the *Poetics* considers truly tragic are situations two and three, where the protagonist is in ignorance of the victim's identity. If he kills him and then finds out who it is he has killed, 'the discovery will serve to astound us'. But the best of all possible plots is the one in which A does not know B's identity but becomes aware in time to step back. It appears, then, that Aristotle considers material recognition to be a powerful source of tragedy. We must remember that, when making his comments, he had only the experience of fifth-century B.C. Greek drama to go on, with its masked characters, stylised action and vast open-air theatres. In these circumstances the question of physical identity can be seen as a legitimate part of the dramatist's concern. What is perhaps more surprising is his desire to avoid unhappy endings. Although Chapter 13 of the *Poetics* envisages the possibility of death, Chapter 14 includes examples of avoidance of it, as when in *Cresphontes* Merope, on the point of killing her son, recognises him in time to draw back. But as John Jones comments in *On Aristotle and Greek tragedy* (1962), 'mutability is Aristotle's tragic focus, not misfortune . . . The alternative of upwards or downward movement is ultimately open, what matters is that the action shall have room to display life's bottomless instability.'

Two-thirds of the way through his career, Corneille, in his *Discours de la tragédie*, summarises Aristotle's arguments about situations productive of tragedy and relates them to his own ideas and plays. As he points out, the very actions condemned by Aristotle are the ones he, Corneille, frequently uses. His *Horace* depicts the title-character killing others, fully aware of the relationship. In *Le Cid*, *Cinna* and *Nicomède*, to name but three other major tragedies, death is avoided when those contemplating it draw back from the brink. Not only does Corneille favour this kind of plot; he considers it to be a new type of tragedy, more attractive than those recommended in the *Poetics*. If a character acts in full awareness of the situation and with the audience's knowledge, then 'le combat des passions contre la nature, ou du devoir contre l'amour, occupe la meilleure partie du poème, et de là naissent les grandes et fortes émotions qui renouvellent à tous moments et redoublent la commisération'.

Our pity, Corneille says here, our *commisération*, is increased by our witnessing the struggles in the characters between the passions and human nature, between duty and love. And this pity leads us, the spectators, to fear that we may fall into a comparable plight, in proportion to our experience, in accordance with our particular natures and failings. There but for the grace of God go we . . .

Elsewhere, as we have noted, it is not *la pitié* nor *la crainte* that Corneille advocates but a third emotion, perhaps the one he was thinking about in the example just quoted: *admiration* or awe. The fight the characters in a play put up, even if they end by losing it, amazes and astonishes us. We *may* go as far as to admire it, but that term implies a moral approval not necessarily contained in the French. In the *Examen* to *Nicomède*, Corneille does indeed invite his audience to feel genuine admiration at the great-heartedness of his title-character, but this is an isolated instance. More often, the audience's reaction is at least ambiguous. As in the case of, say, the great train robbers, we know the deed was wrong but still have a sneaking desire to praise the competent way it was carried out. We admire their skill, although there is no moral quality present that we can approve of. And what of Racine? Significantly he would wish to emend Aristotle's description of his second-favourite plot—'A better situation . . . is for the deed to be done in ignorance, and the relationship discovered afterwards.' In his annotation of Vettori's edition of and commentary on the *Poetics*, he writes: 'But the best by far is when a man carries out some horrible act without knowing what he has done and then afterwards comes to recognise what he has done.' Not only does Racine, then, make this discovery-after-the-event his favourite rather than his number two plot; he substitutes ignorance of the nature of the act for ignorance of the identity of the victim. As Professor H. T. Barnwell comments in a 1965 article, 'the substitution . . . seems to me not only . . . an expression of Racine's retention of discovery in tragedy, while giving it a moral and psychological twist, but also a rejection, no less clear than Corneille's, of *material* discovery'. Recognition of the true nature of the deed, Racine claims, has nothing 'wicked or monstrous' about it; but it does make the audience shiver with fear.

The three responses to tragic events which we have been looking at, pity, fear and *admiration*, may seem incompatible. Indeed writers, including Mairet in the preface (1635) to his *Sophonisbe* and the critics La Mesnardière, in his *Poétique* (1639), and d'Aubignac, in *La Pratique du théâtre* (1657), try to separate the first two and even see them as operating independently of each other. For La Mesnardière,

> the poet must try to see that terror is much less than feelings of pity. This is not to say that terror is not useful on stage. But as it is unpleasant, and should only rule in humble subjects . . . it is preferable that compassion, which is a gentler feeling arising from the misfortunes of imperfect people, unfortunate rather than guilty, should leave its impressions on men's minds and even rule them to such an extent that tears are shed.

Corneille, in his mid-career theoretical writings, is prepared to countenance pity without fear, failing to see that *la pitié* or *la compassion* and *la crainte* or *la terreur* are in fact complementary. John Jones, as well as Humphry House in his commentary on the *Poetics* (1956), are among recent critics who stress the need to hyphenate Aristotelian pity-and-fear, which are successive stages in an audience's response, not alternatives.

The question of whether a play whose effect depends entirely on our acceptance of *admiration* is truly tragic remains an open one: few tragedies, if indeed any, in seventeenth-century France rely exclusively on producing this emotion, although it is often an important element, and, as we noticed, even Aristotle's second-favourite tragic situation is one where murder is followed by a discovery which 'will serve to astound us'. Corneille and his contemporaries, attacked in the twentieth century as being 'untragic', would retort that a character's fight against great odds can produce a response just as significant as that of a Racinian character's apparently less single-minded struggle, and that the tragedies of the second quarter of the century include more emotion, less rational choice and unfettered optimism than many blinkered critics are willing to see. Indeed, both dramatists could be brought quite close together if we accept that it is often the action itself, rather than the outcome of that action, which generates most of the tragedy. But the spectacle offered to audiences in the respective generations of 1630 and 1660 *is* very different: rarely indeed in the plays of Corneille, Rotrou or Mairet do we find anything approaching that 'majestic sadness' which we saw Racine describing as 'the whole pleasure of tragedy'.

Finally, we must look not just at the tragic emotions and their possible effect but at the aims a dramatist has when arousing them in his audience. Aristotle, allusive as ever, says that a tragedy should excite 'pity and fear, wherewith to accomplish its catharsis of such emotions'. This is the only time the word 'catharsis' is used in the whole *Poetics*. Then again it is not entirely clear from the original Greek, far less from later glosses, what is meant by 'such emotions'. Is Aristotle here referring to pity and fear alone, or extending the range to include other similar emotions which disturb a reader or spectator?

Part of the answer (and most of the problem!) lies in the interpretation of the term 'catharsis'. Influenced by the *purgatio* used by translators of the *Poetics* into Latin, seventeenth-century France commonly described the effect of tragedy in terms such as *purger* and *purgation*. Thus Chapelain, for example, writing in 1630: 'The principal aim of any theatrical performance is to move the spectator's soul by the forceful and concrete portrayal of the various passions on the stage, and purge it by this means of the evil habits which might cause it to fall into the misfortunes which these passions produce'. The passions, which he refers to elsewhere as unruly, are not defined, but clearly they are not limited to—and may not even include—the Aristotelian pity and fear.

But does the tragic experience really resemble the remedies inflicted on, say, Argan, the self-styled invalid in Molière's comedy *Le Malade imaginaire*? Does the audience, individually or collectively, have to undergo a course of intellectual enemas and tragic bloodlettings? Surely not. For one thing, few if any theatregoers are unfortunate enough to possess all the 'various passions' which Chapelain refers to.

His adversary Corneille is only slightly more helpful in his definition of catharsis. As he points out, Aristotle explains in detail what he means by pity and fear but has 'not a word' to say about catharsis. For Corneille, the pity we feel at seeing our equals fall into misfortune makes us fear a similar fate; such fear causes us to want to avoid it; and this desire leads us to 'purge, moderate, rectify and even uproot the passion in us which visibly plunges into misfortune those whom we pity'. The passion, here unspecified, seems to be of the same order as Chapelain's, a general one rather than pity and fear, and its eradication will serve a useful purpose. We should note, however, that 'purging' is seen as only one of several possible courses: indeed, Corneille's 'and even uproot' appears to him to be a drastic step, to be envisaged as a last resort, so that by 'purge' he may mean something much more benign, akin to the 'moderate' and 'rectify' which he offers as alternatives.

Corneille is ill at ease when discussing catharsis in 1660. Having seemingly decided that Aristotle's phrase 'such emotions' means that the audience will benefit from tragedy only if it brings into the theatre attitudes and passions similar to those of the characters in the play, he soon afterwards demolishes this theory by admitting that he cannot see it ever working out in practice. 'If purging of the passions occurs in tragedy,' he writes in the second *Discours*, 'I maintain it must do so in the way I explain, but I doubt if it ever does so.' As H. T. Barnwell notes in his edition of Corneille's *Writings on the theatre* (1965), the difficulty lies in confusion between the therapeutic nature of catharsis, which is what Aristotle was hinting at, and the strictly moral associations which Corneille wishes to attach to the term:

The moralistic interpretation, largely prevalent in sixteenth-century Italy and seventeenth-century France, stems from Plato's contention ... that the emotions are harmful and that the arts which excite them should not be practised. While it might be possible to demonstrate that fear is harmful, the same could not be said, especially against a background of Christian teaching, of pity. There is the added difficulty of reconciling the idea of *arousing* pity and fear with that of *purging* these emotions, both of which effects would seem to be produced simultaneously and by the same means.

What Corneille has interestingly introduced, though, despite his confusion, is a concept seized upon and clarified by two other seventeenth-century critics, one English and one French. In his preface (1671) to *Samson Agonistes*, Milton writes that the aim of tragedy is not to purge emotions in the spectator, but rather to 'temper and reduce them to just measure with a kind of delight, stirr'd up by reading or seeing those passions well imitated'. Racine, in thinking about catharsis, uses language very similar to Milton's but perhaps makes his position even clearer. In the marginal notes he added, probably in the 1660s or early 1670s, to his copy of Vettori's late sixteenth-century Latin translation-cum-commentary of the *Poetics*, Racine glosses Aristotle's definition in this way: tragedy arises through 'une représentation vive qui, excitant la pitié et la crainte, purge et tempère ces sortes de passions . . .'

It is pity and fear, then, not a wide range of general emotions, that tragedy stirs up in its audience. And he adds that, having aroused the passions of *pitié* and *crainte*, tragedy 'leur ôte ce qu'elles ont d'excessif et de vicieux, et les ramène à un état modéré et conforme à la raison'—it removes all that is excessive and defective in them and restores them to a moderate and reasonable state.

The dramatist's aim would thus not be to entice into the theatre an audience as wicked or unfortunate as the characters which the action represents and to submit them to an ordeal which, after five acts, will leave them exhausted but totally cleansed and renewed. Rather, the tragic experience consists of allowing the spectators' emotions to be stimulated through identification with the characters on stage and then laid to rest again by the end of the play, through the resolution of the plot. The audience leaves, in Milton's words, 'calm of mind, all passion spent'. At most it has undergone purification rather than purging, and even this may be overstating the case.

Racine's and Milton's approach to the tragic emotions seems a plausible one, within the experience of theatregoers both of their time and ours. Corneille's, while rather different, is not wildly implausible. For example, he rejects some contemporary views, according to which a lower or middle-class public could not feel fear for tragic characters because of their high status: 'These kings are men like the audiences, and they fall into these misfortunes by the heat of the same passions of which the audience is capable.'

But having cleared a path for fear, Corneille fails to see how it can apply
when catharsis, as he believes, means moral purification. He is thus inevitably led to separate the two emotions and, indeed, as Louis Herland suggests, to look on 'fear' (that is, the audience's fear of punishment) not as an
emotion at all but as *une réflexion*, a thinking about the character's action
some time after the event. Furthermore, believing that the suffering of a
good person may on occasion arouse more pity than indignation, while
the punishment of an evil man can correct some imperfection in us, the
audience, Corneille is prepared to incorporate such characters into his
range of plays.

This, in turn, leads to the more forceful, generally more optimistic
characterisation we find in Cornelian tragedy and to the new emotion of
admiration which he adds to Aristotle's pity and fear. If, as I feel we should,
we are prepared to grant that it is the nature of the dilemma and the
quality of the struggle which the character puts up that is the central issue
of tragedy, rather than the outcome itself, then Corneille's version of the
tragic is a valid and interesting addition to that favoured by the more conventional Racine.

What both interpretations and even other, less coherent ones serve to
show is that tragedy makes demands on both its actors and its audience.
In comedy, as has been remarked, our response to the stage action is
detached—we stand aside and look on, laughing at rather than with the
characters. To borrow Bergson's terms, 'the insociability of the character' in comedy must be accompanied by 'the insensitiveness of the spectator'. Tragedy, on the other hand, requires the active participation of all
concerned.

In most if not all tragedies, the fate of even secondary characters is significantly altered in the course of the five acts. Their own deeds and the
influence of others or outside forces change their lives, usually in an unexpected way, and they are brought to understand and accept the new
situation which results from their ordeal. On the other side of the footlights, the audience is invited to share in the enactment, identifying with
(which does not always mean morally approving of) the problems and
emotions of the figures on stage.

The paradox of the ordinary spectator being asked to share the
experiences of men and women of much higher social status is only a
superficial one, for tragedy is the great leveller, making heroes out of
common people and, more significantly, revealing to those who wield
power the frailty of their position and their essential humanity. Perhaps it
is only through this communion of actor and audience, character and
spectator, that the tragic element can be fully brought home to both.

13 Criticism

Although in some ways a dramatist's task is complete when his play is finally written, we have seen the importance that should be attached to the next two steps in the production process: staging and publication. At each of these points the playwright can, if he so desires, make his influence felt, by instructing the actors on how their parts should be played and by revising his text for publication in the light of criticism or his own second thoughts.

There remains one final stage to be considered, the rôle of contemporary critics and commentators and the pressure they could exert on dramatists and the kind of plays that were written. The range of writings here is a vast one, including literary gazettes, treatises by non-dramatists, prefaces by practising ones, private correspondence between people outside the theatre, and the attitude of the Church to drama in seventeenth-century France. We can only look briefly at any of these but each contributes a particular element to the overall picture.

As with many other aspects of French classical tragedy touched on in previous chapters, we must first of all rid ourselves of some ingrained twentieth-century habits and ways of thinking. For example, the France of Louis XIII and Louis XIV had no daily newspapers; it was only shortly before the Revolution, one hundred years after Racine wrote *Phèdre*, that the first daily began to appear. Indeed the earliest regular French paper of any kind started to come out, weekly, as late as 1631, and the inclusion of literary news was catered for in a series of rival publications which began in 1650. If we are so much more poorly informed about theatrical life and stage performances at the time of Hardy, Mairet, Rotrou, Tristan and the early Corneille than we are in the Racinian period, it is due not just to the chance non-existence or subsequent loss of important documents but also to the almost complete absence of a literary press.

Initial criticism of tragedies, as of other plays, occurred orally, in the salons or at pre-performance readings which dramatists might give to private aristocratic audiences. The readings in select private houses, in which Corneille and Racine indulged, could provide helpful criticism for the dramatist but also gave him and his current play free advance publicity.

When Théophraste Renaudot, encouraged by an 800 livres subsidy from Cardinal Richelieu, brought out the first number of the *Gazette* in 1631, an important step forward had been taken. This weekly quarto-sized publication, issued first on Fridays, later on Saturdays, consisted of four, then eight and afterwards twelve pages of political and social news from France and abroad. But there was no news of literary happenings apart from the occasional Court performance, and certainly no comment or analysis; journalism was still regarded as a descriptive trade, the passing-on of more or less official information, uncontaminated by editorial matter.

The Cardinal's support of the press was continued by his successor, Cardinal Mazarin, who offered his protection to Jean Loret, founder of an all-purpose newsletter called *La Muse historique* which he wrote from 1650 to 1665 and which, after his death, was continued in the late 60s and the 70s by others, including Charles Robinet. Loret's often appalling doggerel verse gives invaluable details of politics, society news and cultural events, but apart from the dates of some performances and information about who took what parts, his comments on tragedy are disappointingly superficial. In a January 1655 number he reports, then counters the recent rumour that Corneille had passed away. 'The wonder of Parnassus', 'divine genius', 'my illustrious compatriot' (both were Normans) is 'restored to life' in two dozen typical octosyllables.

At least this is a piece of hard news. The day after *Oedipe*'s first performance in 1659 at the Hôtel de Bourgogne, the *Muse historique* offers over thirty lines praising the play and its author Corneille to the skies. But the account is hearsay: 'I wasn't there, but I've been told . . .' Four years later, in January 1663, Loret mentions Corneille's *Sophonisbe*, first played a week earlier at the Hôtel. The 'incomparable' tragedy is the usual complete success, but the journalist says he does not intend to analyse its contents for his readers: the only way to appreciate the merits of the play is to see and hear it.

On the very day of the première of the same dramatist's *Sertorius* (1662), the *Muse historique* reports that Paris society has been discussing the great

Corneille's 'latest marvel' for the past week, saying that it surpasses *Le Cid* in 'beauty', *Horace* and *Pompée* in 'strength and graces', the 'inimitable' *Cinna*, as well as *Rodogune, Héraclius* and *Oedipe*, in 'seductiveness'. When *Othon* is played for the first time, before the Court at Fontainebleau in August 1664, Loret pens a few lines, hoping to have a first-hand account to offer his readers in the near future. But the report in the issue of 8 November 1664, a few days after the first public performance at the Hôtel de Bourgogne, is still based on others' impressions of the 'incomparable' tragedy by 'this inimitable genius', Corneille.

Robinet, in his *Lettres en vers*, carries on the *Muse historique*'s tradition: every new play is greeted in ten or twenty lines as the 'latest marvel', a 'rare work', 'a true artistic masterpiece'. The same indiscriminate praise is heaped on the newcomer, Racine. Plot summaries of his plays and eulogies of the actors and actresses are provided (ninety lines are devoted to *Andromaque* after Robinet sees it in November 1667), and short accounts are included of the deaths of Montfleury, who played Oreste and died of apoplexy, and of Racine's mistress Mlle du Parc, who took the part of Andromaque and passed away in December 1668, leaving the author 'half dead'.

Another potential source of criticism from 1665 onwards is the *Journal des savants*. But it reviews plays as works of literature rather than as drama-in-performance. Commenting a fortnight after *Othon* was first published in February 1665, the *Journal* writes that none of the twenty-seven plays that Corneille has had played to date has been greeted with less than applause; this latest one 'cannot be bad', since the author says as much in the preface. Few interested Parisians have not yet seen the play; the *Journal*, by mentioning it, hopes to arouse enthusiasm in foreigners and provincials, who can now read the text. Similar attention is drawn to Racine's *Athalie* in 1691, since the play, apart from a couple of Court performances at Versailles, had only had restricted private performances at Mme de Maintenon's girls' school at Saint-Cyr, for which it was written.

The main rival to the rhymed newssheets of Robinet and others is the *Mercure galant*, a monthly founded by Donneau de Visé in 1672. This contains society news rather than serious political comment, although there are a number of genuine pieces of literary and dramatic criticism, but since de Visé was joined by the playwright Thomas Corneille in 1681, the comment tends to be slightly biased in favour of the latter and of course his elder brother. Thus de Visé writes in March 1672 about Pierre Corneille: 'He is the only person whose works one can praise without having read them and from whom, despite his great age, one must always expect perfect plays, such as his latest tragedy, to appear next winter under the name of *Pulchérie*, will certainly be found to be.'

But Corneille stops writing two years after the start of the *Mercure*, and the journal is generous with its praise of Racine, already an established dramatist by 1672. That year it defends the relative Turkishness of *Bajazet*, commenting, as we have seen, that characters in love are realistic and more appropriate than barbaric ones, and placing Racine at the summit of Parnassus, as a French Sophocles or Euripides. 'This famous author' manages to please, instruct and touch, says the *Mercure galant* with reference to *Mithridate*, while *Phèdre* is found incomparably better than Pradon's play, largely because Racine, unlike his rival, has shown Phèdre as Thésée's wife, with all the consequences, rather than as his fiancée. 'Racine is still Racine', de Visé proclaims when the play is published; the lines are as beautiful in print as they were in performance. And twenty-two years later, on the dramatist's death, the journal can write that 'we have lost one of the most excellent men of this century'.

The limitations of these gazette and newsletter accounts are obvious. Most reports describe the actors and the set, but usually in such uniformly ecstatic terms that readers who had not seen a particular play could have little idea before they read it of how it really compared with previous works by the same author or other contemporary plays. There is no criticism of the structure or content of tragedies, and an analysis of the overall talent of a writer and the quality of his work has to await his obituary. Even here, minor dramatists often receive more extended treatment than playwrights of genius, reflecting the harsh reality that the most popular plays are not always written by the most talented authors.

This embryonic press was, of course, centred on Paris; provincial journalism was almost non-existent, with local gazettes in Toulouse and Besançon in the 1660s and at Grenoble in the closing years of the century. But as we have noted, all plays of any merit at all were first staged and then published in the capital, so the restriction is only relative. It is outside the gazettes that we find comments from writers living in provincial France or abroad. The letters of Guez de Balzac and Mme de Sévigné and the critical works of Saint-Evremond provide some of the most interesting material. All three will be stout defenders of Corneille in what, given the chronology of events in seventeenth-century drama, inevitably becomes a contest between the ageing Corneille (already fifty-eight when Racine's first tragedy is performed) and the young author of *Andromaque*, *Bérénice* and *Phèdre*, the main body of whose plays are all staged within a twelve and a half-year period while he is in his twenties and thirties.

Before the arrival of Racine in 1664, the plays of Corneille were, naturally, submitted to much examination, as we have seen in earlier chapters.

The *Cid* quarrel and a series of treatises which appeared a year or two later (La Mesnardière's *Poétique*, Sarrasin's *Discours de la tragédie* and Scudéry's *Apologie du théâtre*, all published in 1639) would seem to establish once and for all the triumph of 'regular' tragedy. But as early as August 1637, halfway between Scudéry's *Observations sur le Cid* and Chapelain's *Sentiments de l'Académie Française sur le Cid*, Corneille writes defiantly in the dedication to his comedy *La Suivante*, to be published the following month:

> The rules of the ancients are very religiously observed in this [comedy]. There is only one main plot to which all the others are subordinated. The place does not extend beyond the area of the stage, and the duration is no longer than the time taken to act it, if an exception is made for lunch which occurs between the first and second acts. I have even ensured that there is a link between the scenes, which is merely an embellishment and not a precept . . . I like following the rules, but, far from being their slave, I relax or tighten them as my subject requires, and I even have no hesitation about breaking the one regarding the duration of the plot when its harshness seems to me completely incompatible with the finer points of the events described. To know the rules and to possess the secret of taming them skilfully for use on stage are two very different things. To make a play succeed these days, it is perhaps not enough to have merely read up one's Aristotle and Horace.

What attracted a writer like Jean-Louis Guez de Balzac to Corneille was not just the realism but the idealisation of certain characteristics. In a letter of January 1643, he tells the dramatist that *Cinna* cures the sick, causing paralytics to clap their hands and restoring speech to the dumb. The Rome which Corneille depicts is Livy's Rome, 'as magnificent as it was at the time of the first Caesars'. Indeed, where Rome was constructed in brick, you rebuild it in marble, Balzac writes. You fill voids with masterpieces, and what you lend history is always better than what you borrow from it. The following month, in another letter, he does not hesitate to compare Corneille to Sophocles. Guez de Balzac, author of a voluminous and stylish correspondence much appreciated in his day, understands that a literary work must be judged not by its adherence to a strict set of rules but by how far it pleases its public.

The view that Corneille not only equals but improves on his source-material is echoed by later writers. In his *Théâtre français* (1674), Samuel Chappuzeau, reporting that eleven years earlier Corneille's *Sophonisbe* had found less favour than Mairet's version, talks of Corneille's skill in making Carthaginians, Greeks and Romans speak as they ought to and even better than they did in real life. Saint-Evremond also comments on

Sophonisbe: the various citizens are shown to be more authentic than their originals and, if Corneille's play failed, it was precisely because he retained the flavour of the source-material, whereas Mairet had sought, and managed, to please the ladies and courtiers. Like Balzac, Saint-Evremond was a confirmed Cornelian. In his *Défense de quelques pièces de théâtre de M. Corneille* (1677), for instance, he refutes criticisms that Rodogune should not have asked Antiochus and Séleucus to kill their mother, Cléopâtre, and maintains that the captive princess is doing no more than securing her own safety against a much greater criminal. In *Sur les tragédies*, published in 1684, the year of the dramatist's death, he says that Corneille does not just present us with characters in action; he looks for the principles which lie behind their acts, and goes into their hearts to see the passions taking shape and to reveal what is most hidden there. What pleases him is that everything which propriety does not forbid is shown: Corneille is not as barbaric as the ancients, for he has incorporated some love-plots, 'judiciously placed', but has succeeded in giving priority, as is right, to truly tragic subjects which can arouse fear and pity.

Yet Saint-Evremond is not an indiscriminate admirer. Looking back in 1674, perhaps with the advantage that since 1661 he has been exiled, mainly in England, he criticises *Polyeucte*, saying in *De la comédie ancienne et moderne* that religion and tragedy cannot be successfully combined. The conversations between Pauline and Sévère add interest to the martyrdom scenes with Polyeucte, which by themselves would have made a fine sermon but a wretched tragedy. By the late 1660s, indeed, Saint-Evremond and other supporters such as Mme de Sévigné were realising that for all his great talents Corneille was beginning to lose popularity.

When Racine's second tragedy, *Alexandre*, was published in 1666, Saint-Evremond claimed in a letter that everything in it was mediocre, a worse thing than extravagance in a heroic subject. Alexander the Great was recognisable only by his name, for the author had no sympathy with antiquity. This same last point is repeated two years later, when Saint-Evremond hopes that Corneille can pass on to his successor his skill in character portrayal. Yet that is now the only talent that Racine lacks. The same year, 1668, Saint-Evremond admits that *Andromaque* 'seemed to me a very fine play, but I think one can go further into the passions and that there remains something deeper than what is there'. According to the letter-writer, however, Racine must, all things considered, be more highly regarded than any other author . . . after Corneille. Almost simultaneously Saint-Evremond writes to Corneille, reassuring him that he is the only French writer to make an impression in England: Ben Jonson is seen by his hosts as the 'English Corneille', and he assures the author of *Le Cid* that the 'bad taste' of those who prefer the young Racine will soon pass. The late 1660s, as we shall see shortly, was a period of rather acrimonious debate between Church and stage. It was also a time when Racine, increasingly secure in his reputation, could launch barely veiled attacks on his predecessor through the choice of Roman subjects in *Britannicus* and *Bérénice* and the content of the prefaces to both plays. The Cornelian camp could do little to retaliate. Although Saint-Evremond criticises the criminality of Narcisse, Agrippine and Néron in the former play, he has to admit that the characterisation has been well handled and believes that *Britannicus* is superior to *Alexandre* or *Andromaque*. One day Racine might almost rival Corneille. Titus in *Bérénice* is too desperate a character, Saint-Evremond writes in *Sur les caractères des tragédies* (c. 1671–5); the audience or reader should be made to feel grief, not despair. But Corneille's *Tite et Bérénice* is no better, the author contravening both truth and verisimilitude in showing the emperor ready to leave Rome simply in order to follow Bérénice to Judea. The abbé de Villars, in his *Critique de 'Bérénice'* (1671), finds Antiochus superfluous, a rôle created for the actor Champmeslé whose wife had played the title-part, while in trying to be different from Corneille Racine has created a play which from start to finish is purely elegiac.

Like Balzac and Saint-Evremond, Mme de Sévigné, although a habitué of précieux salons, was forced by circumstances to spend long periods away from Paris. This cultured woman, able to read Italian and possibly Latin, steeped in the *moralistes* and a lover of nature and music, was an ardent admirer of Corneille and La Fontaine. Many of the numerous letters she wrote to her married daughter in Provence contain approximate quotations from Corneille's plays, even after the dramatist had stopped writing. Her reaction to *Bajazet* is typical of her reluctant acceptance of the 'new' playwright. Writing in January 1672 after seeing an early performance, she praises the tragedy, finding it better than *Bérénice* but not as good as *Andromaque*. 'Believe me,' she assures Mme de Grignan, 'nothing will ever approach (I do not say surpass) the divine passages in Corneille.'

Two months later, when she has had a chance to read the play, printed in February, she claims that without Mlle Champmeslé to play Atalide, the text loses half its attractions. 'I am mad about Corneille ... Everything must yield to his genius.' A week later, her opinion of *Bajazet* has sunk even lower. The title-character lacks warmth; Turks are not all that worried about marriage; the dénouement is poorly prepared. Although there are satisfactory elements, the reader is not carried away: there are none of those tirades which send such pleasant shivers down the spine in a Cornelian tragedy.

Things are different when Mme de Sévigné is invited to a performance of *Esther* at Saint-Cyr. 'If I were devout, I would aspire to see it', she writes to her daughter on 31 January 1689; within ten days her name has been whispered in Mme de Maintenon's ear. In the meantime Mme de Grignan is informed by her mother that Racine 'loves God as he loved his mistresses: he is in favour of things sacred as he was of things profane'. Later in February Mme de Sévigné finds herself in the second row at Saint-Cyr, seated behind the duchesses. She cannot summon up words to describe the play and assures her daughter that it will never be imitated. Her speechlessness is increased when the King deigns to have a brief and hardly more than banal conversation with her. It may be unfair to see this high spot in Mme de Sévigné's social life as the cause of her conversion to Racine, for Corneille had been dead and buried for over four years. But preferences and prejudices *are* created by such strictly irrelevant events: what happened to Mme de Sévigné at Saint-Cyr early in 1689 is not untypical of the less than rational response to drama and dramatists earlier in the century.

Between Corneille's death and that of Racine (1699), a number of works appear, comparing the respective merits of the two playwrights. Adrien Baillet, in the *Jugement des savants* (1685–6), says that the quarrel will last as long as it has not been decided whether the public wants heroic figures from antiquity, shown with the character and behaviour of the appropriate period, or characters brought up to date and given qualities and feelings which agree with seventeenth-century French ones. The dramatist Longepierre, in his *Parallèle de M. Corneille et de M. Racine* (1686), finds much in favour of the younger man. Racine's greater tenderness and grace is not without the necessary grandeur; he is as skilful a constructor of plots as Corneille ever was; he depicts love better; his style and versification are more competent; and he has the immense advantage of having stopped writing while still at the peak of his career.

The balance is restored, not unexpectedly, by Corneille's nephew Fontenelle in a similar *Parallèle* (1693). He points out, among other things, that his uncle had no guide to follow, whereas Racine did; he had the greater task in removing vulgarity from the French stage; his characters are true, although not common, while Racine's are true only because they are common; audiences wish for self-improvement after seeing a Corneille play, whereas a Racinian audience is merely happy to have witnessed characters as weak as themselves; Corneille has a surer talent for depicting historical characters, Racine's being basically modern French-men; despite his much larger output, Corneille repeats himself less often than does Racine; Corneille can equal Racine's poetry, if only sporadically. Of course, comparisons like this could have no direct influence on Racine, although Baillet and Longepierre wrote before he composed *Esther* and *Athalie*. Other authors, too, publishing in the 1670s, came on the scene too late to do more than sum up the achievements of the 1660 generation and its predecessors. As far as tragedy is concerned, Boileau, for example, is hardly 'the legislator of Parnassus': the laws had been established and accepted long before his *Art poétique* appeared in 1674. But then the comments of early journalists, correspondents and various part-isans mentioned previously were also more expressions of current opinion—and the opinion of a restricted group of people—than an attempt to seriously analyse, far less question, the structure, content and aims of French classical tragedy. Nor is it just in the field of drama that seventeenth-century 'criticism' proves largely disappointing to the modern reader.

One pressure-group which could have affected the kind of plays shown—or indeed the very existence of the live theatre—was the Church. The situation was more than slightly paradoxical. Two successive cardin-als, Richelieu and Mazarin, actively encouraged drama along with other artistic forms; the abbé François de Boisrobert, a contemporary of Cor-neille, and the abbé Claude Boyer, active in the second half of the century, wrote for the theatre, as did the abbé d'Aubignac, author of *La Pratique du théâtre* which, for all its rather conservative views, is certainly not an attack on drama itself. A decade later the abbé de Pure, admittedly a rather worldly cleric, could bring out his *Idée des spectacles anciens et nouveaux* (1668)

It was in the early 1660s, just before Racine's arrival, that the trouble started. On the secular front, Corneille, as we know, published his import-ant *Examens* and three *Discours* in 1660. Many of their arguments were a re-statement of positions he had held ever since the 1630s. But they can also be seen as a denial of the stance adopted in 1657 by d'Aubignac, whose name and work Corneille is careful never to mention but which he is clearly keen to attack. Annoyed by this opposition, d'Aubignac lost no time in criticising Corneille's *Sophonisbe* (1663) and to that *Dissertation* added three others, against *Oedipe, Sertorius* and the author's 'calumnies'. The arguments are familiar to readers of the *Pratique* or of Mairet's or Cha-pelain's comments on *Le Cid: Sophonisbe*, for instance, breaches the rules, does not follow history and contains characters who act in an unedifying manner. In a preface when the play is published in April, two months after d'Aubignac's first *Dissertation* was printed, Corneille has little difficulty in demolishing the abbé's arguments. It was his predecessor Mairet who was historically inaccurate; he is simply following an unimpeachable source, Livy. Love, as he had found when composing *Oedipe* and *Sertorius*, is certainly needed in contemporary drama, but it should not be the sole or main interest. Corneille above all is determined to reject d'Aubignac's attempts to turn characters taken from antiquity into seventeenth-century Frenchmen and women, perfect sighing lovers.

The *Sophonisbe* controversy, like the *Cid* quarrel a generation earlier, did not involve the Church directly. But d'Aubignac's insistence on acceptable characters can be seen to fit in with a moral and religious criticism of drama which encompassed not just tragedy but also comedy in the 1660s. Molière's *L'Ecole des femmes*, first performed in December 1662 and published the following March, was attacked for several reasons, but in part the criticisms were based on mere prudery and social prejudice. The passage in Act II in which the naïve, innocent Agnès hesitates to tell her ward Arnolphe what it was the young man who loves her, Horace, took hold of was judged by some commentators to verge on the indecent. 'There is nothing more scandalous, for example, than the fifth scene of Act II of *L'Ecole des femmes*', wrote the Prince de Conti in the preface to the *Sentiments des Pères de l'Eglise* (1666).

Much more open to attack were two of Molière's subsequent comedies, *Tartuffe* and *Dom Juan*. The hoodwinking of Orgon by the religious hypocrite Tartuffe and the latter's skilful use of ambivalent language combining lechery and apparent saintliness contributed to the play being banned before it could be published. In the circumstances (it took Molière five years to have a revised version of *Tartuffe* accepted), it is hardly surprising that *Dom Juan* (1665), with its title-character openly admitting to atheism and with the conventional Christian view entrusted to a well-meaning but inarticulate valet, was also denied the right of performance.

At the same time as plays were being banned for the reasons stated, treatises were appearing in which drama itself came under attack. The Prince de Conti, whom we have already encountered—a near contemporary of Molière at the Jesuit college in Paris and one of the dramatist's patrons during his tour of the south-west of France but converted to Jansenist views in the late 1650s—wrote a *Traité de la comédie et des spectacles selon la tradition de l'Eglise*, printed in 1666. His aim is to prove that drama is not an innocent amusement and that Christians should look on it as evil. Early tragedies were perhaps acceptable, but now love is to the fore, demanded by the audience. Tragedy no longer aims to instruct; indeed spectators are unable to restrain the passions stirred up by it. Even virtue is not always shown to advantage, being represented often by an elderly king played by a third-rate actor with uninspiring lines to deliver. Hence audiences at *Cinna* are much more interested in the 'tender and passionate things' which the conspirators Cinna and Emilie say to each other than in the clemency of Auguste, to which they barely give a second thought. Drama, aiming to 'stir up the passions', is incompatible with religion, designed to moderate and destroy them as far as possible: *Polyeucte* is a dry and unpleasant tragedy. Finally, plays are performed on Sunday, the Lord's day, which belongs to Him and not to actors.

The rigorous views of Conti, who died in February 1666, are shared by the Oratorian Father J-F. Senault, whose *Le Monarque ou les devoirs du souverain* is published in 1661. In it, Senault sees the pleasure of drama as 'this agreeable poison', 'the bait covering the hook to which it is attached'. The theatre seduces the mind after bewitching the senses. Only those made of bronze or marble could resist such temptation; the average man, a victim of sin and inclined to vice rather than virtue, must be advised to steer clear of the reef which the theatre represents.

Better known are the words of the Jansenist moralist and theologian Pierre Nicole. In his treatise *De la comédie* (1667), he states that drama is based on love, pride and honour, three pernicious concepts which flatter the corrupt inclinations of readers and theatregoers. Writers justify 'damnable maxims' like Rodrigue's (and, one might add, Polyeucte's) 'I would do it again if I had to do it' by simply saying they are 'in character'. For Nicole, all the plays of Corneille (the best of a bad bunch of dramatists) are representations of pride, ambition, jealousy, revenge and especially of Roman virtue, another term for self-love. The more grandeur and *générosité* Corneille gives to these *vices*, the more dangerously acceptable they become.

A few months earlier, in a letter of December 1665, Nicole had crystallised his views into a single, pungent sentence 'A novelist and playwright are public poisoners,' he wrote, 'not of the bodies but of the souls of the faithful, who should look upon themselves as guilty of an infinite number of spiritual murders, which they have actually caused or which they could have caused by their pernicious writings.' Feeling directly attacked by his former teachers at Port-Royal, Racine replied early in 1666 with a stinging letter, asking what plays and novels had to do with Jansenism and suggesting that the *solitaires*, with their austere moral doctrine, should concern themselves with things of the next world and not of this.

At the end of 1667 Corneille in turn answers the criticisms of Conti and Nicole. In the *Au Lecteur* to *Attila*, he submits everything he has written or will write to both secular and ecclesiastical authorities; would that his critics did likewise. And as Racine had done, he points out that a translation of some of Terence's comedies had been published some twenty years earlier from Port-Royal itself. This legitimises Corneille's own efforts, which are moderate anyway. Love is certainly an important element in his tragedies, but unhappy love arouses pity and purges us of passion rather than stimulating it in us.

The quarrel continues until the closing years of the century. In the preface to *Phèdre* (1677) Racine remarks that a tradition of didactic drama would enable tragedy to be acceptable to 'a number of people famous for their piety and doctrine who have condemned it recently'. In the mid 1690s, in answer to Father Caffaro's *Lettre d'un théologien illustre* arguing in favour of the stage, Bossuet puts his considerable weight behind religious opponents of drama and publishes his *Maximes et réflexions sur la comédie* (1694). But this falls outside our period, and indeed we must not exaggerate the influence of the strictly religious criticism of French classical drama. What is important is to have followed, through this chapter and in some of the earlier ones, the range of comments which tragedy in general, and certain types in particular (sacred tragedy, the heroic tragedy typical of Corneille, and so on), gave rise to in seventeenth-century France.

While plays similar to *Polyeucte* had died away from the commercial theatre by 1650, their disappearance was more a natural phenomenon than a response to attacks by Jansenist rigorists. In the case of secular plays, loyalty to Corneille remained strong among gazette writers and private correspondents, even after the advent of Racine, whose very different talents were quickly acknowledged. Corneille himself, after an initial period of doubt, stuck by the type of tragedy he had begun with, in *Médée* and *Le Cid*, conforming to the essential requirements of the genre but demanding for himself more latitude than many of his rather short-sighted critics were willing to grant him. After such largely unorthodox plays, those of Racine, in all their perfection, must have seemed conventional indeed. But as Fontenelle was to suggest, his task, after a generation and more of regular French tragedy, was in many ways a less difficult one.

Conclusion

There can be none. On the one hand, we may choose to stress the artificiality of French classical tragedy, which cannot be an 'exact copy' or imitation of an action (no drama can), but is, rather, a transposition of material, a re-arrangement—as Aristotle says, a heightening of certain traits as in a painting, a playing down of others. In short, an idealisation, an improvement on what nature offers. And this enhancement of the subject-matter is reflected everywhere else—in the choice of words, the arrangement of acts, scenes, speeches, entrances and exits. It is achieved in large part through a strict selectivity, partly on moral grounds (if the dramatist has any intention at all of writing didactic theatre), partly for aesthetic reasons (by limiting or removing entirely those elements which could shock or simply displease). Within the topic chosen, the keynote is self-restraint and economy: restricted, often claustrophobic space and a neutral setting; restricted time, from Corneille's thirty hours to Racine's rationed minutes; restricted gesture and movement; restricted language.

On the other hand, provided one accepts the convention of eighteen hundred or so twelve-syllable lines of verse grouped into rhyming couplets and divided into five acts and some thirty scenes (and without that acceptance one might as well return one's text to the bookshop or ticket to the box-office), then all the limitations can be seen for what they are: not drawbacks, but opportunities for the playwright to spotlight the essentials and leave in shadow all that is unimportant. A neutral set gives added significance to any outside detail or dash of local colour. Absence of movement makes all the more meaningful the occasions when, for instance, Phèdre sits down (in her first scene) or Bérénice stands up (in her last). A basic vocabulary need not and does not rule out an infinite range of tones—revealing passion, hate, fear, ambition, revenge—and the seemingly inflexible alexandrine can convey a host of effects, ranging from the vigour and majesty of Corneille's speeches to the subtly suggestive, poetic evocations of Racinian verse.

Of course, when it came to the stage, the Elizabethans and Jacobeans had much in common with the inhabitants of seventeenth-century France. 'Private' theatres like the Blackfriars in London shared the structural disadvantages of the *jeux de paume* and buildings modelled on these oblong, indoor tennis-courts, while on theoretical matters the unities were also to be found in England—in Sir Philip Sidney's *Apology for poetry*, which was written in the early 1580s and followed Castelvetro's lead in discussing time and place, or in the prologue to Ben Jonson's comedy *Every man in his humour*, performed in 1598. But this was not the whole story, for the Globe was not rectangular and Shakespeare did not feel constrained to abide by the theories propounded by Sidney or Jonson, who wrote before any of his plays were performed. Add to this the apparent lack of influence which English dramatic texts had on seventeenth-century French drama, and it becomes clear that, beyond an extensive core of necessarily common elements, Britain enjoyed a very different theatrical tradition from that of its closest neighbour.

If this little book has done anything at all to make more understandable the aims of French classical tragedy, the conventions which its authors accepted, often willingly or perhaps unconsciously, sometimes against their literary judgement, and the problems which the genre presented them with, then it will have more than served its purpose.

Further reading

The theories and rules of seventeenth-century French tragedy are most fully explored in René Bray's *La formation de la doctrine classique en France* (Paris, 1927). Their practical application is studied in Jacques Scherer's *La dramaturgie classique en France* (Paris, 1950), an indispensable storehouse of facts, figures and examples which examines the technique of French dramatists of the period.

H. C. Lancaster's *A History of French dramatic literature in the seventeenth century* (Baltimore, 1929–42, 5 parts in 9 volumes) remains the 'monumental' achievement his successors refer to; it provides an analysis of every extant play from the seventeenth century and much else besides. Again for English-speaking readers, the late Geoffrey Brereton's *French tragic drama in the sixteenth and seventeenth centuries* (London, 1973) offers a survey of the period designated, with chapters on Corneille, Racine and the most important of their respective contemporaries, a summary of the main plays and a compact bibliography. Jacques Truchet's *La tragédie classique en France* (Paris, 1975) is a skilful and thought-provoking summing-up of current thinking about the genre and includes an excellent bibliography and index.

R. C. Knight's seminal article 'A minimal definition of seventeenth-century tragedy' is to be found in *French Studies*, X (1956), pp. 297–308. H. T. Barnwell's inaugural lecture *The tragic in French tragedy* (Belfast, 1966) complements his invaluable edition of Corneille's *Writings on the theatre* (Oxford, 1965), a fully annotated collection of what are undoubtedly the most interesting and important seventeenth-century critical works on French tragedy. Peter France's *Racine's rhetoric* (Oxford, 1965) is a pioneering study in a field which is as yet inadequately explored.

Finally, Peter D. Arnott's *An introduction to the French theatre* (London, 1977) 'attempts to take plays which are now more commonly read than seen, and place them in a living theatre context'. Its scope, despite its title, is limited to the seventeenth century, but it includes chapters on dances and machines and on Molière.

Index